CUSTOMARY LAWS OF MEITEI AND MIZO SOCIETIES OF MANIPUR

MANIPUR

Showing Areas Inhabited by
the Meiteis and the Mizos (Kukis)

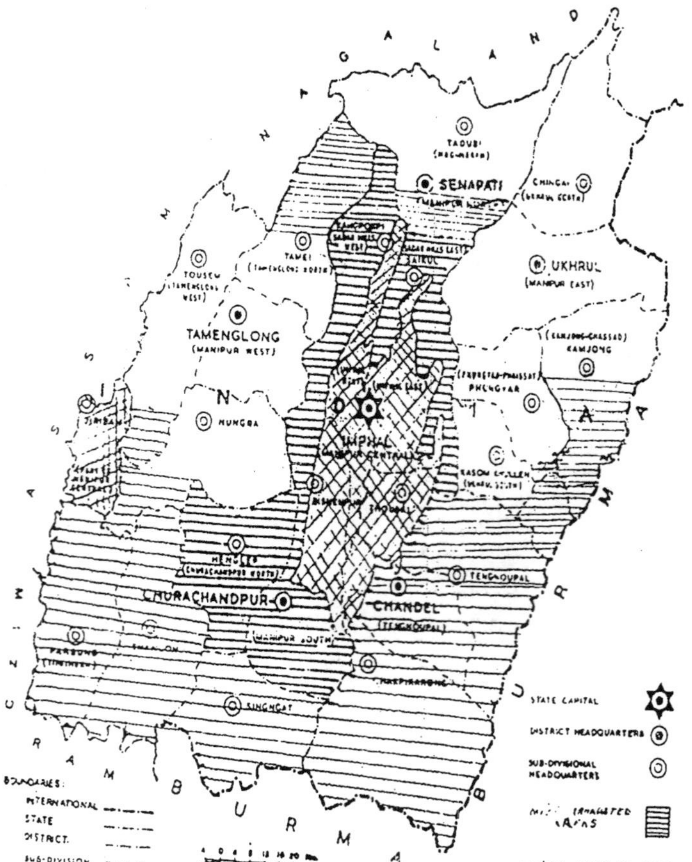

CUSTOMARY LAWS OF MEITEI AND MIZO SOCIETIES OF MANIPUR

Priyadarshni M. Gangte

AKANSHA PUBLISHING HOUSE
NEW DELHI - 110 002 (INDIA)

AKANSHA PUBLISHING HOUSE
4649/21-B, Ansari Road
Daryaganj, New Delhi - 110 002
Phones: 23263193, 9811582579, 9435116718
E-mail: ektabooks@yahoo.com

Customary Laws of Meitei and Mizo Societies of Manipur

First Published, 2008

ISBN 978-81-8370-130-3

PRINTED IN INDIA

Published by Akansha Publishing House, New Delhi - 110 002 and Printed at Capital Offset Press, Delhi

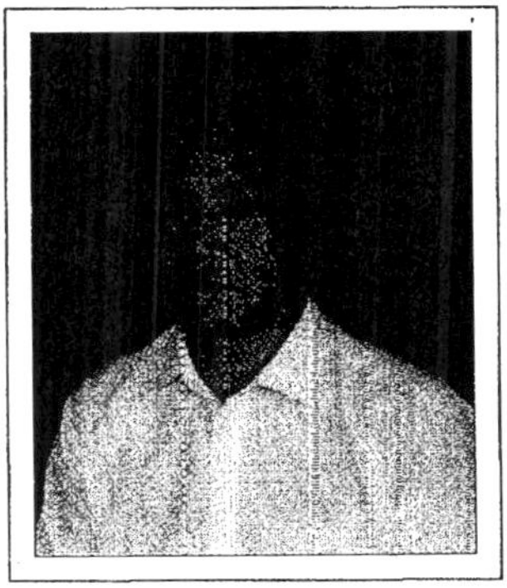

Dedicated

in

Cherished Memory

of

my beloved husband

Dr. T. S. Gangte

(30th November, 1932-29th July, 2007)

whose unstinted support, inspiration & encouragement throughout has been my source of strength.

The author with her husband
Dr. T.S. Gangte

Contents

Foreword

'Custom' is indeed an important key for the historian in profiling the stages in the growth and development of a community, particularly in the context of such societies which were in preliteracy until only two to three generations ago. The role of customs has been found to be stronger in such societies which are basically traditional, and the tradition continues despite the modernity. The 'dos' or 'don'ts' and the ritual practices are supposed to have originated in a society under compelling situations at particular points of time in history. The moments of glory and ignominy — the prides and prejudices — are meticulously showcased in the social behavioural patterns enjoined by the customary beliefs and practices. The challenge for the historian is to catch the 'point of time' and the 'situation' of the origin and sustenance of a customary practice to explain the landmarks in the history of the community. And such landmarks are always very important in the historians' craft in computing the stages in human social development. The legal semantics no doubt distinguish between 'custom' and 'customary law', but by the time the customary laws come into existence the society has had already outlived pre literacy and reached a stage of development when it is capable of codifying the customs and making and enforcing laws for its own governance. Many other sets of data are by then likely to be in command of the historian for studying the society in its new form. In the mean time, the society has already traveled a long way and some of its customs have survived the stresses and strains of time and circumstances. The customs have also played a role in holding the community together in course of that arduous march of the humanity for survival. The effort of the historian is to chart this long way' or the 'course of journey' through the key of customs and customary laws, to evaluate the historic role of the customs in various stages of social growth, and to reflect on the futuristic behavioural relevance of all or some of the customs. The customs or practices that hindered the growth and development of the society in the past might not be considered progressive and relevant for the future and might call for serious consideration of the community for modification or substitution. What is most important in the context is to objectively appreciate the fact that a practice can attain the status of a custom by the logic of its being a very long usage and its universal acceptability within the society. Like the living or practicing customs (say, 'custom that still holds good'), there may be some obsolete ('used to be' or 'no more relevant) customs that the elders in the society may. recall and such 'used to be' or 'no more relevant' customs may indicate spectacular changes in life and conditions and the value system of the community. The rhetoric of 'long usage' and 'universal acceptability' or 'no more relevant' or 'used to be' are expected to be insightful paradigms in retrieving the grass-root 'history from below'. The prospects pre-empt the historian's interest in customs and customary laws.

Dr Priyadarshni M Gangte has made a great beginning in interpreting the history of the indigenous communities of Northeast India by her study of the customary laws of the Meiteis and the Mizos of Manipur. Her formal education in History and Law and her personal affiliation to the two societies, namely, Meiteis and Kukis (a tribe within the Mizo group), are understood to have been to her advantage in studying the published as well as the unpublished materials on the concerned communities both in English and vernacular languages and in generating additional information through her own field investigations and in interpreting both the sets of materials. I am happy that she made the best use of the advantage to academically serve the social interests of both the communities. The book that emerges from the author's doctoral dissertation in History of the Manipur University is important not only as a commendable collection of the customary laws of the Meiteis and the Mizos of Manipur but also for its significance as a research work in the history of Manipur. In fact, the focus on historical and cultural perspectives of the customary laws has significantly enlivened the study. It addresses the aspects of the Meitei and the Kuki social and community life and reflects on the importance of the customary laws for the ethnic societies in managing their corporate life, despite the on-going processes of social modernization. The task was stupendous, but the author accomplished it with zeal and labour.

I strongly feel that Dr Gangte's book will inspire many more studies on the subject; it will contribute to the increasing appreciation of the importance of customary laws for the ethnic societies, and it shall be handy for the judiciary to refer. It is indeed my pleasure to recommend this keenly researched publication to all those who are interested in history and society of the peoples in India's Northeast and their customary laws.

J B Bhattacharjee
Chairman
Institute of Northeast India Studies,
Kolkata
Formerly, Vice-Chancellor,
Assam University, Silchar

Kolkata
August 1, 2007

Acknowledgements

It is with a sense of exceeding gratitude to my Guide, Professor K.K. Das, that I say "Thank You, Sir". He has been the source of inspiration to put my 'research work' in order, and to make it a 'thesis' worth-presentation. Indeed, words fail me to express my sincere gratitude for his invaluable guidance in giving direction and shaping my work. I shall ever cherish his profound scholarship and his concern for the scholars working under his guidance.

My special thanks go to Professors Laldena and Jacob Luirum who have been source of strength in my quest for higher academic pursuit. I am also thankful to Professors N. Joykumar Singh, M. Jitendra Singh, Salam Irene, L. Kunjeshwari Devi and all other members of the Teaching and Non-teaching staff of the Department of History, Manipur University, for their encouragement and moral support. I thank Professors Ksh. Bimola Devi and N. Lokendra Singh with gratitude.

I am deeply beholden to Prof. J.B. Bhattacharjee, Chairman, Institute of Northeast India Studies, Kolkata, formerly Vice-Chancellor, Assam University, Silchar for going through this study and contributing a Foreword to this book.

I thank Indian Council of Historical Research, New Delhi, for awarding me Junior Research Fellowship for my Research project, which proved a great financial help to me.

I sincerely thank the Librarians of Manipur University and the L.M.S. Law College for the help extended whenever required and for allowing me to utilize the facilities extensively.

I am thankful to Prof. L. Sadananda Singh and Dr. Mangshatabam Lokendra, for their invaluable assistance extended in securing rare research data materials and translating them for my work.

Similarly, I thank Shri Naorem Nobinchandra Singh who has not only typed the dissertation but has endured to make the entire printed materials take a final shape.

I thank with love, and gratitude to Smt. M. Sumila Devi and Kumari M. Binaton Devi, my younger sisters, for their financial help and their untiring labour in preparing the bibliography. I am extremely thankful to my daughter, Kikim, who has been the source of constant inspiration to me.

I express my gratitude to my late parents. It is in reminiscence of their loving tender kindness that I shall ever remain indebted for they cared and really loved me and brought me up to get educated. I extend my respect to my husband for his loving kindness and concern and the keen interest that he took in my well-being and research work. He has always stood by me and my whims. I indeed cherish his thoughtfulness.

—Priyadarshni M. Gangte

Introduction

Customs are not customary laws. They are not synonymous either. There may be various customs without any legal authority whereas customary laws have sanction of the bulk of society and, if not obeyed, such violator is liable to be punished. Custom, like law, in its widest connotation, is a body of rules which regulates the conduct of human beings with each other and the society as well.

As a matter of fact, Paton, an eminent jurist, while defining origin, nature and growth of customary law, said, "Custom in any early society was not only the main but also the only vehicle of legal development".

When man first started to live together constituting a society among themselves, they adjusted among themselves of their different individual nature so that they might live in harmony. This was the beginning of creating social behaviour with various activities conducive to their diverse nature. Such nature, which has the greatest possibility of acceptability by most of them, gradually became accepted law which duly became Customary Law on account of being practised repeatedly within and without that particular society or social group.

Keeping the Customary Laws and the "evolution theory" thereof in view, studies in origin, growth development and changes brought about only Customary Laws of the Meiteis and the Mizos of Manipur, are undertaken with reference to their historical, traditional and cultural perspectives. Particular focus is given to the tenacity to endure or otherwise in respect of political and social functionaries, such as, Chieftainship, Social Structure, ethnicity, and some social institutions, such as, birth, marriage, death, feast, festivals, rites, rituals, etc, that have direct bearings on customary laws especially since the 18th century which is considered as a watershed in anthropo-historical considerations.

One of the crucial questions that have emerged from the very beginning in our study has been to focus on understanding the reconciliation processes among the indigenous populations of the ethnic communities identified as the Mizos and the Meiteis in the Northeast and the meaning they attach to the term 'law' and its customary aspects. Our aim has been to look into their genesis of common origin – a point which has been made by several scholars but has never before been investigated thoroughly.

In both the societies – the Meiteis and the Mizos – conflict is more readily observable than integration. Consequently discussions for or of integration or stability is more implicit rather than explicit. As researchers we are aware of the fact and that has been well brought out in our work that the absence of conflict and presence of cooperation and coordination are sometimes used as indexes of integration and social stability. Whenever any social disruption or aberration of deviant behaviour is observed laws are needed to settle disputes, disagreements or conflicts arising out of it because it impedes successful integration of society and harmony in it. It is, therefore, that detailed records of the course of disputes, their causes from their origin to their attempted settlement are events that follow upon this attempt become crucial for our study. In our research work, therefore, we have tried to understand the sociology of the customary laws wherein the ethnic communities – the Meiteis and the Mizos – are seen to have slowly progressed towards establishing systems of organized authority – e.g. the state formation or the jurisprudence in it – on the basis of their customary laws.

During the course of our investigations through field work we observed that if jurisprudence is full of controversies centering on how law should be defined and applied, the terminological disputes are increased when tribal societies e.g. that of the Kukis and by extension the Mizos – with their not so different cultures are investigated, which in fact should decrease. The reasons are bit difficult to understand. Perhaps the answer may lie in the fact that since our own words for law and related phenomena are already loaded with meanings the researchers are found with paradoxes. In fact, the researchers belonging to tribal ethnic backgrounds find it difficult as soon as they try to apply these words to activities of their own cultures vis-à-vis other cultures. So, in general terms customary laws or law per-se should be viewed as social control through the systematic application of the force of politically organized society. However, if by the term 'Politically organised' we imply the existence of courts, then there may be societies without law and where lawlessness may prevail or where aspects of law may be rather loosely interpreted and applied to societal situations.

We are, therefore, to be aware of indications and indicators that in tribal societies the system of dispute settlements often defy the standard format available in advanced societies or culture groups. It may once again be reiterated that the analysis of customary laws requires a more flexible approach.

In fact our research has revealed that any analysis of the reasoning of reconciliation mechanisms in involving customary laws involves considering the types of social relations out of which disputes have emerged. We understand here that in tribal societies like that of the Mizos or even in settled and well established ethnic community of that of the Meiteis most transactions take place between closely related persons, usually Kinsmen or in-laws, disputes in such societies are qualitatively different from those societies when persons are linked in a rather indirect or in different ways by contract or through some favour or through matrimonial alliances. The Chief in either case is more of a conciliator than an arbitrator. In fact, we have often found, he is both and acts as such. Sometimes he even acts as a ritual mediator and settles disputes by threatening to curse the disputing parties and there is no suggestion that he listens to and weighs evidence.

Among the Mizos in their society the Chief settles conflicting issues on the basis of customary laws and in terms of a complex process of sanctions, compensation and sacrifices for cleansing and atonement. It is similar to many of the Hindu and Jewish measures wherein the impression that the Chief judges the case and compels the acceptance of his decision to the feuding parties then perhaps it is not factual because when he appears to force the aggrieved party to accept compensation by his insistence even to the point of threatening to curse them, it is an established convention through customary laws that he should do so in order that the bereaved party or relatives may retain their prestige. What seems really to have counted are the acknowledgement of community ties between the parties concerned are hence of the moral obligation to settle the affair/dispute by the acceptance of a traditional payment and the wish on either sides to avoid for the time being at any rate, further hostilities. Normally vengeance in corporate life of a village, among the villagers, is not allowed because general opinion is expressed for an early settlement. Often the feuding parties have frequent social contacts in village gatherings or feasts of merit so, eventually the mechanism of the Chief's intervention has to be employed to prevent their complete social dislocation and open hostility. It was considered wise act to bring about a thaw in a relationship and conclude an active state of feud. Evans-Pritchard has written,

> "... the disputes including the role played in it by the Chief is thus a mechanism by which the political structure maintains itself in the form known to us."

It is in this background that the customary laws of the Meiteis (a conglomerate of clans) and the newly politically formalized group of Kuki fraternity (an ancient group of people with widespread diaspora) under the nomenclature of Mizo or Zomi have been studied by us. The customary laws of these two groups have revealed the existence of closer ties in not so remote past between them which clearly suggest towards a common genesis in a commonly held territory. It appears rather difficult to comprehend these facts which we have looked into and examined thoroughly because of our sectarian biases and the increasing chasm between the groups for reasons of political expediencies and other socio-religious and economic factors but it remains a fact that earlier traits have revealed a vibrant relationship within the folds of cultural similarities and inter-personal relations including interactive language learning processes in the midst of even hostile socio-political conditions.

The 18th and the 19th centuries in the northeast have been one of tumultuous conflicts, raids on each other followed by reconciliations among the several groups of ethnic origin – The Kukis, the Nagas and the Meiteis for obtaining tributes, territorial dominance and cultural superiorities. In many community decisions customary laws took a back seat, politics dominated and genocides were frequent. The interplay of power games become more complex with the British ideas of diplomacy and indulging in petty politics to continue to divide and rule through emphasis on dissimilarities and suppression of truthful facts which had continued since the remote past or when the ethnic communities had come to settle in several parts of this region. On the one hand we observe the fragmentation of the Kuki ethnos, the Nagas, which got formalized by the frequent projections of the group of tribes by the British. The Kukis too were used as buffer tribes. Consequently, the Kukis were seen as a domineering group existing in the region which could act effectively in conflicting situations. As such they became the tribal group to bear the animosity of both the Naga groups and the Meiteis. And this was played upon by the British which ultimately disunited the three major peoples and by the time the three realized what had happened it was already too late and the British had emerged as a major player. The politics in subsequent phases after 1870 became murkier with the active introduction of missionary activities. At almost every level – political, social, religious and economic – the social groups in the North east lost control of their system governance which was endemic based upon customary laws and historical traditions to externally motivated rules of governance and administration. Though this was accepted at superficial level the tribes retained their customary laws despite their conversions to Christianity. Many splintered tribal ethnic communities commenced social movements to identify and retain their identities, individually and collectively. The beginning of the early 20th century witnessed it.

When during the course of our research we applied historical analysis to customary laws conflict and reconciliation often focused on the manner in which situations of conflict revealed the structural alignments and divisions within the groups and in the group itself. It was not surprising therefore, that the differences and inner contradictions which were masked in everyday interactions were generally laid bare in the conflicts that had abounded where persons had been subjected to pressure to define their loyalties. The Kukis had on several occasions revealed their loyalty when they had acted or supported the British and Meiteis alike. It was only during the Anglo-Kuki War, 1917-1919 that they had exhibited their loyalty to their fraternity, as in the past, to take on their conviction to a higher plane of loyalty, remain united, and go all out for ousting the British imperialism from this region. They carried the struggle on the basis of their customary laws and at the end, defeated, demoralized yet bravely faced the aftermath of it in terms of suppression and tortuous treatments meted out to them they survived and grouped against the British once again and supported the INA movement in the hope that freedom would come through the demonstrative use of warfare as a medium of force. The Kukis joined the war to oust the British but they never lost sight of their culture and tradition – customary laws, religious belief systems and traditional administrative set up in their social milieu. In our work we have emphasised upon these aspects – that disputes through the applied customary laws revealed the features of social and cultural organisation and the mechanisms which existed for their settlement likewise indicated points of authority and cohesive power within social and political systems. It is therefore that a critical study of the existing customary laws of the two culture-groups, the Meiteis and the Mizos, helped us to penetrate deeper into the social systems and unravel the true working of mechanisms that really matter at the social-plane. As we progressed in our research we went on understanding and examining the life cycles of conflicts waged within these groups at different levels and realized that the customary laws give us a more comprehensive approach towards understanding social dimensions of varied kinds and the mechanisms of reconciliations. We also realized that the process through which a conflict may pass may be found to be inherent in the type of conflict itself. In fact various mechanisms are found and employed within the same society to heal the breaches of peace and satisfy aggrieved minds. These actions range from the informal arbitration to formal legal machinery to the performance of public rituals.

Those who deal with customary laws believe mystical beliefs and ritual actions rather than judicial machinery, are particularly effective in dealing with disturbances arising from processes inherent in the life cycles of groups. Among both the groups the Meiteis and the Mizos we have observed that traditional groups even today give much attention to their customary laws as they are more familiar with them and as they have an inbuilt desire to avoid cumbersome process of modern law and its arbitration. In fact everybody who takes their case to a village council or to the chief is aware of the facts, knows and understands that he can be affected by the chain of relations and dispute which lie behind it. It is here again that we can say that the principal task of moving towards social harmony and individual composure or the groups' composure is of paramount importance and what disposition of issues is all about.

Dissonance is suppressed or neutralised. Through the customary laws it is the mechanism of decision making, procedures of reconciliation and re-correction that occupy the centre stage of attention rather than techniques of determining what happened. This is where historical understanding steps in where we have to make an objective assessment of subjective local concerns and consensus of unanimity of thoughts. So in customary laws what matters finally is that unanimity of mind is demonstrated in public process by which it has been generated. Here the propriety to be preserved must be seen to be preserved, for legal sensibility draws its sustenance from the culturally given norms and precedents of practices of law which have often an uneasy relationship with the local knowledge which acquire a specific character depending upon the social and cultural formation of that society.

While we understand that the modern law is based upon a detailed categorization of rules, offences, punishments etc the legal sensibility that we talk about is more unfocussed normative order with very broad parameters. In one sense we can understand the instrumentality of legal sensibility as a counter hegemonic strategy used by communities to protect their limited and conditional autonomy, in another sense there exists on over arching sensibility which govern peoples' judgement about reconciliation procedures of modern systems. Hence, legality presumes the emergence of authoritative norms whose status as such is guaranteed by evidence of other consensually validated rules.

In stepping from the prelegal to the legal world a society develops special rules for curing the defects of a social order based on unofficial norms. A plethora of unofficial norms has a number of inherent limitations including the difficulty of resolving uncertainties as to the existence or scope of norms. No criterion or procedure is available for settling such issues. The distinctively legal emerges with the development of secondary rules, that is rules of authoritative determination. These rules, selectively applied, raise up the unofficial norms and give them a legal status. The customary laws thus emerge and give to itself a legal status. Herein we see the place of authority, consensus, and rationality in the legal order. In a developed legal order that of the Meiteis and the Mizos authority transcends coercion, often accepts the restraints of reason, and contributes to a public consensus regarding the foundations of civic obligation. To the extent that Customary Law is the enterprise of subjecting human conduct to the governance of rules it can be said that it aims at a moral achievement – the rule of laws. Its distinctive contribution is a progressive reduction of the arbitrary element in positive law and its administration.

Our research as an intellectual discipline in customary laws or the sociology of law has a far broader compass then the study of the requirements of justice. Not every society gives equal weight to the ideal of control by rule as against other ideals. The customary laws are so intimately associated with the realization of these special values that study of 'the rule or law' among the Meiteis and the Mizos must have become a chief preoccupation of legal sociology. Indeed our research has established this preoccupation beyond any doubt.

II

The Meiteis which comprise of Seven Clans and several sub-clans and the Mizos which constitute of Lushai (Rokhum, Zadeng, Palian, Sailo and Thangluah or Rivung), Thadou, Rangkhol, Zou, Paite, Hmar, Anal, Aimol, Lamgang, Maring, etc., are some important tribal groups in Manipur. A study of these societies on comparative basis has not been undertaken by anyone, thus far. While Meiteis predominantly embrace Hinduism, Mizos have accepted Christianity increasingly. Their historical legacy is deep-rooted, and their social contribution apart from their culture is too significant. There lies their importance.

In explaining social reality of a society, be it a tribal group or an advanced community, relevance of customs and customary laws is of decisive importance. Mizo society, and for that matter any tribal society, has always been characterized by egalitarian values. And so is the Meitei society. The customs and customary laws of the Mizos and the Meiteis are, indeed, embodiment of this phenomenon. They provide convenient mechanisms through which the webs of social relationships can be understood in their deeper meanings and correct perspectives. While customs command a special dignity and relevance, customary laws embody the bonds that hold the multitude together in celebrations or otherwise, in functional rites and rituals at times of birth and or death.

A study of customs and customary laws affords relevance of unusual dimensions of dynamics of change through historical events and crucial concerns that confront elements of sustainability of social assertions expressed in the form of institutional concerns and credibility. A comparative study of customs and its laws seeks to investigate historicity of highly complex problems associated with social changes brought about by agents of modernism and evolve analytical framework for a true appreciation of the extent to which the social institutions contributed towards the continued existence of traditionalism.

In the course of research we have explicitly emphasised upon the importance of the principles of social organizations, highlighting how kinship, marriage and other ritual ties have gone in shaping the structure of the societies of both the Mizos and the Meiteis. The processes of historical growth and cultural dynamics of customs and customary laws to identify the trends of social change and show how far they influenced the traditional life in the face of modernism and onslaught of Christianity are also minutely examined and stressed in the light of the fact that evolution of customary norms and procedures in these societies have taken place in the course of their interaction with streams of moderation in a very dynamic manner which have undergone radical changes without creating corresponding social tensions. It is characteristic of a situation where forces of tradition and modernity confront and conflict with each other. And so it is obvious that in a complex society of today, such as, the Meitei or the Mizo, customary norms and procedures are apt to loose certain amount of sanctity. However, interestingly it was observed that relevance of customary norms and procedures especially in the context of emerging new social orders and codes among the Mizos as well as the Meiteis had many consequences.

It is also amazingly true that structure and function of the Meitei and Mizo societies attach certain inherent prerogatives to the office of Chieftainship. As a matter of fact, such institutionalized traditional offices are considered custodians of customs, perennial source of customary laws having mechanism of interpretations thereof, despite introduction of various legislations to do away with such traditional institutions. Commensurate with the position of eminence enjoyed in their traditional society, concern of the Chiefs for welfare of the masses was particularly noteworthy. Despite this, the winds of change brought about by growth, change, development, etc, importance of customs and customary laws cannot be overlooked and marginalized.

III

The focus of our research work is concentrated on the premises of historical perspectives commencing from the eighteenth century to 1947, tracing the origin, growth, change, development, etc., of customs and customary laws in the two major communities of Manipur in the North East. The methodology of our research is on inter-disciplinary line, adopting 'Observant Participation'. This was supplemented by evaluating facts from original written books, journals, Seminar papers, documentaries, etc., from Libraries of Universities and several research centres. There are some classic writings of historians, sociologists, anthropologists, British administrators, scholars, academicians on various aspects of social life which touch upon similar issues of our research work. In brief, we have not only looked into the primary and secondary sources but have also relied upon oral traditions and subsequent interviews with living personalities in both the communities.

The work is divided into six Chapters, each dealing with different aspects on the subject matter.

The first Chapter, "Historical and Traditional Background of Customary Law", highlights historical times so as to fathom the origin, growth, practices, etc., of customary laws in the backdrop of earlier writings among the English commentators on African and Indian societies. Its functional acceptability in the countries where customary laws confront modern world views and their acceptability as law applicable to gentry and the common folks are dealt with. Its centrality to the Mizo and the Meitei societies are also focused.

The Second Chapter which deals with "Historical and Cultural Background of the Mizos" has become expedient because of the 'Mizo' terminology having been developed in recent times. Its origin, connotation, growth, development, etc., has become relevant to be put in right perspective. In doing so, historicity and cultural background of the people it signifies needs to be highlighted for which it has to be traced as far back as possible and not simply from the 18th Century. This reference to the pre 18th century leads to the paradox of the origin that ultimately leads to the terminology "KUKI". Earlier research works reveal that MIZOs are none other than the Kukis. And, as per their customary laws, rites, rituals, religious beliefs and traditions, the claim of certain sections of Mizos appears to have some strong reason for their group being one of the 'ten lost tribes of Israel' who ultimately claim of being the children of Joseph, which may be termed as "Putative Judaism". A deeper look brings out several dormant inner contradictions which have been also discussed.

The Third Chapter is in regard to "Historical and Traditional Background of Customary Law of Meiteis". It is observed beyond doubt that the foundation of the present day Meitei society was laid down by the coming together of the Seven Clans and several sub-clans which had resulted into the evolution of 'Loyumba Shinyen' as a common treatise on Customary Laws with the formation of Meitei State under the Dynasty of Ningthouja. It is interesting to note the evolution of the 'Loyumba Shinyen' to be converted into a written Constitution despite several certitudinal and incontrovertible criticism.

Chapter Four deals with "Historical Tradition on Social Institutions of the Mizos". As we are aware, in societies, particularly with small tribal societies, social institutions are indispensably intertwined with their daily-life activities, functioning of social mores, customs and customary laws. So social institutions are the core milieu of the society. For this purpose, such various social institutions as are practiced among different Mizo tribal groups are taken into account for correct exposures.

Chapter Fifth concerns with "Chieftainship among the Meiteis and Mizos". It touches upon the basic foundation on which administration of a society, be it advanced or backward, has to lay its strength and sustain existence in the face of inter-tribal hegemony and inter-village rivalry constantly. 'Loyumba Shinyen' was developed as a written constitution for the people inhabiting the Chiefdoms in the valley and its adjoining areas. The Hills were governed separately on the basis of their ethnic laws.

Unlike that of the Meitei society which has rich antique materials and *Puyas* (Manipuri manuscripts in original), the sources from which this work is prepared, the Mizos do not have such primary sources to depend upon. Whatever one could secure as pieces of source materials from the Mizo society, it is only of oral tradition. For this purpose, extensive field study was undertaken to meet aged and knowledgeable persons in the hill areas.

The Sixth Chapter concerns with "Social Structure of Meiteis and Mizos". We know that social structure is the foundation or base central to any study which makes systems analyzed. Inclusion of social structure, interwoven in customary laws is *sine qua non* from our analysis. The Seven Salais of the Meitei Society among which the

Ningthouja Clan ultimately emerged as a royal dynasty of the Meiteis is indicative of the indispensability of existence of social structure, the result of inter-clan rivalry and hegemony. It is also true among the Mizos from where emerged the dominant clan among the Thadou speaking groups and the Sailo clan among the Lushai (Dulian) speaking group based on their customary laws.

IV

In our conclusion we would with certitude specify that despite differences, slightly in details, general similarities on the two, the Mizos and the Meiteis, systems are observed in various social, religious, customs, rites and ritualistic activities and are in existence till date.

It is incumbent to drive home the fact that several of the customary laws with the passage of time became part and parcel of social system. The institutions of Joking Relation, Mother's Brother's Daughter (MBD) marriage, Konglo marriage, purification rite of the bride and the groom before entering their conjugal home, etc., got deep-rooted in the Mizo psyche to the extent that without these rituals and their customary significance no marriage could be genuinely performed. Similarly, the performance of rituals as part of cleansing ceremony of persons who were involved in digging graveyard of the deceased or who had participated in the burial service for the deceased or even in erection of memorial stone over graveyard of the deceased had become part and parcel of the Mizo Customary Laws. To a larger extent barring a few of these ceremonies, the Meitei culture also reveals similar practices. Both the communities are proud of their cultural and traditional antecedents.

Lastly, it must be said here and now that Mizos are part of the Kuki tribal ethnic groups. The people who were originally called Kuki by the Bengalees and borrowed by the British, were subsequently called LUSHAI who are now using the term MIZO in substitution thereof were among the first groups of KUKIs. Now, MIZO terminology has been well received with recognition all over India and the world, having got a State of their own by the name, MIZORAM, meaning thereby the land of Mizos. The term LUSHAI now being synonymously called MIZO has a simili, in that, in much the same manner as ISRAEL was God-given-name to the people of HEBREW origin so is the term MIZO to the people of KUKI origin.

It must also be brought home the fact that the 'Meiteis' and the 'Kukis' have a common origin, sharing the same territory and a having shared perception through give and take attitude of a progressive society, their future is stressed not in isolation, but in togetherness.

In order to understand the genesis of the Meitei and Mizo customary laws and their cultures, some of the sources need to be consulted quite often as these have been deemed as pioneer works – among many others.

Cheitharol Kumbaba by L.M. Ibungohal and N. Khelchandra

Loina Shinlon by O. Bhogeswore Singh

Pancthoibi Khongkul by M. Chandra Singh

History of Manipur: Vol-I : Pre-colonial period by Gangmumei Kabui

The Kukis of Manipur by T.S. Gangte.

The Monograph of Lushai Customs and Ceremonies by N.E. Parry.

The Lakhers by N.E. Parry

Zo History by Vumson

Lushai-Kuki Clans, Part I & II by J. Shakespear

Emergent Women by Bonita Aleaz; and

Status of Women in Mizo Society by N. Chatterjee

which have thrown critical light on several aspects of these two communities. In course of our research we brought into the ambit of our research many more sources which are equally significant (See Bibliography).

1

Historical and Traditional Background of Customary Law

'Customary Law' is the term most commonly used to describe the largely unwritten indigenous laws of the indigenous people especially the tribes recognized by European powers in their colonial territories. The basis of validity for these laws, which are similar to the "custom" of the western legal systems, lies in social practices accepted as obligatory.

Bekker[1] observed that when lawyers write about customary laws, they have professional concern to reduce the typically undifferentiated repertoire of principles, adages, maxims, and folk proverbs of an oral tradition to a systemic code of rules. For this he exemplified court precedents, statutes, ethnographies and colonial commissions of enquiry so as to make use of them in the courts and legal practitioners. Such approach suffers because of defects in the rules which are abstracted from social context, and are frozen in precedents and other formal legal sources, their function is obscured as is their standing in relation to the reality of current social practice.

It must, however, be kept in mind that from an early date, the task of writing about customary law was mainly the task of anthropologists. In doing so, they took care to place law in its social context by developing a separate scholarly tradition. Schapera[2] was one such a distinguished scholar as could be evidenced from his account of the Customary Laws of the various peoples of the Bechuanaland Protectorate (now Botswana) which is considered a model of the gentry. He described Tswana law against a background of Tswana Social and political institutions and the tensions between tradition and the influence of modern world. His work had been commissioned for use in the Colonial courts.

Following closely the approach of Schapera, Holleman[3] while writing sought to avoid pitfalls. As an anthropologist, Holleman, explained the institutions of marriage and succession of a Shona people in Southern Rhodesia (now Zimbabwe) primarily with reference to their system of kinship. The works of both Halleman and Schapera are best considered as representative of a high point in functionalist anthropology despite the fact that law and societies they described have long since succumbed to the forces of capitalism, under-development, urbanization etc. not to mention such post-colonial concerns as national unity and gender equality.

Among the third group of scholars who undertook such studies on Customary Law, Simons[4] may be mentioned. He tried to show as to how social, economic and political policies regulated the status of women in South Africa. In doing so, he placed the law, be it customary, statute or precedent, in the historical framework of South African politics in the then existing social context when colonial authorities were highly conscious of their "Civilizing mission", they sought to suppress bridewealth and polygamy on the ground that these practices degraded the position of women.

Later, when policies of segregation and apartheid came into force, the courts and government revived African culture and with it the tradition of patriarchy.

A leading anthropologist, Gluckman[5] stands in a class on his own and acquired a reputation as "the father of African jurisprudence". His main interest was primarily to reveal the universality of legal concepts, such as ownership, contract, delict, crime, and his argument was based on a study of Lozi in Zambia comparing it with early English and Roman law. Many have criticized Gluckman for imposing English terms and concepts on his materials, but his works are still fruitful sources of ideas about the effect of Social Structure on legal institutions.

Since the second half of eighteenth century, "legal pluralism" had been adopted which contended that law should be seen to be derived from social practice, not state authority. Thus, a valid study of customary law has three versions –

(i) Used by the legal profession;

(ii) Academic variety (found in scholarly texts on the subject); and

(iii) The "living" law (rules actually observed in social practice).

Confining her enquiry into the disputes arising out of women's claims to property in a small village in Botswana and how these claims are pursued through the fora of traditional ruler, the local magistrate's court and the High Court, Griffith[6] analyzed the pluralist manner of state law and the various manifestations of Customary Law.

This work is related to the theory of legal pluralism as about revealing new social practices. She stresses the dynamics of process and exposes the fallacy of certain conceptual destinations, such as, that between living and official laws and that between recognized courts and unofficial fora. Her other concern, a dominant theme in Customary Law today, is about gendered world in which individuals live. She explores the ways in which gender affects women's access to law, how women exploit rules (and contradictions between rules), and how they shop for sympathetic fora.

Bennett[7] in his work on 'Sourcebook' concedes the tenets of legal pluralism that aims at the law student and practitioner rather than the social scientist. He collected all the major legal and anthropological sources of Customary Law in South Africa and provides extensive commentaries upon them. Topics include the various tribunals applying Customary Law, choice of law rules governing application of customary and common law, marriage, divorce, the status of women and children, and succession. A sub-text on the current debates about legal and cultural theory, comparative family law reform, and human rights runs through each topic.

In another work aimed at lawyers, Bennett[8] addressed the growing interest in contradictions between systems of Customary Law and human rights in his book on Human Rights and African Customary Law under the South African constitution. While dwelling on problems of conflict and reconciliation in terms of South Africa's Bill of Rights, it has wider relevance to all constitutional and international instruments, guaranteeing fundamental rights. Important preliminary questions are the right to pursue a culture of choice, suggesting that the State is obliged to recognize systems of customary law, whether culture may limit individual rights, how local culture may influence the interpretation of bills of rights, and whether such rights are applicable in personal relationships as opposed to relations between the citizen and State. Therefore, specific issues are considered, notably, the patriarchal tradition of Customary Law versus the principle of equal treatment and the inherited authority of traditional rulers versus the principle of democratic accountability.

The work of Albott & Woodman[9] in additing 'People's Law and State Law', "The Bellagio Paper", deals with the general theory of legal pluralism with its application to desperate committees, ranging from Peru to Zambia to the U.S. Two introductory chapters define "folk" (or living) law, its regulation of Semi-autonomous social fields and its relationship with official systems of law. Leading writers in the field consider matters such as the interplay between official and folk procedures, the implications of applying a common-law doctrine of *Stare decisis*, and the tensions between secular and Islamic law.

Customs and Customary Laws are not synonymous. There may be various customs without any legal authority whereas the customary laws have the sanction of the bulk of the society and if not obeyed, such violator is liable to be punished.

Custom, like law, in its widest connotation, is a body of rules which regulates the conduct of human beings vis-à-vis each other and vis-à-vis the individual and the society as well.[10]

It is now well recognised that in all early societies, custom has been not merely the main, but the only, vehicle of legal development. Indeed, custom is coeval with the very birth of community itself. The moment man started leading some organized life, whether in small nomadic groups or in small settled or semi-settled ways, the stage was set for the evolution of customs. Today, this merits reiteration for understanding of the origin and growth of customs. As human beings engaged themselves in multifarious activities, there emerged certain uniform patterns of human behaviour. These patterns are perpetuated either on account of belief in their propriety or on account of sheer necessity of living together. As men gained experience in group life, they learnt that a particular mode or behaviour or conduct was conducive to collective living. While others were not so relevant in useful hence these needed to be rejected or dropped so that they went into disuse and ultimately get eliminated. Universal recognition made modes of human behaviour well established and accepted. Simultaneously, as new individual and complex social needs arose, new patterns of human behaviour emerged. This dialectics gave endless impetus to the behaviour patterns, probably, this process continued in all human societies till they evolved a conscious law making machinery. It is dialectics of human dynamism which needs to be tempered in a society on the move which brings about deserved social acceptance of norms and the dynamics of social changes that legal codes bring about social changes rather fast was understood than belatedly. But subsequently the need for codifying the Customary Laws was strongly felt and many societies formulated the codified laws. Manu's Dharmasastra illustrates codification of laws or for that matter the cultic codification of laws all reveal the need for a social change and social regulations through laws.

Paton,[11] an eminent jurist, in his attempt to define, origin, nature, growth of customary law has said that 'custom in any early society was not only the main but also the only vehicle of legal development'. When man first started to live together constituting a society among themselves, they adjusted among themselves of their different individuals nature so that they might live in harmony. This was the beginning of creating social behaviour with various activities conducive to their diverse nature. Such nature, which has the greatest possibility of acceptability by most of them gradually, became accepted law, which duly became customary laws on account of being practised repeatedly within and without that particular society or social group. In this connection, it may be of relevance to note that Maine[12] in his celebrated work, Ancient Law, propounded the theory that in the evolution, first were Themistes, the judgements of inspired Kings, then was the custom which was according to him, created by judgment and finally were the codes. But it is now well established that custom was exterior to Themistes. Now, there is not much scope to doubt that the first stage of evolution of law was custom.

It is critically appreciated that the group habits collectively lead human beings to get accustomed to doing certain things in a certain regulated manner. The adherence of the group or of the individuals to these modes of behaviours, gives rise to customary laws.

Llewellyn and Hoebel[13] have contended that the people concerned accepted or approved them as model behaviour saying that it is of greater interest to the jurists since it raised the question of how factual occurrences developed into prescriptive models of behaviour of the group commensality that have a degree of sanctions behind them. These prescriptive models of behaviour or settled patterns of human behaviour are given the name of custom which cover practically all the aspects of individual's life.

Customary Laws command obedience since disregard of them will involve some kind of penalty whether imposed in the realm of conscience or by the collective will of the group or the community. In early societies these customary rules were enforced by social reprobation. But all customs do not have the force of law.

Modern anthropological research in customs has constantly showed that, in fact, it is the enduring character and the binding force on custom, which have challenged the very foundations of the analytical system of jurisprudence. One of the most outstanding features of customs is its essentially non-litigious origin. They arise not from any conflicts of rights adjusted by a supreme court, not from any claim of *meum* and *tuum* but from any practices prompted by the convenience of society and of the individual, so far as they are prompted by any conscious purpose at all.

Concept of Law vis-à-vis Custom:

Of all scholastic searches in regard to various concepts of social and other sciences, search for appropriate definition of 'Law' and its concept is still the highest. Yet, no definite and satisfactory concept and definition of 'Law' could be arrived at so far. Sophisticated scholars such as Cohen and Hart[14] in their attempt to define the concept of law have been driven either to write treatises on the art and pitfalls of definition. Similarly, Stone[15] defined it as to give the reader a set of mnemonics to remind him what has been talked about. This was followed by Kant[16] saying that lawyers were still seeking a definition of their concept of law. But after a century and a half later, Stone[17] stated that 'law' is necessarily an abstract term, and the definer is free to choose a level of abstraction; but by the same token, the choice must be such as to make and be significant in terms of the experience and present interest of those who are addressed.

In the effort to define 'law', some modern scholars like Hart[18] conclude that there are three 'basic issues'. They are – (1) How is law related to the maintenance of social order? (2) What is the relation between legal obligation and moral obligation? (3) What are rules and to what extent is law an affair of rules? As against it, some others such as Stone[19] said that law is (1) a complex whole, (2) which always includes social norms that regulate human behaviour. These norms are (3) social in character, and they form (4) a complex whole that is 'orderly'. The order is (5) characteristically coercive and (6) institutional Law has (7) a degree of effectiveness sufficient to maintain itself.

In view of the above, there are two aspects of legal institutions that are not shared with other institutions of society. First, legal institutions alone must have some regulated way to interfere in malfunctioning, and perhaps, the functioning as well, of the non-legal institutions in order to disengage the trouble case. Secondly, there must be two kinds of rules in the legal institutions, those which govern the activities of legal institution itself called 'adjectival law' by Austin and 'procedure' by most modern lawyers and those which are substitutes for, or modifications or restatements of, the rules of the non-legal institution that has been invaded, called 'substantive law'. These are the only minimal aspects that are shared by all known legal institutions. In the backdrop of this, the distinction between law and custom is fairly simple in that – (i) customs are rules more or less strict and with greater or less support of moral, ethical, or even physical coercion about the way in which people must behave if social institutions are to perform their tasks and society is to endure. All institutions including legal institutions develop customs. Some customs in some societies are reinstitutionalized at another level. They are restated for the more precise purposes of legal institutions. When this happens, therefore, law may be regarded as a custom that has been restated in order to make it amenable to the activities of the legal institutions. In this sense one of the most characteristic attributes of legal institutions is that some of these 'law' are about the legal institutions themselves, although most are about the other institutions of society, such as the familial, economic, political and ritual.

Malinowski[20] has influenced lawyers widely with a faculty mode of distinguishing law from non-law through his work on "Crime and Custom in Savage Society, 1926". He claimed that law is "a body of binding obligations regarded as right by the other, kept in force by the specific mechanism of reciprocity and publicity and publicity inherent in the structure of ... society". His error was in equating what he had defined with the law. It is not law that is "kept in force by ... reciprocity and publicity" (1926: 1961, p. 58). It is custom as is defined here. Law is better thought of as "a body of binding obligations regarded as right by one party and acknowledged as the duty by the other" which has been re-institutionalized within the legal institution so that society can continue to function in an orderly manner on the basis of rules as maintained. In short reciprocity is the basis of custom; but the law rests on the basis of this double institutionalization.

Anthropological Meaning

"Custom" refers to the totality of socially acquired behaviour patterns, which are supported by tradition and generally exhibited by members of society. For indicating this sense, the more current expressions are 'culture' and 'tradition', one area of anthropology in which expression 'custom' still has currency is the comparative analysis of legal and political systems in which it is distinguished from law. Custom is supported only by psychological constraint, when the individual violates the customs. In contrast, laws have the additional coercive support of specific individuals or groups who have an institutionally vested charge to enforce conformity.[21]

Thc concepts of custom and tribe seem to go together. 'Tribe' is a group of families who have a feeling of community through occupying a territory and following similar customs. 'Tribe' and 'tribal' are convenient terms for indicating that a people still follow custom, rather than law.[22]

If we go through anthropological literatures we find more than 150 definitions of tribes, some contradicting each other and others tallying one in one way or the other. The most acceptable and standardized definition may be the definition[23] that tribe as small in scale restricted to the spatial and temporal range of their social, legal and political relations, and possessing morality, religion and world view of corresponding dimensions. They execute a remarkable economy of design and have compactness and self-sufficiency. They have unity and coherence of their own values that are ultimately related to social institutions. They are extremely ethnocentric.

The main criteria for definition of 'custom' and 'tribe', therefore, are homogeneity, self-sufficiency, cultural and customarily rigidity and ethnocentricity. It is interesting to note in this regard that the Government of India while categorizing different types for the purpose of Scheduled listing tribes in India did not conform to the criteria mentioned above as are being standardized for definition of 'tribe'. This has resulted in many instances of discrepancies in categorizing tribes. Bhowmick[24] observed that criteria relied upon by the Government in determining whether a group is a tribe and those used by the academicians do not tally with each other. Thus, disharmonious categorisation is found to prevail with regard to the definition of a tribe. The same group of people may be considered as Scheduled tribe in one state and is not considered to be so in a different state. Instances are many. We may give one example: The Bhumijas of West Bengal are not considered as Scheduled Tribe, whereas the Bhumijas in the adjoining areas in Bihar are regarded as Scheduled Tribe. Bhowmick[25], therefore, attributed categorization of tribes by the Government of India as having been done without 'valid scientific definition' applicable to a tribe.

This has certainly resulted in the differentiation of choice for adopting common nomenclature particularly among those who are protagonists for retention of the traditional generic term called Kuki* on the one hand and antagonist of the same on the other. This differentiation is strongly apparent between the dominant tribes and the minor tribes. Among the dominant tribes are the Thadous and their cognates who speak the Thadou-Kuki language as against the minor tribal groups such as the Anals, Marings, Moyons, Monshangs, Chirus, Chothes, etc., who were at one time categorized as belonging to the 'Old Kuki' tribes. It still went further that some of the said minor tribes had taken extreme steps not only abandoning their nomenclature called 'Kuki' but switched over to Naga tribe with the intention to take political shelter under the

* Ref. 1777 A.D. in the Tiperah (Tripara) territory wherein Hill people fought with the British.

dominant group[26] and emergence of new nomenclature such as Zomi or Chin or Mizo or Khul or Khur as counter productive of posture of traditional dominant groups and politicization[27] of minor tribal society by the proletariat groups.

A report of the International Labour Organisation on dispute settlement in African countries points out that the success of the institutions set up under the modern law in those countries is largely due to their kinship with their customary institutions and to the scope which was allowed for the traditional institution known as "Palver"[28] The same phenomenon is, in substance, witnessed in other countries as well, whenever the question of super-imposing 'modern' institution upon the traditional structure has had to be dealt with.[29]

Salient Features of Customary Laws of the Mizos

On juristic analysis, certain customary law will be found to reveal at least the following features that have considerable theoretical importance:

(I) In the first place, customary law is the law of a group, while the law elsewhere has an individual oriented basis. This does not, of course, mean that tribal is exclusively by group feeling or by a groupist philosophy – a caveat which several anthropologists have also entered. What is meant is that group life and communal living and a sense of belonging to a social unit are much more predominant in tribal life than law in non-tribal social institutions.[30]

(II) Secondly, customary law is deeply rooted in history and pays homage to the past. Like all other laws, customary law also changes but the change is gradual and imperceptible and it is not accompanied by the jolts that are usually experienced when by statute a rule is changed substantially or by judicial decision a proposition is laid down in terms different from the position that had been understood on a particular point in the past.[31]

(III) Thirdly, tribal customary law is the special law applicable to a place where closely knit communities live together. This proposition emphasises not merely the identity of the group, its individuality, linkage with the past, attachment thereof, and integral association with a place. In fact, this aspect has been well recognised in the statutory provisions in India dealing with the law to be applied by tribal courts.[32]

(IV) Continuity is as essential a characteristic of custom as its antiquity.[33] May be it is established that a custom has an antiquity of 400 years or more. But if it has not been followed since then, this fact may be a sufficient indication that it has ceased to exist. Continuity of existence without interruption refers not to its active exercise but rather to the claim to enjoy it.

(V) Custom must not be unreasonable, immoral and contrary to public policy and law. Interpretation of custom should have doctrine of justice, equity and good conscience without which it cannot be enforced because, it is bad on the test of morality, reasonableness and public policy. An instance in this regard may be recalled when the Punjab Laws Act, 1872 was enacted which clearly stipulated that custom must not be contrary to law.

(VI) A valid custom has to be observed continuously. Abandonment of custom by the people is abrogated or repealed.[34] In the words of Brown, "As the will of

> the community establishes custom in the first instance, so the same community may, by the expression of its collective will as evidenced by not being in usage abrogate it"[35]

To sum up, the salient features of customary law enumerated above, it is not suggested that everything in customary law is dominated by 'Group'; philosophy. As has been pointed out by Malinowski,[36] the assumption that the primitive individual is completely dominated by 'group', i.e., the thinking and opinion of the group is wrong.

Custom as Neither of Logical Deduction, Analogy Nor Theory

Custom is a fact, which must be proved by authoritative pronouncements or by instances in which it has been followed, or by some other evidence. It cannot be established dialectics.[37] It cannot be established or extended by logical deduction or analogy. Custom should not be enlarged beyond the usage because it is usage and practice that make the law in such cases and not the reason, though reasonable custom is void. No reason, even the highest whatsoever, would make a custom or law, and therefore, custom cannot be enlarged by any parity or reasoning since reason has no part in the making of the same.[38] While enforcing custom or while reconsidering the question whether a custom has been proved, the court should not draw any analogy or quest what the custom is or should be; it should go by evidence and see what the custom really is and whether it has been proved. Custom must be proved by evidence and courts are not permitted to deduce the existence of one custom from another. It is not the function of the judge to customize what custom should be; its duty is to see whether, as alleged custom has been established by evidence, failing which his observation may be otherwise.

Similarly, while considering the question whether a custom has been proved or not, the court should take cognizance of actual facts instead of being swayed by theories. Custom can never be a matter of mere theory but must always be a matter of fact and like any other matter of fact must be established by cogent evidence.

Proof of Custom

Rattigan's Digest lays down that a custom may be proved by anyone of the following modes.[39]

(I) By the opinion of persons likely to know of its existence, or having special means of knowledge thereon.[40]

(II) By statement of persons who are dead, or whose attendance cannot be procured without unreasonable delay or expense, provided they were made before any controversy as to such custom arose and were made by persons who would have been likely to be aware of the existence of such custom if it existed.[41]

(III) By any transaction by which the custom in question was claimed, modified, recognized, asserted or denied, or which was inconsistent with its existence.[42]

(IV) By village oral traditions;

(V) Written memorials, such as the Chatlam Lutin.

(VI) By judicial decisions, and

(VII) By authoritative manuals of customary law.

Importance of Customary Law and Pre and Post Independence Studies

The administration of justice in Nagaland, Meghalaya, Manipur, Tripura, Mizoram and Arunachal Pradesh prior to the introduction of British administration was carried on according to local customs and laws as ordinated by the kings or chiefs of different areas.[43] During the early part of British administration in the Brahmaputra Valley, the ordinary criminal and civil duties were performed by councils of the local gentry, designated Panchayats, of which were some half a dozen. More heinous cases were tried, with the assistance of a Panchayat, by the Commissioner's Assistants, who also disposed off appeals from the panchayats, and from whose decisions both appellate and original a further appeal lay to the Commissioner himself.[44] Gradually, the British system of law and administration of justice was introduced in the Brahmaputra Valley and in the districts of Cachar and Sylhet which were also part of Assam prior to partition of India in 1947.

The administration of other areas, such as, Nagaland, Meghalaya, Manipur, Tripura, Mizoram and Arunachal Pradesh was carried on by the Rules of Administration of Justice and Police passed by the British Government.[45] After Independence also the administration of justice was carried on in these areas substantially on the same line and on the basis of same interpretation, which had been carried out in the past.

The legal position of the districts of Goalpara, Kamrup, Darrang and Nowgong was defined by Act 2 of 1835 which placed all functionaries employed in them under the control and superintendence of the Sadar Court in civil and criminal cases, and of the Bengal Board of Revenue in revenue matters.[46] When the semi-independent tracts in Upper Assam were resumed a few years later, the provisions of this Act were extended to them also.[47]

As regards judicial administration, in 1880 a Judicial Commissioner was appointed for Assam.[48] In 1903, the post of Judge-Commissioner was split up and a separate officer was appointed as Judge. Thus, there was a whole time Judge.[49]

In the post-Independence context, it may be pointed out that in pursuance of the Constitutional commitment of the Government to ameliorate the condition of the tribal communities, attempts had been made to study their culture and ways of life. A number of Tribal Research Institutes were set up. The Anthropological Survey of India and the Census Organisation of the Government of India contributed a lot to tribal research by publishing a number of valuable papers and articles on the tribal cultures of different parts in India.

However, legal studies relating to the tribal areas, dealing at length with their customary laws, are scarce. The sanctity of customs among the tribal people is very great. This is particularly so in the case of those customs that have a bearing on their family life and kinship – such as inheritance, marriage, divorce, maintenance, adoption and guardianship.

To be ignorant about the laws and customs of own people is not a happy situation from any point of view. If we lack knowledge about them, we cannot understand the people of these areas. Such a situation not only acts as a hindrance in creating a sense of oneness and integration, but also hampers the understanding the problems by the administrators and needs of the people. They are paid to take suitable action to deal with such problems and to meet those needs. Further, such a study may also help us in understanding the laws, and customs better in the rest of the country and even in adopting correctives wherever needed.

There is yet another aspect – juristic one. There is a crisis challenging the law as a defensive mechanism and as a protection against undesirable activities. An anthropological understanding of the working of laws in the special areas with which this study is concerned might help in understanding the problems and evolving solutions in a much wider area.[50] Thus, the cause of advancing the science of jurisprudence may itself be promoted by a study of the tribal laws, even though the geographical range of the study may be a narrow one.

In the past the numerous tribal groups living in Manipur had been placed under the administration of their respective customary laws. These were gradually replaced partially by ordinances for better effective administration. At the threshold of Indian Independence, the Manipur State Hill People (Administrations) Regulation was enacted in 1947. However, we understand that the customary laws were not totally abandoned, but the same were retained to deal with various tribal social and political problems the lowest law enforcing agencies at the Village level. This was subsequently improved by another Act called the Manipur (Village Authorities in the Hill Areas) Act, 1956. [51]

This Act created strongly a sense of opposition, generated a great amount of discontentment, apprehensions of Government's intention to do away with the rights of chiefs over the land and vehemently resented application or extension of the Act in the hill areas. Protests of all kinds were launched by the public and within the then Territorial Council of the State, by the Kuki members of the Manipur Territorial Council that resulted at times in the instability of Government due to change of sides (defection) to topple the political party that held the reign of Government.

Thus, with insecurity looming large over their heads like 'Democles Sword', the Kuki National Assembly[52] decided to take a political decision to demand a Kuki State[53] in 1960 by submitting a Memorandum addressed to the first Prime Minister of India, Pandit Jawaharlal Nehru, on the 24th March, 1960.

Though these are the immediate resultant consequences of the Act enacted relating to the administration of the Hill areas, the main provisions of the said Act are highlighted below that gradually eroded the authority of the customary laws among the hill tribes of Manipur including the Mizos, in particular.

Manipur State Hill Peoples (Administration) Regulation, 1947

In Manipur, the Manipur State Hill People (Administration) Regulation was enacted in 1947, containing provisions for administration of justice in the hill areas. It provided that the criminal and civil justice should be administered by the court of a village authority, the Court of the Circle Authority, the Hill Bench at Imphal and the Chief of Manipur State.

The Court of a Village Authority was empowered to try any criminal case, involving the offence of theft, mischief, cattle lifting, simple hurt, assault, using criminal force or illegal slaughter of cattle.

In civil matter the Village Authority could try any suit of values below Rs. 501/-

The Circle Court could exercise the powers of a magistrate of the first class.

The Hill Bench at Imphal exercised the powers of the

Session Court. It was composed of a judge of the Chief Court as Chairman with two hillmen as judges.*

Except the Village Authority the other Court had appellate powers.

The provisions about powers, procedure etc, under 1947 Regulation were more or less the same as those in 1937 and the series of Rules for the Hill-Districts of Assam.

The Manipur (Village Authorities in Hill Areas) Act, 1955

In 1956, the Manipur (Village Authorities in Hill areas) Act, 1956 was passed, modifying the provisions of the 1947 Regulation, so far as the Village Authority was concerned.

It was represented to the Sub-Group that the Village Authorities set up under this 1956 Act had failed to command the same respect as the earlier traditional village authorities. So this was further amended and the same was called, "The Manipur Hill Areas (Acquisition of Chiefs Rights) Act 1967". This gave rise to increasing speculation that the Government of Manipur was bent on evicting the Kukis from their land. Enhanced, it justified the inevitability of representation submitted to the former Prime Minister of India in 1960 demanding "Kuki State".[54] The effort of the Government to belittle the customary laws was clear and it can be seen in subsequent years. The amended Act in 1967 made more stringent provisions to make it 'a more firmly empowered act'. However, it weakened the rights of the Chiefs hitting directly on the customary laws as amended in 1983.

* Mr. Thangkhopao Kipgen and Mr. Kathipri Mao were the Judges who were subsequently nominated to the Indian Administrative Service and ultimately retired as Chief Secretaries of Goa and Nagaland respectively.

Coupled with this, introduction of the District Councils Act, 1971 have failed to meet the needs of the tribal people. Added to all these the All Manipur Students' Union pressurized the Government of Manipur by submitting a memorandum[55] and urging them to extend the ML&LR Act, 1960 in the hill areas of Manipur. Under the circumstances the Mizos in particular and for that matter the Kukis in general felt very insecure and their mindset was restless with absolute hopelessness of their future political destiny. And so, a gradual but radical approach to solve social disputes etc evolved in which not economic matters but customary laws could be marginalized. We will see this in subsequent chapters.

REFERENCES

1. Bekker, J.C., Seymour's Customary Law in Southern Africa, 5th Edition, Cape Town, Juta, 1989.
2. Schapera, I.: *A Handbook of Tswana Law and Custom,* 2nd Edition, London and New York, Oxford University Press, 1955.
3. Halleman, J.F: Shona *Customary Law with reference to Kinship marriage, the family and the Estate, Cape Town and New York, Oxford University Press, 1952.*
4. Simon, H.J.: *African Women: Their Legal Status in South Africa, London; Hurst, and Evanston, Illinois: North-Western University Press, 1968.*
5. Gluckman, Max: *The Ideas in Borotse Juresprudence, New Haven, Connecticutt: Yale University Press, 1965.*
6. Griffiths, Anne M.O.: *In the Shadow of Marriage: Gender and Justice in an African Community, Chicago University of Chicago Press, 1997.*
7. Bennet, T.W.: *A Sourcebook of African Customary Law for Southern Africa, Cape Town, Juta: 1991.*
8. Bennett, T.W.: *Op. cit.*
9. Allott, Antony N. and Gordon R Woodman (editors): *People's Law and State Law: The Bellagio Papers, Dordrecht: Foris, 1985.*

10. Paras Diwan: *Customary OLaw of Punjab and Haryana Publication Bureau, Punjab University, 1978; p.*
11. Paton: *Jurisprudence (4th Edition); p. 191.*
12. Henry Sumner Maine: *Ancient Law, 1907;* Chapter 1, London (John, Murray: 1897, 1st edition).
13. K.N. Llewellyn and E.A. Hoebel: *"The Cheyenne Way"*, Chapter X, 1941, Norman (Okla).
14. Cohen, Jonathan and Hart, H.L.A., 1955: *Symposium: Theory and definition in Jurisprudence,* pp. 213-264 in Aristotelian Society, proceedings, supplementary Vol. 29: Problems in Psycho-theory and Jurisprudence, London: Harrison.
15. Stone, Julius: *1964: Legal system and Lawyer's reasonings,* Stanford University Press.
16. Kantorowicz, Hermann: *Definition of Law: Edited by A.H. Campbell,* Cambridge University Press (Published posthumously: 1958)
17. *Stone Julius:* 1964: Op. Cit., p. 177.
18. Hart, H. L.A.: 1954: *Definition and Theory in Jurisprudence:* Law quarterly Review: 70: pp. 37-90.
19. Stone: Julius: 1966: *Social Dimensions of Law and Justice;* Stanford University Press.
20. Malinawski Bronislaw: 1926: *Crime and Custom in Savage Society: London: Routledge* – A paper back edition was published in 1959 by Littlefield.
21. Stanley Wilkin: *"Custom" in Encyclopaedia of Anthropology:* 1976, p. 113.
22. Elizabeth E. Bacon, *"Tribe" in 27 Encyclopaedia Americana:* 1969, p. 98.
23. Lewis: *International Encyclopaedia of Social Services,* Vol. XVI, pp. 146-150.
24. P.K. Bhowmick: *Some Aspects of Applied Anthropology:* 1980; p. 28.
25. *Ibid.,* p. 2.
26. Gangmumei Kabui: *The Anals: A Transborder Tribe of Manipur:* 1985; p. 50.
27. Andre Bettelle: *"Castes; Old and New,* 1969, p. 139.
28. I.L.O., *"The Evolution of Labour disputes settlement procedures in certain African countries" in 91(2), International Labour*

Review, 1965, p. 102, 103, 119. Palver means a free wide-ranging discussion between the interested parties, witnesses, elders and the general public, leading not so much to judgement as to freely accepted settlement.

29. L. Nader (ed), *Law in Culture and society,* 1972.
30. Kusum and P.M. Bakshi: *Customary Law and Justicein the Tribal Areas of Meghalaya under the auspices of The Indian Law Institute,* New Delhi: 1982; p. 63.
31. *Ibid.*
32. *Ibid.*
33. Paras Diwan: *Op. Cit., p. 16.*
34. *Ratiram V Shararam, 1938, PLR 900.*
35. *USAGES, 122.*
36. Malinowsky: *"Forces of Law and order in a Primitive Community" in C.K. Meek, Law and Authority in a Nigerian Tribe, XIII, 1950, footnote: 3.*

2

Historical and Cultural Background of the Mizos

For study on any aspect of Mizo society, it is imperative that its historical and cultural background need be understood in its right perspective. For this purpose it is all the more imperative to know that the appellation. 'Mizo' is comparatively a new phenomenon that should be understood in that in as much the same manner as 'Israel' signifies the people of 'Hebrew' origin, so, is the word 'Mizo' for the people of 'Kuki Origin'. Therefore, historical and cultural background of the 'Kukis' need to be well established first in order to study 'Mizo' society profitably as reflected through their customary laws.

The study of History and Culture together of any society is of rare combination, more so, in the case of Mizos whose history, in the real sense of the term and with due regard to the people directly concerned, is no history but anecdotes of population movements for generations together except that one group or the other of the Mizo tribes are engaged in sporadic encounters with enemies of their allies or supporters of one authority or principality. There had not been an instance of an independent Mizo authority engaged in a warfare with its independent counterpart either to defend his political territorial integrity or to wage war against any neighbouring authority in the entire length of their *en masse* population movements except that there were incidents wherein there were isolated raids and skirmishes with the subjects or armies of some independent authorities, over whom they either won or lost in such encounters that resulted in no question of annexation or subjugation of enemy's territories or possessions thereon.

This is mainly so due to absence of a Central Authority under whom several Mizo tribal groups subordinated themselves as constituent segments in an organized hierarchical order. Notwithstanding, British anthropologists, colonial bureaucrats, army Officers, in their various writings at different period of times collectively called them KUKI who were found to have occupied certain areas in Tripura, North Cachar Hills District, Lushai Hills District, Naga Hills District, Manipur, etc., in India and in Arakan and Chittagong Hill Tracts of Bangladesh. Similarly, same groups of Kuki tribes are given the name CHIN when they are in Burma. They did so exclusively in view of their homogeneity in regard to their culture, customs and customary laws, tradition, rites, rituals, beliefs, linguistic affinity, uniformity in their system of administration, method of cultivation, etc. However, after Lushai Expedition in the Lushai Hills District in 1872-73, use of the term KUKI was superseded by LUSHAI, the dominant clan which took prominent role against the British during the Expedition.

Thus Shakespear[1] in his work on LUSHAI KUKI CLANS divided the entire Kuki tribes into six groups as detailed hereinbelow:

1. In the first group he put the Lushei Clans, based

from Thangura the pedigree of all the living Chiefs who were accurately established to have been included under six lines of Chiefs. They are –

(i) Rokhum, (ii) Zadeng, (iii) Thangluah, (iv) Pallian, (v) Rivung and (vi) Sailo.

2. In the second group are included the Clans[2] that are included under the term Lúshai though not Lusheis, having been absorbed. They are -

(i) Chawte (Chothe in Manipur), (ii) Chongthu, (iii) Hnamte, (iv) Kawlni, (v) Kawhring, (vi) Khiangte, (vii) Ngente, (viii) Rentlei, (ix) Roite, (x) Vangchhia and (xi) Zawngte.

3. In the third group are included Clans[3] which, though not absorbed, have been much influenced by the Lusheis. They are –

(i) Fanai, (ii) Ralte, (iii) Paihte or Vuite, (iv) Rangte (Gangte in Manipur).

4. In the fourth group are included the Old Kuki Clans.[4] They are –

(i) Aimol, (ii) Anal, (iii) Chawte, (iv) Chiru, (v) Kolhen, (vi) Kom, (vii) Lamgang, (viii) Purum, (ix) Tikhup (Mantak), (x) Vaiphei, (xi) Rhangkol, (xii) Khelma, (xiii) Biate and (xiv) Hrangchal (Hallam).

5. In the fifth group are included the Thadou Clans[5] among whom were –

(i) Doungel, (ii) Sitlhou, (iii) Singson, (iv) Kipgen, (v) Haokip, (vi) Chongloi, (vii) Hangshing and some non-Thadou groups who have been absorbed among the above mentioned Thadous having for all practical purposes embraced all customs, culture, language, religious beliefs, rites, rituals, etc. Yet, they are the only groups who do not claim to be the descendants of Chongthu with a tradition of Khul or Khur origin, instead, posing as from 'Celestial origin'. They are – (i) Lianthang and his brother Thlangum (Lhangum), and (ii) Lunkim and his brother, (iii) Changsan who also claimed to have survived the 'Thimzin' trauma.

6. In the sixth group are included only the Lakhers[6] or Mara. They are closely allied to the Southern Chins. They call themselves Mara, Lakher being the name used by the Lushais. The Chins call them Zo, and the Arakan name for them is Klongshai.

The languages of all the above clans are very similar[7]. As per classification of Grierson, these languages are termed "KUKI-CHIN", YET ADDED THAT "Meitei-Chin would be a better appellation, as the whole group can be sub-divided into two sub-groups, the Meitheis (Manipuris) and the various tribes which are known under the name of Kuki-Chin".. are considered as belonging to the Burmese branch of the Tibeto-Burman family which he sub-divided as follows:

(i) Meithei or Manipuri.

(ii) Chin Languages:

1. Northern Group: Thado, Sokte, Siyin, Ralte and Paite or Vuite;
2. Central group: Tashon, Lai, Lakher, Lushai, Banjogi and Pankhu;
3. Old Kuki group: Rhangkhol, Bete (Biate), Hallam, Langrong, Aimol, Anal, Chiru, Lamgang, Kolren

(Kolhen), Kom, Purum, Mhar (Hmar or Khawtlang) and Cha;

4. Southern group: Chinme, Welaung, Chinbok, Yindu, Chinbon, Khyang or Sho, Khami.

Under the situation thus obtained, it should be understood that the term KUKI would denote the clans mentioned above collectively. All the same, it must also be noted that while KUKI as a common nomenclature has rapidly declined, abandoned and disused by a good number of them, MIZO as a new phenomenon has become increasingly dynamic in popularity and accepted as a National identity in the backdrop of contemporary political situation as it exists today. Therefore, while the nomenclature 'Mizo' would be mainly and prominently used in this research work as its sole terminology for the purpose, the appellation 'Kuki' would as well be used intermittently as per relevance of the context to mean equivalent expression of MIZO.

BACKGROUND

The hardship one may encounter in the study of history of the Mizos is absence of historical evidences. Whatever sources that could be counted as historical, belong to the post-colonial period left by the colonial rulers of the pre-independence days. Thus lack of conventional data is the greatest hindrance to tracing the early history of the Mizos in a precise manner. Secondly, heterogeneity of the Mizo society as is briefly narrated above is another limitation. Therefore, usual division of historical periods into ancient, medieval and modern is not possible, overlapping in tracing history an inevitability under such a situation. Despite this, attempts are being made to construct history of the Mizos. In doing so, sources of history may, however, be classified Oral, Inscription, Literature and Archival for the purpose of our research work.

1. Oral Sources

Romila Thapar[8] contended that sources of history are necessarily divided into historical and traditional so as to make history well founded and authentic. But in the case of history of the Mizos this may not wholly be possible. Mainly the Mizos did not have their own scripts to reduce their languages in written form earlier than later part of the 19th century so as to use the conventionally recorded indigenous sources of their history. The only feasible means, therefore, is the traditional non-conventional sources, such as, folklores, folksongs, beliefs, superstitions, ceremonies, hymns, rites, rituals, etc., which are, as Bhattacharjee[9] contended, always important for the people as they reflect on the needs and aspirations of the common people at various points of time. Under the situation, oral traditions are the only and indispensable sources for which our research work in this regard will be placed to the minimum possible limit

(a) Khul or Khur or Chhinlung or Sinlung Tradition

Traditionally, all Mizo tribes claimed that they came out of a very big cave called 'Chhinlung' by the Dulian (Mizo) speaking tribes. 'Sinlung' by the Hmars, 'Khur' by the old Kuki tribes, such as, Aimol, Anal, Chothe, Chiru, Maring, Lamgang, Kom, etc., and 'Khul' by the Vaiphei, Paite, Gangte, Simte, Zo, Thadou and cognate groups of New Kukis[10] etc., with the exception of Changsan, Lhangum, Thangeo, Lunkim, etc., who claimed that they were of "Celestial Origin". By this, we know that the Mizo tribes in general are the people of "Cave Origin". This tradition is supported by folksongs and legends that were handed down from generations together. One such folksong as rendered in English version runs as follows (only one stanza):

> My mother land, famous Khul,
> Home of my own ancestors,
> Could it be called back like Chongzil,
> Home of my own ancestor.

(b) Khampat Tradition

Khampat is located at its traditional or original location close to the Manipur border, and was the oldest town ever built by the Mizos. The town was said to have been divided into more than ten sectors. The Central block was considered as the palace site where the King or the ruler was believed to have resided. The Mizos had to move from this place due to pressures of the enemies coupled with the on-going process of movement of population to the west.

As evidence of their having sojourned at the place with a firm belief that they would reoccupy this place one day[11], they planted a Banyan Tree at the palace site so that it would bear witness to the effect that when one of the branches thereof touched the ground it would be indicative of fulfilment of their cherished hope.

It is a fact, believe it or not, that Khampat is, as of now, being inhabited by the Mizos and that by the time a section of Mizos returned to Myanmar and settled in the areas in the beginning of 20th century A.D., the branches of the Banyan Tree thus planted had already touched the ground.[12]

Now many a people assume that this was a manifestation of fulfilment of the prophecy forecasted by their forefathers as the folktale related above was handed down from generation to generation.

II. Inscriptions

For a historic period where written documents are not available, epigraphic evidence to make history authentic is indispensable. But no such dependable inscription has been discovered for a genuine early history of the Mizos either in Manipur, or Myanmar or Mizoram, except the one recently discovered at Suangpuilawn, about 150 kilometres North-East of Aizawl, where an inscription on a stone tablet could not be properly deciphered as yet. The same is now installed at State Museum, Aizawl. According to some, the inscription was either in the *old Meitei script* or the *old Bengali script*. When it is properly deciphered it is expected that history of the Mizos might be different from what is now being current[13].

In addition, there is one copper plate inscription wherein the name of *Mizosthanan* (land of Kukis) was written. Suhas Chatterjee[14] contended that Dharmadhar (Swadharmapa, or Chengpha) was the Raja or Kailagadh, who invited a Kanauj Brahmin, Nidhipati, to his principality and granted him real estate as Brahmottar land. The land given to him was inscribed in the copper plate, at the second verse of the Sanskrit couplet as follows:

> Sri Nidhipati Vipraya Vastsya Gotraya Dharmine, Prahayang Longai *Kukisthanan* Pratichyan Gopala nade.

According to Chatterjee, the English rendering of the verse runs as follows:

> To Sri Nidhipati, the Vatsya Gotra Brahmin, the land bound in the east the Longai and Kukiland and in the west the Gopola river.

The land grant to Nidhipati was dated as 1195.[15]

III. Literature

The Mizos have no literature of their own. Tradition has it that once the Mizos were given a book (script), but due to carelessness, a dog carried away. That was how they lost the script. The scripts written in Roman Characters now being used were introduced only in the late 19th century with the advent of Christianity coupled with introduction of western education among the Mizos. Therefore, availability of literary evidence as source of Mizo history, the Rajamala or the Chronicle of Tripura Rajas may be cited as one of the main sources.

According to Rajamala, there arose a quarrel during the reign of Dhanya Manikya (A.D. 1490 – 1515) between him and the Kukis over possession of white elephant[16]. Therein it was also narrated as to how the Raj Kumar, the 57th in succession fell in love with a Kuki woman which

Secondly, the Hindu literatures, such as, the epics, the Puranas, etc., have so much potential historical evidences that should invariably contribute in the reconstruction of early history of the Mizos, because Chaterjee[19] contended that in them we find references to the Chins as Mizos, Chins and even Lushais. Analytical study of these literatures would immensely help us in understanding more of the Mizos and their history.

IV. Archival sources or Contemporary Records

The annexation of erstwhile Lushai Hills District of Assam by the British in 1890 and conclusion of the Anglo-Kuki War, 1917-1919 in Manipur and Chin Hills, Myanmar, marked the beginning of modern period of the history of the Mizos, which covers, as is the case with all parts of India, till it attained independence from the yoke of British imperialist regime in August, 1947.

During the process of consolidation and analytical investigation into the indigenous form of government, history and culture, the British did commendable service to the Mizos when they brought out a huge mass of historical materials of immense value for which one cannot but thank the British imperialism. These materials are now available in the National Archives, New Delhi (though partially closed), State Archives, West Bengal, Kolkata, Record Office, Dispur, Assam and Record Office, Aizawl (known as State Archives), etc.

Early Phase of Mizo History

Now, in view of preceding paragraphs it is clear that the Mizos are known under different names, such as, 'Chin' in Chin Hills, Myanmar, 'Kuki' and thereafter 'Lushai' in erstwhile Lushai Hills which was ultimately replaced by 'Mizo' though the people of the same groups who bear different names as per geographical areas occupied mentioned above, the nomenclature KUKI is still prevalent in Manipur, Nagaland, North Cachar Hills of Assam, Tripura and Arakan and Chittagong Hill Tracts of Bangladesh.

Most scholars think that Mizos made their first appearance in China. Burkitt[20] thought that the later Stone Age people made their movements from China to Central Asia and thence to Europe. Therefore, while searching for the original habitat, our attention is focused on China, particularly the southern part, because our tradition points to it. The Mizo tradition has it that 'Chhinlung' or 'Sinlung', or 'Khur' or 'Khul' is their original habitat[21]. believed located somewhere in Szechuan Province in southern China[22].

Burma Phase

They are grouped as Tibeto-Burman Family[23]. Chins are akin to Kukis and in Myanmar 'Kukis' are known as Chins. They came to Burma in the second half of the 9th century A.D. But Luce[24] puts in between the 4th and the middle of the 8th century A.D.

According to Lehman, Luce derived the 4th century from the fact that the Chins by this time had already used the word 'tangka' (coinage) which is believed to be the name of a Gupta coin of India. It is firmly believed that the coin was brought to the East by Samudra Gupta (C.320-380 AD) in the middle of the fourth century A.D.[25]. The 8th century A.D. is, however, derived from the fact that the ancient land route used by the Caravans and traders from China to India was not mentioned in literature. This convinced Luce to believe that the route was presumably closed after AD 300 until AD 750 and as such no major westward movement was noticed, otherwise it would have been recorded in the annals or literature[26]. He, therefore, strongly believed and concluded that most of the hill people arrived in Myanmar between the two dates. Harvey[27] has, however, believed that many of the immigrants must have settled in Burma before Christian era. It may, therefore, be concluded that the Mizo people occupied the present Chin Hills before the end of the 8th century A.D.

From the account given above, it may be conjectured that the Mizos came to Myanmar along with the people who are akin to them.

The North-East Phase

The North-East India has been the seat of multi ethnic abode since time immemorial and is therefore known for its diverse ethnic mosaic from the waves of immigrant racial elements[28]. Kiratas, Cina and other primitive tribes were earlier inhabitants[29]. Kiratas means wild non-Aryan tribes connected with Cinas and the Chinese, said Chatterjee[30], and people living in the cave of the mountain according to MacDonald and Keith[31], are the Mongoloid origin who migrated from South-east Asia and Burma according Sanskrit term[32].

The epics and the Puranas refer the 'Cinas' as Kuki-Chins or Lushai[33]. The Geography of Ptolemy, a work of about A.D. 150 deals with the geography and peoples of other parts of Assam. But many of the words and places mentioned are difficult to identify. The word Kirrhadae, for example, is identified as Kiratas. In the same way another work of the Greeks – The Periplus of the Erythrean Sea[34] which mentions about Assam in different descriptions also refers a number of tribes as Kirrhadae[35]. In this connection, the work of Gerini, Researches on Ptolemy's Geography, is commendable. He rightly identifies Ptolemy's Alosong with Shillong and Tiladai with the Kuki-Chin[36]. Tiladai was located to the north of the Moirandos near the Garo Hills and Sylhet[37].

In the Mahabharatta, the Puranas and Tantras the ancient Assam is referred to as Pragjoytisha and Kamarupa respectively. The Mahabharatta mentions one Bhagadatta as one of the four sons of Naraka. He was a powerful ruler who ruled in the west. The Sabha Parvan, from Hindu literature, relates the war between Bhagadatta and Arjun. In the war, the latter defeated the former after eight days of war.[38] It also mentions that Bhagadatta had a host of Kirats and Chins and other numerous warriors who dwelt on the sea cost.[39] The Hindu literature like the two epics and so many others makes references to the Kiratas.[40] About the proper home land of the Kiratas, the Vishnu Purana says that the Kiratas are in the east of India.[41] Therefore, Chatterjee concludes, "the Kiratas were known to the Hindu world as a group of peoples whose original home was in the Himalayan slopes and in the mountains of the East..."[42] History of the arrival in India (North-East

India) of the various Mongoloid groups speaking dialects of the Sino-Tibetan family is not known but their presence in India was noted by the tenth century B.C. when the Veda books were compiled.[43] The result of their participation in the history and culture of India in the areas where they had established themselves, has been their assimilation and absorption with the other peoples.

The migrations of the Mongoloid tribes to Assam took place through the North-Eastern and Southern routes of Assam from Burma. They entered Assam through the courses of the river Brrahmaputra, Chindwin, Irrawaddy, Salween, Mekong and Menam. Some of them also entered Assam through mountain passes of Assam and Burma through the north-east and south-east[44]. When they arrived in Assam the Mon-Khmer tribes had already occupied some hilly regions but they had been driven out later by the newly arrived tribes into different directions[45]. Therefore, some occupied the foot hills of the Himalayas from Sadiya to the Punjab in the West, and the rest occupied the hills of Assam such as the Garo Hills, Naga Hills, Lushai Hills, Khasi Hills and so on. It was only after their distribution and occupation of particular areas that they came to be known as Nagas, Bodos, Kukis, Khasis and so on and the areas of their occupation were known by their tribal names. The Sesatae of the Periplus and the Besadae of Ptolemy were also the same hill people of Assam allied to the Garos, Nagas and the Lushai-Kukis or the Mishmis[46].

The Lushai Hills Phase

Like the previous movements, the migration of the Mizos (Lushai Kukis) from Myanmar or the North-East took place in three phases and as such, the people were for the sake of convenience identified under the three names as 'Old-Kuki', 'New-Kuki' and the 'Lushai'.

The 'Old Kuki' or Hrangkhawl, Biate, Langrawng, Pangkhua and Mug (Mawk) was the first batch in migration. They were followed by the so-called 'New-Kuki' and then the 'Lushai' followed them as the third batch in migrations. It is not precisely known, like the previous movements of the people as to when did they come to Lushai Hills but what is known definitely is that the first two batches had been pushed, causing them to go as far as what is now known as Tripura State of India and the present day Bangladesh. A good number of Mizos(Kukis) are still living in Bangladesh. But history of their migration indicates that the first two immigrants, or at least some of them migrated back to Hiramba and made their settlements at the hills now known as North-Cachar Hills District of Assam.

Soppitt[47] brings the date of their migration to the middle of the sixteenth century A.D.. But this conclusion may be disputed on account of the fact that mention is made in the annals of Tripura under the Raja Chachag or Roy Chachag who is said to have flourished about 1512 A.D.[48] Chachag or Roy Chachag[49] was the military commander of Dhanya Manikya who ascended the throne of Tripura in 1490A.D. In 1513 A.D. the Raja issued a coin in his name and in the coin it is written as "Conqueror of Chittagong"[50]. During his reign a quarrel arose between him and the Mizos(Kukis) over the possession of a white elephant. The Mizos occupied the deep forest lying to the East of Tripura and the West of Lushai Hills[51]. The Rajamala, the Chronicle of the Tripura Rajas, also mentions the Kukis. The Chronicle speaks about the services rendered by the Kukis to the Tripura kings[52]. The Chronicle also narrates how the Raj Kumar fell in love with a Kuki woman[53].

There is also evidence to indicate that the Mizos had

already arrived in Tripura late in the twelfth century A.D. As had been said hereinabove, in the history of Tripura mention is made that once Raja Dharmadhar of Kailagadh invited Nidhipati, a Kanauj Brahmin to his court and granted him an estate, known in history as Brahmottar land. The inscription in the copper plate marking the event bears the name of Kuki-land. The land bounded in the east of Longoi (Langkaih) river and the date is mentioned as 1195 A.D.[54]. The theory is that the Kukis, who are known in Tripura as Halam, sneaked into Tripura due to ethnic pressures, possibly perhaps, long before the coming of Palian and Zadeng ruling clans of Zahmuaka who had been pushed down by the Sailo Chiefs of the same ancestor. They entered Tripura not from Lower Burma, but from Upper Burma passing through the area known as Lushai Hills. We cannot place them far behind the Kukis of the first batch said Sangkima[55]. Hence, they are said to have arrived in the land in the period between fourteenth and fifteenth centuries A.D.

The last batch of migration, which were identified as 'Lushai', like the first two groups, consisted of many clans. The most prominent among them was the Lusei tribe of the Sailo clan. They were the direct descendants of Thangura who is believed to have existed in 1580 A.D. As noted before, Palian and Zadeng groups came before the Sailos and they are said to have come in 1610 A.D.. The Sailo clan are believed to have migrated to Mizoram beginning from the second half of the seventeenth century and might have continued till the beginning of the nineteenth century, Sangkima further said[56]. McCall has asserted that Lallula occupied Mizoram around 1810 A.D.[57] Whatever the case may be, from the dates given above, a genealogy of the Sailo Chiefs and others and their respective periods, may be worked out. Though this may seem to be a difficult task, an attempt has to be made to string together the story of ancient ruling clans of the Mizos.

The Manipur Phase

As for the Kukis of Manipur, Johnstone[58] convincingly contended that the Kukis were inhabitants of Manipur since time immemorial and commented with appreciation that his predecessor, McCulloch, was Cool and Considerate that having confirmed that the new wave of Kuki immigrants who came to Manipur in 1843-1845 in great numbers were mainly with the main intention to secure land for cultivation that prompted him to place them at various strategic places all over the Hill areas of Manipur to meet the quest of Kukis for land which had no intention whatsoever with conquest of land. This became a very convenient policy framework to create 'Buffer Group' out of the Kukis as 'human shield' to protect the Raja of Manipur and the British from their enemies. The Government of India in Bengal appreciated highly and created Kuki 'levies' at various strategic places. Johnstone further praised him stating that McCulloch extended financial assistance to the Kukis from his private pocket money that won the confidence of the Kukis and their allegiance, placing themselves available by his side in any manner their services were required. These complementary notings were fully corroborated from McCulloch's[59] own accounts of the Kukis in Manipur.

Modern Phase

(i) Concept of 'Zo' (Jo) Unification

At this juncture, it may be relevant to briefly describe the meaning of 'Jo' which was generally considered as necromancers and sorcerers for which the Burmese were not accorded ill treatment for fear of being revenged with some enchantment.[60] In this connection it is significant to note that Father Sangermano was sent as a missionary in 1782 who arrived in Rangoon in July, 1783 and proceeded to Ava directly the same year. Herein, it is pertinent to refer to the letter from Vum Hau[61] (Vum Ko Hau) to Haokholet.

In this letter he emphasized the fact that the nomenclature of the 'Mizos' and 'Zos' should be retained. There was no iota of doubt on the truth of their nomenclatures. In doing so, he indicated the equations between 'Mizo' and 'Zomi' stating that more than 200 years ago a most learned Italian missionary had recorded the fact that the 'Kuki' and 'Zo' people were either Mizo or Zomi. These people lived on the west of the Chin Mountains between 20° and 30° longitude and 21° and 30° N latitude and that area was called 'Jo' in course of time becomes Burmese.

He further claimed that he read most of the books concerning the 'Jo' from the British Museum, the National Library of France, the Museums in the Hague and Leyden and Utracht, and also the Indian Office Library, the London Library and National Library of Scotland in Glasgow wherefrom he could confirm that Father Sangermano was the first author to record the word 'Jo' (Zo).*

In consideration of the above contention it may be concluded that the tribes who are known broadly as Kuki, Zou and Mizo in Manipur reveal a common origin in their

* Father Sangermano was an Italian Catholic Missionary who worked in Burma from 1783 to 1807 during the reign of King BowdowPaga (1782 AD – 1819 AD) He wrote a number of books on Burma.

These so-called claims of Vumkhohau as having gone through the records from various Libraries of European countries that confirmed Father Sangermano as the first author to record the word 'Jo'(Zo) need proper verifications and confirmations.

customary laws and many prevalent traditions. Such concept equating Mizo and Zomi will not be incorrect or an underestimation of their socio-political or religious status.

In this connection, the terms 'Zo' 'Kuki' and 'Mizo' signify a common social and cultural group of people. This idea is not a new thing. It is a global phenomenon caught under the ethnic explosion the world over. This had been termed as "*political creed*".[62] Instead, it could be more appropriately termed as '*ethnic consciousness*' prompted by revolutionary movements to consolidate the said group of people led by Vumkhohau under the banner of 'Zo' unification.[63] He met General Aung San[64] in February, 1947 in the historic 'Panglong' Conference as the Chief delegate of the 'Zomi' and entered into an agreement with the latter for the full fledged Chin Hills State in the event of Burma being granted independence. Herein, the fateful disastrous day of 19th July, 1947, may be mentioned that when the entire prospective Cabinet Ministers of the Constituent Assembly on the threshold of Burma being given independence were murdered including General Aung San. As luck would have destined, Vumkhohau survived the ugly incident. This ultimately brought him into political prominence in independent Burma when he joined the first Cabinet of the Thakin Nu (U Nu) which had been constituted after the death of General Aung San. And so he along with Prime Minister U Nu signed the Burma Independence Treaty in London on 17th October, 1947. This was a momentous land mark in the regional geo-political history of contemporary Burma and Manipur as it gave impetus to Zo national movement for their unification.

It is comparable to the movement of nationalism that had awakened the leaders of Italy and Germany to unify their respective countries.[65] in the 19th Century. During the same period Bismarck of Prussia consolidated more than three hundred states together and constituted one nation.[66] Likewise, Zo people presented a united far sightedness in their approach. Nationalism was reflected in their socio-political insights and movements in the 20th Century.

(ii) Concept of Hebrew Origin(Israelite Concept)

While tracing the origin of the early history of the Mizos, one of the sources that cannot be overlooked or sidelined as totally baseless and unfounded, is the culture and tradition which claim that the Mizos are descendants of a tribe of Israel in the House of Ephraim, the tenth tribe. According to the Old Testament of the Bible, the Israelites were the chosen people with whom God entered into a covenant[67]. But the people were unfaithful to God and consequently God dispersed them among the people from one end of the earth to the other and there they served gods of wood and stone which neither they nor their fathers had known[68].

In doing so, God dispersed the Israelites as a punishment by means of Assurians and Nabukadnazzar, King of the Babylon in 720 B.C. and 587 B.C. respectively. This was beginning of the diaspora of the Israelites, the dispersion of the Jews to the different part of the world. This lasted into the 20th century AD. The Jews also came to the east in ancient times[69]. By following the foothills of Himalaya the 'lost tribes' then arrived in China. According to one estimates, when Israel attained Independence in 1948, about 5000 Jews migrated back to Israel and have settled in the Kubbutz[70].

On the basis of culture, tradition, customary laws, etc. it could be identified that the Mizos have Israelite religious and social connections. The culture, customary laws, etc.

are important in these groups as their identity is based upon it. As a result of this, the Welsh Presbyterian Church banned all revivalist manifestations, including 'listening to voices, prophecy and speaking unknown tongues'.[71] This ban could not, however, be enforced. Revivalism has remained a potent force in religious practice. Impact of Revival has been still more dramatic. McCall commented that revivalist movement was fairly widespread and that the Missions were trying faithfully to keep it within the bounds of decency.[72] In a progressive way these groups have retained their past culture, which have got manifested as a living tradition.

On the basis of existing culture, tradition, customary laws, religious belief systems, rites and rituals, some groups of Mizos have been identified as the children of 'Manmasi'. The term itself is distorted form of 'Manasseh' of the Israelites who was the son of Joseph.

In the backdrop of such a situation, Lalbiaktluanga[73] recorded that a revivalist named Saichhunga from Hlimen village claimed that Mizos were 'the lost tribals of Israel'. This statement was confirmed as true by Chala of Buallian village in 1951 which was substantiated by those who accepted the claims[74] saying,

"In the year 1936 the word of the spirit of our Lord came to Pu (honorific title similar to 'Shri' in Hindi or 'Sir' in English) Kapa and Pu Saichhuma, telling them that "we are Israel". Also in 1946 the same message was received by Pu Chala of Buallawn village. Henceforth from every part and every corner of Mizoram we cried longing for our homeland, Israel ... and searched every possible way for contacting Israel". It is observed that while Liabiaktluanga speaks of one Saichhunga, Benjamin calls this man 'Saichhuma'. Similarly, Lalbiaktluanga tells us that Chala of Bualawn "confirmed" Saichhunga's statement in 1951 as against which Benjamin offers 1946 as the appropriate year. These contradicting names and years need to be rectified.

From this account and several others it is clear that the connection with the Israelites had not been realized until "the word of the Lord came out to our prophets since 1936", even though this revelation explains a history that would stretch back over two and a half thousand years. In this connection it has to be understood that as per historic events the biblical Northern Kingdom of Israel was conquered by Assyrians in 720 B.C. Its inhabitants were taken into exile and banished from history. The fate of these people, "the Lost Tribes of Israel", has inspired many legends and much wild conjecture.[75]

There are such other local persons as Khuplam Milui Lenthang,[76] who propagates Mizos being the children of Manmasi (twisted form of Manasseh of the Israelites). Here one sees, though very likely concocted or allegory, an element of evolution in the identification of the "putative Israelite" tribal origin of the Mizos. When Chala first claimed that the Mizos were Israelites,[77] he did not clearly indicate to which of the Ten Lost Tribes of Israel they belonged.[78] By 1972, however, one group asserted that Mizos of Manipur were originally descended from one of the ten lost tribes of Israel whose name was called 'Manasseh'[79]. But such identification arose by deduction rather than prophecy.

In support of this it may be observed that in many of the chants, rites, rituals, exclamations, used in various sacrifices and other sacred incantations as per Customary Laws the terminology, Manasia or Manase or Manmasi, is used. These names have come to be equated with that of Manasseh in the Bible.[80] Some such instances are that:

(i) when earthquake takes place, people run out of their houses and exclaim aloud, saying, - "Calm, Calm, we the children of Manmasi are still alive." It is said, whosoever might have been responsible for the earthquake, on hearing the name of Manmasi, stops the earthquake. This has been all along the tradition before Christianity came to hold its root among the Thadou Mizos and is still believed and practiced spontaneously whenever earthquake takes place;

(ii) When *'Ai Kawngpui Sial'* occasion (*pre-Christian sacrifice for success in hunting*) takes place, the priest, followed by his party chants, "Those above and those below, go away, flee, we the children of Manasia are coming". This practice among the Lushai Mizos was given up after Christianity came in the area.[81].

(iii) There lived a legendary heroine called 'Lenchonghoi' as was current in the folklores of all the Mizo tribes. She was known for her beauty. She was kidnapped by one Monster called 'Topipa' in the absence of her brothers. Her youngest brother who happened to be the strongest and bravest went after his sister to rescue from her captor. Finding her in a corner of thick jungles they came homewards. 'Topipa', on his return home found 'Lenchonghoi' missing and immediately went in pursuit of her. As they met, 'Topipa' and Lenchonghoi's brother struggled for her. In the course of struggle, Lenchonghoi's brother beheaded 'Topipa' several times. Yet, the head of 'Topipa' rejoined the body each time beheaded.

While the struggle was fiercely fought without either

of the two men the victor, two Angelic sisters watched the fight from their celestial abode who sided with Lenchonghoi's brother. At last they planned to help him won the struggle. In doing so, the elder sister advised her younger sister that the latter should tie one butterfly-like object made of thin wooden-plate and to tie it at the one end with a cotton thread so as to drop it, holding at the other end of the thread. In doing so, the younger sister should advice Lenchonghoi's brother to cut the same hanging his overhead by addressing him "Manmasi" (twisted form of Manaseh or Manase). But Lenchonghoi's brother did not pay heed to what she repeatedly said, not knowing as to whom she addressed as "Manmasi". At last 'Topipa' told him that he was advised to "cut the thread with which the object was hung over your head, addressing you as Manmasi". Then Lenchonghoi's brother did as he was asked to do. Now, as he cut the thread, Topipa's head was severed from his body and died.

Thus it is said, 'Manmasi' is the 'God-given name' of the Mizo people among whom the legend had been current in the past many generations before Christianity came and is current till date. Therefore, the concept that Mizos are the 'lost tribes of the Israelite origin" is no new invention or make-belief of some fanatic protagonists of the 'lost tribes of Israel' theory. It is nothing but 'God given name', it is said, with an overtone of finality, quoting their tradition and customary law of the Mizos as evidence of their culture.

Similarly, there are a host of cultural and traditional instances where Manmasi among the Mizos in Manipur is conspicuously made manifest as their ancestor. One such customary instance is when a grave is about to be dug. A libation is poured into the ground and the priest chants, "Make way, o stones and trees, for the children of Manmasi have gone to claim their own possession".[82] With the claim of Manmasi as used in Manipur or Manasia or Manase as used in Mizoram to identify their ancestor, some Mizo groups adopted a new name as 'Bane Manasseh', meaning thereby "children of Manasseh" in Hebrew. Sawngtindaṁ observed[83], "The significance of the new identity is far reaching for it ... dovetails elements in cultural and traditional religion with a significant force in the Jewish religion", namely the fate of the Lost Tribes and the hope that some day they would once again be returned with the Jewish people. The belief is fulfilled and the customary law lives on.

It is a fact today many groups have accepted the Mizo Manasseh identity and are attempting to follow 'Judaism in some form.[84] This may be called conventional "Orthodox Judaism" or the so-called "Messiamic Judaism", a cult which associates observance of precepts from the 'Old Testament', such as circumcision, observance of Saturday as the Sabbath, dietary restrictions and the Jewish festivals, with the Christian's faith in Jesus as the Messiah.

Our research in this sphere has shown that there is an ironical aspect in these developments. Of all the elements of their traditional culture, animal sacrifice was one practice, which initially led to the identification of Mizos with the Israelites in the Bible, as it led also to identify group with similar practices as their associates or primary/segmentary groups.

Conclusion

That historically the Mizos are a Mongoloid race of the Tibeto-Burman group of tribes and that the mountainous region of Southern China the original home of these people is unquestionable because their tradition, myths, legends and the historical facts based on research all point to it.

But it is extremely difficult, perhaps impossible, to definitely give the correct date of their settlement and beginning of their migration from them. Therefore, to this aspect of the Mizo history, no conclusive research can presently be made.

Having found their new homes in Burma the Mizos are believed to have been there for a number of centuries. Unlike other Kiratas who reached Assam following the course of the Brahmaputra river and still others who reached the other hill areas through mountain passes, the Mizos arrived in their present habitats. The evidence is that Mizos arrived here from the Chin Hills of Burma through the present Chawnchhim popularly known as Champhai. In Chin Hills of Burma till now there are so many Mizo villages and the main route appears to be the land route via what is popularly known as Rihdil, the Rih lake. It is certain that when they moved westward they moved in small number. One group under the command of one Chief moved from one place to another.

Among the Mongoloid tribes whom the classical writers and modern authors refer to as Kiratas as having found their ancient settlements in the plains and the hills of Assam with whom the Ahoms had contacts with, the Mizos had no part to play because they were distinctly different from them.

CULTURE OF THE KUKIS

Culture is that complex whole which includes knowledge, belief, art, morals, law, custom and any other capabilities acquired by man as a member of society, says Tylor[85], so said Malinawski[86] that culture is the handiwork of man and the medium through which he achieves his end, and, in like manner Mazumdar propounds culture as the sum total of human achievements, material as well as non-material, capable of transmission, by tradition and communication, vertically as well as horizontally[87].

Thus, we can surmise that there are certain characteristics of culture that may briefly be given as follows:

(i) that culture is an acquired quality, learned through socialization, habits and thoughts;

(ii) that it is social and not individual heritage, a social product which is shared by most members of the group;

(iii) that culture is idealistic, embodying the ideas and norms of a group, a sum-total of the ideal patterns and norms of behaviour of a group;

(iv) that it is the total social heritage that links with the past which endures because it lives in culture passing from one generation to another through traditions and customs;

(v) that it fulfils those ethical and social needs of the groups which are ends in themselves;

(vi) that it is an integrated system, its various parts being integrated with each other and any new element introduced is also integrated; and

(vii) that language being the chief vehicle of culture, living not only in the present but also in the past and future, it transmits what was learnt in the past and enables further to transmit the accumulated wisdom.

Now, as has been sufficiently made clear in the preceding paragraphs, the Mizos are of Tibeto-Burman Family group of people. They arrived the Chin Hills of Burma from Southern China as a result of population movements. They lived there for centuries and formed themselves into a homogeneous group of varying clans. They developed their culture into different dimensions.

Chieftainship was instituted as a single source of authority in society. They also developed their economic system adopting the method of cultivation called "Slash and burn", the oldest method of cultivation and the most dreaded system the world over today. They cannot do away with it till this day among the Mizos wherever they might settle, either in the Chin Hill, Burma (Myanmar), or Manipur, or Nagaland, or Tripura, or Mizoram, or North-Cachar Hills in Assam or Arakan and Chittagong Hill Tracts in Bangladesh. The reason is not far to seek. It is due to non-availability of better alternatives. Their religious life also improved considerably with innovative rites, rituals, methods of propitiations, etc., to the then existing ones. The cultural life of the people showed all round marked development from their rudimentary stage of social institutions which are components of culture.

The humming activities of year round tribal life among the Mizos revolve within the ambit of earning bread for survival without consideration for future growth and development on an agro-based economic system which has no place for concept of 'Saving', consumption being conspicuous and community bias. Such a life of routine nature becomes obviously monotonous which must find expression in various forms of social celebrations to give vent to their longing for a life away from sacrosanct. In doing so, their structural functions of life are made often manifest in more than one way which have become social institutions that are major components of their culture. Two such Institutions are briefly given below:

I. Sawm or Zawlbuk (Bachelors' Dormitory)

"Sawm" or "Zawlbuk" is an institution[88] of the youth which concerns only with able-bodied young boys of the village. It is a bachelors' dormitory in which all the young boys of the village sleep together at night. The nature of hostility and practice of inter-tribal feuds necessitate existence of this institution so that in times of emergency the services of all able-bodied men might be available at short notice.[89] They have to offer their free and compulsory services to the Village from external dangers. In times of peace they render every possible service to the Village community whenever required. Moreover, it is an institution for recreation of the young boys. In the 'Sawm', younger boys are taught all sorts of things from cutting jokes to taking responsibilities. Stories are told by the elder members and sometimes topics ranging from girls to war become subject matters of great interest. This institution is also connected with the 'Thih-Kheng' office because the efficient mobilization of the village youth for defence depends mainly upon the ability of the 'Thih-kheng' to produce weapons. In a nutshell, it may be equated with modern system of 'Informal Education' and may as well be likened with that of Defence and Home Departments of modern administration.

The Mizo society is such that during the days when intertribal feuds were part of their way of life, every able-bodied youth of a village slept together as called for by customary law so that they might be readily available for deployment in times of emergency. 'Sawm' or 'Zaulbuk' is also considered as a place of learning. Boys of different age-groups are assigned various jobs and other sundry chores. The boys of younger age-groups learn things from the older groups. They also learn social customs, customary laws and manners. It serves as an institution of learning discipline and other essential character formation necessary for a man to be responsible in future life. It has thus been considered as a very essential part of the village administration among the Mizos. This is an organisation responsible for mobilization of the services of the youngmen to meet exigencies of situations. In this connection Roy[90] describes the bachelor's organisation as :

> ... archaic form of economic, social and religious organisation. It must have been effective economic organisation for purposes of food gathering a useful seminary for training youngmen in their social and other duties, and an institution for magico-religious observances calculated to secure success in hunting and to augment the preventive power of the youngmen so as to increase the number of hunters in the tribe.

Thus, the young boys of the village are concentrated at a place for emergency service. In this connection a story is current, which runs as follows:

There was a time when every tribe was scared of the Pawis (Lakhers) because of their ferocity in warfare. But the Sitlhou Chief of Jampi village, the head of all the Sitlhou clan of the Thadous, arranged things in such a way that he and his collateral brothers must not move out from their place for fear of the Pawis[91]. He asked his two junior collateral Chieftains of Lhungtin and Aiyang villages belonging to the Hangsing and Chongloi clans to remain in their villages on condition that he as a senior collateral cousin would remain together with them. So, the three villages forming a confederacy remained in union where they were based. Now, having stood their ground unitedly, Lhungtin and Aiyang villages acting as buffers between the Pawis and the Jampi village, became the thorn in the flesh to the Pawis, who could not stand any longer in the face of such combined force of the three confederate villages.

In order to relent situation and with a view to living side by side in peace and amity, the Pawis sought for the concurrence of the Jampi Chief to pacify his junior collateral two cousins of Lhungtin and Aiyang Chiefs. As a token of peace and amity of the proposed pact, the Pawi Chief came to him pleading that the Pawis were no longer able to live in peace because of fear for 'Your brethren Singhangs[92] (Hangsings). Please be kind and pacify them and ask them not to trouble us any more, so that we all might live in peace as good neighbours." In proposing such a peace pact with the three collateral brethren Chiefs, the Pawis brought two shields to be used in front and back – 'Lum Le Phaw' – one big type bead, called 'Khi-chang', one spear, known as 'Tiengcha', one belt which has seven lines of one rare kind of bead, called 'Paigen', to the Chief of Jampi.

It was obvious, when one comes with such a peace and goodwill mission that the proposal was difficult to be turned down. Therefore, accepting the proposal of the Pawis in good faith, the Chief of Lhungtin and Aiyang villages relaxed and were at peace with the Pawis. Obedience and veneration to the senior Chief were the mode of life in those days as formally incorporated in social etiquette per customary law. Thus, when a senior collateral Chief advised them to stand down, there was nothing but to abide by his wishes as provided for in the codes of customary laws, which they thought to be in their best interest.

Accordingly, the Pawis also ceased their hostility against the three villages. But this was a lull before the storm and it lasted only for the first year[93]. Believing in what superficially appeared as being reality of the situation with complete cessation of arms hostility on the part of the

Pawis, the three collateral cousin Chiefs became complacent with over-relaxation. [94]

On the other hand, the Pawis had been surreptitiously planning to attack the Lhungtin village by surprise[95]. It so happened that one night, when all the able-bodied youngmen of Lhungtin village slept* in their dormitory, the Pawis stealthily came and butchered them, killing instantaneously as many as eighty able-bodied youngmen. As a result, the Hangsings were scattered and fled in different directions. Most of them were found to have settled down among the Paites[96]. The one that gave a serious impact besides all other repercussions was that as provided for under customary laws the institution of 'Sawm' has to continue its existence in amended form as part of essential administrative structure of youth-wing of the Village under any circumstances. The institution of 'Sawm' which was centralized took the character of a decentralized form due to defensive strategy. Such a different form of 'Sawm', though still continues, exists on small scale at different houses where there are young unmarried girls. [97]

Sawm Kivah or Sawm Juneh (Feast)

Under the present system, some boys sleep together in different houses, where there are girls who are at the back and call of the boys[98]. They live so closely with the family of the girls that they become almost identified as being members of the family of the girls. The boys of one particular 'Sawm' help the family of the girl in all possible ways, even in the matter of cultivation when the family members of the girl fail to complete it in time. When there occurs a feast of the Lawm of the village, the girl and the boys of her 'Sawm' go together taking care of each other during the feast. Sometimes it so happens that the girl becomes inebriated by over-drinking of rice-bear. In such a situation, all the boys of the 'Sawm' take special care for her and bring her home safely. Likewise, the girl takes care of the boys. Even the parents and other members of the family regard the boys as part of their family.

With the passage of time, a stage came when most of the 'Sawm' members grew up. Some of them pursued diverse interests. Some had grown enough to fall in love with some other girls. Even the 'Sawm' girl had fallen in love either with a boy other than her own 'Sawm' members or with one of the 'Sawm' members[99]. They felt that time had come to part company and that the 'Sawm' be disbanded. Under such circumstances, they considered that it was best to have a farewell party provided the parents of the girl gave consent to the proposal.

When such a situation arose, the question of 'Sawm Kivah', meaning thereby a feast of the 'Sawm' cropped up for consideration. When such a 'Sawm Kivah' is proposed, the members of one particular 'Sawm', the number of which varies between ten and twelve, discuss the proposal with the parents of a 'Sawm' girl. If they agree, a date for it is decided upon and preparations start for the same.

Normally, the young boys buy a small pig which is kept under the charge of the parents of the girl. As the day for such 'Sawm Kivah' approaches, the girl of the 'Sawm' also requests her close friends to prepare a few pots of 'Zu' by way of helping her for the occasion. Those girls will, in their turn, ask their friends to help them. Thus, a chain of help for preparation of 'Zu' for the 'Sawm Kivah' is sought. Ultimately almost all the girls of the village are involved in this function. The same is true in the case of the boys of the 'Sawm'. Each of the 'Sawm' member asks his close friends to join him on the occasion. Ultimately, boys of the whole village are covered. In accepting such invitations each of the boy friend invited contributes one pot of 'Zu' on the day. Finally, it becomes usually the affairs of the whole village, though it is initially thought to be an affair only for a small group of ten or twelve boys[100]. Of course, the particular boy members of the 'Sawm' bear the bulk of the expenditure for the occasion.

In the previous evening of the night before the 'Sawm Kivah', members of the 'Sawm' serve one pot of 'Zu' to the parents of the girl wherein the Chief of the village along with his Council of Ministers, the Priest, the 'Tucha' and 'Becha' relatives of the parents of the girl are invited. The 'Sawm' members will request them all to join them in the feast and to extend all possible help to make the occasion a success.

Early, the next morning, the 'Tucha' and the 'Becha' relatives of the girl's parents do all the needful[101]. They take up the entire responsibility for the function. As the meat is cooked, all the invitees are asked to have it to their heart's content. But the Chief and his Council of Ministers, the Priest and the father of the girl or, in his place, his 'Becha Bul' will take the 'Sapang' or the head portion of the pig. In addition to this group of people, another group of the members of the 'Sawm', which hosts the feast and their 'Sawm-Nu', the girl of the 'Sawm', are given a portion of the meat kept apart by the 'Becha' of the girl's parents. The rest of the people take the feast at random, as normal feasting is done, without any formality.

On this day, drinking method of the 'Zu' is such that apart from all other pots of 'Zu' served on the day, two particular pots are separately kept and these are served at a special place. One of them is the pot contributed by the boys of the 'Sawm', who host the feast. The other is the pot contributed by the parents of the girl. The 'Zu' contributed by the boys of the 'Sawm' is first sipped by the Chief, followed by the Prtiest and then the father of the girl. Sometimes the mother of the girl is also included in this sipping spree. The style of sipping is that one full bottle of water is the measuring level called 'Aleng'[102]. The bottle of water is poured to the pot of 'Zu' without ceasing, and whoever sips the 'Zu' is made to do so without ceasing until his level of sipping is finished. The level of sipping for the above VIPs is made double of the normal level. The same is done to the other pot of 'Zu' offered by the girl's parents, which is given to the boys of the 'Sawm'. The order of sipping among the 'Sawm' members is that the leader of the 'Sawm', called 'Sawm Upa', sips first. He is followed by others in order of seniority.

While the 'Sawm' members sip, they are tied with a rope on their waist and bound to a place upon the rafter of the building, so that they do not run away being unable to do justice to the level of sipping fixed for them. Thus, the 'Zu' contributed by the parents of the girl is sipped by the boys of the 'Sawm' and the girl, while the pot of 'Zu' contributed by the boys is sipped by the Chief and his Council of Ministers, the Priest, the father of the girl or his 'Becha' simultaneously. All the other pots of 'Zu' prepared on that day are served for drinking only and not for sipping.

The next day is meant for the Chief and his Council of Ministers, the Priest and the 'Tucha and the 'Becha' relatives of the Girl's father. A feast is arranged for them only and the pride of place is given to them by offering the head portion of the slaughtered pig. In doing so, each of those who had the privilege of eating the 'Sapang' brings one jar of 'Zu' each. On the other hand, the boys of the 'Sawm' who host the feast provide the meat for the day. They may buy another pig or some of their friends may make a gift of some cocks for the purpose. These are flayed, cooked and eaten along with the leaders who are offered the meat with 'Zu' on the day. After the feast, the elders retire. With the approach of the evening, the young boys and girls collect themselves at one place with a view to passing the night in singing and dancing.

On the stipulated third day of the feast, the young boys and girls, belonging to some other 'Sawm' would come with gifts of 'Zu' and other edibles to help their friends who hosted the feast. In this way, they continue the feast for the third day. On this day, however, the elders do not take part in the feast or in the drinking bout. At the close of this day's feasting and drinking, the 'Sawm Kivah' comes to an end.

Thus, the beginning of gradual dissolution of the old members of the 'Sawm', which has hosted the feast, is initiated. On this occasion some of the boy members get betrothed. In case there is a younger sister of the disbanded Sawm girl, the sister continues to care for the remaining junior 'Sawm' members who may like to continue in the same 'Sawm' where they have so long been junior members, instead of joining some other 'Sawm'.

It is, therefore, in an entirely different situation that the 'Sawm' institution survives today. In view of the fact that the society is changing, most of the boys and girls have started looking for greener pastures of social mobility in the urban areas of the country. Despite this, the old system of 'Sawm' in somewhat decentralized form still survives being bound by customary laws. But among the Lushai Kukis in Mizoram, the institution has been abolished in view of fast changing situation in society.

II. KUT Festival

The people now inhabiting Mizoram, the tribes in the Hill areas of Manipur other than the Naga dominant areas, the Kukis of Nagaland, Assam, Tripura and Chittagong Hill Tracts of Bangladesh and the people in the Chin State of Myanmar are the tribes who have been professing observance of various kinds of Kut Festivals from time immemorial. They all practice Jhum cultivation as the mainstay of economy, growing, Millet, Maize, Sesamum, Job's ear, Cucumber, Pumpkins, etc, etc, as their staple foods prior to their entry into Myanmar from China. These groups of people were said to have taken to rice cultivation only after their entry into Myanmar. Such contentions cannot, however, be substantiated as to the truth of the claims. These are more of legends than of historical facts. They are of conjectural work. In fact, their hoary past is shrouded in mystery. Nevertheless, the fact remains that these people have been observing Kut Festivals for generations.

These people commonly claim to have come "out of the bowels of the earth, a cave called Chhinlung or Sinlung or Khul, believed to be in China". One of the authorities on the Kukis, Shakespear[103], in his book on "The Lushai Kuki Clan" said that they were of many clans, each speaking different dialect and scattering over an area of 25,000 square miles. The then Governor of Assam, Robert Reid[104], in his book on "History of the Frontier Areas Bordering on Assam" said that these people who claimed to have come out of the bowels of the earth speak dialects of the same language". Similarly, Grierson, a linguist, said that they belonged to the Tibeto-Kuki sub-linguistic group in his book on "Linguistic Survey of India".

Origin

During the olden days, the people who observed Kut festivals were not aware of the existence of the great religions of the world, such as, Christianity, Islamic, Hinduism, Buddhism, etc., etc. Thus as were true in all cases of other primitive societies, these groups of people were either atheists, or professed ancestral worshippers (animists) or naturists. In any form of these worships, certain objects as sources of life and of other worldly nature were attributed. Their belief was, therefore, associated either with animate or inanimate objects as the sources of all powers that gave life to mankind with abundance of blessings if particular aspect of life was made subservient to it. Likewise, when the said supernatural object was believed not satisfied or was displeased, all sorts of evil fortunes were attributed to it. With this end in view, the people worshipped the objects with certain prescribed rituals in propitiation as prescribed by the customary laws.

In order to appease not to harm mankind or to praise such objects for the blessings received, propitiation of supposed supernatural objects for the benefit and welfare of the community was performed by a socially acceptable person to intercede between the people and the objects attributed as supernatural. Such person to officiate performance of the rituals was considered 'holy man' called 'village priest'.

Such activities that interceded between the supernatural object and the society being of collective welfare in nature, observance of certain occasions as Kuts and the rituals associated therewith were essentially of community in nature.

Rites and rituals give strong elements of ethnic affinity

and influence on their social cohesion and solidarity. It also symbolizes the integrating force among the community, cutting across tribal boundaries and linguistic differences.

Thus, observance of different kinds of Kut is originated from the worship of various objects considered as supernatural associated with good and evil attributes of life.

Concept

Radcliffe Brown and Emille Dirkheim said that the principal function of communal rituals was to emphasise and to reaffirm the sentiments of collective loyalty. The purpose of such festive function was to create a sense of identity and social solidarity reinforced by the performance of communal rituals which expressed social content and behaviour of a group. This is an essential lifestyle in egalitarian society.

The means of subsistence of the people who observed Kut festivals was agricultural products. Annual communal feasts manifested the type of economy being pursued by the society. The glaring fact that lacked the concept of saving in their economic system could be observed from the practice of conspicuous consumption through the various Kuts in festivity and communal rituals in propitiation to the deities of Kuts. Also, an important aspect that associated inseparably with Kut festivals was religiosity of the occasions that stemmed from obeisance and incantation to the creator of all things which preceded the celebration.

Kut festival is in thanks giving to the almighty creator of the Universe who is believed to have blessed the people through the deities of various crops cultivated. There might have, therefore, been many Kuts celebrated in the olden days of variegated and seasonal ones. However, there are some Kut festivals common to all tribes. They are[105] –

(1) Mim Kut (Job's ear);

(2) Chavang Kut (paddy);

(3) Pawl Kut (Gourd harvest);

(4) Thai or Thak Lop (crops).

Hence, as the names suggest, Kut observance is invariably done with the arrival of the new crops or after harvesting as the case may be.

The basic concept behind such observance is, therefore, that the toiling community has to have a short respite and recreation after the year's work has been reaped and before the new-year's work is begun. It is also an occasion when the village community praise God for the blessings bestowed upon them.

The religious rites that precede the Kut celebration are officiated by the 'holy-man' called, 'Village Priest', who intercedes for the villagers to the deities of the Kuts concerned.

Observance of Kuts by our forefathers was marked by many significant rituals. Some salient features are given as follows briefly –

> In the early hour of the morning of Kut, the man in-charge of information of the village, called, 'Tangsampa' or 'Lhangsampa' or 'Tualteekpa', etc., etc., would herald the advent of Kut, shouting aloud, throughout the village with the words,
>
> "The sun rises, the sun rises;
> the sky is clear, the sky is clear";
>
> and would enter every household, arming himself

with a burning torch of fire-wood in his left hand and a hammer in his right hand, saying[106],

> "Your days are over, you evil spirit!
> Be away from our midst, and
> be with your wife and children.
> We are sick of your filthy waste".

Having performed his part, he will handover the proceedings to the 'Village Priest'. Then, the 'Village Priest' shall arrange jars of 'Ju' (rice bear) for all the villagers to sip, and shall intercede for all the villagers to the deities of harvests.

The common ritualistic rites for this purpose are the offering of a cock and a bawl of rice placed at the altar of the deities. The rice is crushed to turn it into powder. The neck of the cock is throttled and cut with a sharp knife, and that the blood that oozes out therefrom is strewn on the altar and on the powdered rice.

Thereafter, the village priest shall start sipping the 'Ju' from the 'Jar' prepared for the occasion. The priest shall spit out the first mouthful of 'Ju' he thus sipped which is called 'Juphi' (spraying of the 'Ju') in symbolic offering to the deities. He then shall invite the Chief of the village, followed by the eldest villager present to start sipping of the 'Ju'. The sipping-bout continues by turn till the last person. With it, the celebration commences being followed soon by drinking, singing, merry-making, dancing, sporting and feasting.

It is time when even the poorest man of the village forgets his state of poverty.

Growth

With the passage of time, contacts with outside of

their own homogeneous communities entered into the fibre of their social life. People who observed such Kut festivals became aware of the world beyond their own small community. Gradually, western education began to hold its roots followed by Christianity that propagated to dispense with hitherto known 'culture and tradition'. Ultimately, when increasing number of people started embracing Christianity, observance of Kut as provided for by their customary laws, became less and less important and ignored, culminating into complete abandonment of the same. People have almost forgotten even existence of such a 'cultural heritage' as the Kut festivity[107].

Identity of a community is known by its rich cultural heritage and perpetuation thereof. Rapid vanishing of the age-old tradition and direction placed the resurgent generation at a loss, and became aware of the vacuum that had been created by such abandonment of the Kut culture due to Christianity. It was dreaded that with such relegation of the rich cultural heritage into oblivion, posterity would be at the cross-road of life.

It was found that there was no conflict whatsoever between Christianity and culture. The two could go hand in hand without being encroached upon each other. While the part of 'village priest' can be appropriately substituted by the role of Christian Pastor, the glamour of 'Ju' and its resultant pleasantries can be replaced by tea and snacks, fun and frolics of all kinds, etc. More innovatives can be incorporated into the system retaining the intrinsic social values.

Modernized items, such as, beauty contest and fashion show are changes that have been fed into the new fibres of Kut culture.

Likewise, with a view to harmonizing the festival with modernity and new way of life which are completely divorced from the traditional homogeneous village life, the many Kut festivals observed in the days of yore have been moduled into a single occasion of Kut on November 1 of every year.

Radcliffe Brown[108] contends that such changes reflect the changing aspects of society signifying creation of new aspects in the form of new tradition or redefinition of an old one.

Tradition and culture should not be static. It must be dynamic in its growth, assimilating what good things have been provided by a living society, absorbing local and outside elements in its vibrant whole so as to enter into uncharted areas to make it possible to withstand the winds of change from all directions without the original framework and values being sacrificed at the altar of change and dynamism.

REFERENCES

1. Lt. Col. J. Shakespear : *The Lushai Kuki Clans;* 1912, Part -I; p.3
2. Lt. Col. J. Shakespear: *Op. cit.,* Part –II, pp. 127-132.
3. *Ibid.,* pp. 132 - 145.
4. *Ibid.,* pp.146 - 186.
5. *Ibid.,* pp.187 - 210.
6. *Lt. Col. J. Shakespear : Op. cit.,* p. 211.
7. *Ibid.,* p. 224.
8. Romila Thapar: *A History of India,* Vol. I, Penguin Books, New Delhi, 1990 (Reprint), p. 29.
9. J.B. Bhattacharjee: *Keynote Address delivered at the Seminar on sources of the History of North-East India,* organized by ICHR -- NERC, Guwahati, on March 12-14, 2002.
10. Lt. Col. J. Shakespear: *The Lushai Kuki Clans,* 1912; p. 147.
11. Sangkima : *'Oral Sources of Mizo History' – Paper presented at the Seminar on Sources of History of North-East India,*

organized by ICHR – NERC, Guwahati, on March 12-14, 2002.

12. Sangkima : *'The coming and settlement of Myanmarese in Mizoram: – Paper presented in the National Seminar on cross border movement of people......, 25.4.02.*
13. Sangkima : *Essay on the History of the Mizos : 2004,* p.9 : *Spectrum Publications Pan Bazar, Guwahati, Assam.*
14. Suhas Chatterjee : *Early History of the Mizos : Proceedings of North-East India History Association,* 9th Session, Guwahati, 1988; p.102
15. Suhas Chatterjee : *Op. cit.,* p.102.
16. Rev. James Long : *Analysis of the Rajamala or the Chronicles of Tripura* (Reprint), 1955; p.11.
17. Rev. James Long : *Op. Cit.,* p. 7.
18. *Ibid.*
19. S.K. Chatterjee: Kirata – Jana-Krti: *The Asicatic Society,* Calcuta, 1974, pp. 26-36.
20. M.C. Burkitt : *Our Early Ancestors: Cambridge, London,* 1929, p. 79.
21. Rev. Liangkhaia; *Mizo Chanchin,* Aizawl (Reprint), 1978, p. 1.
22. Sangkima: *A study of the Mizos with reference to their early Home;- Paper presented at the International Seminar held on 7-9 April, 1992 at Aizawl on the studies on the Minorities Nationalities of North-East India : The Mizos.*
23. Peter Kunstadter: *"Burma" in South-East Asian Tribes; Minorities and Nations;* Peter Kunstadter, Princeton University, 1967, pp. 79-84.
24. G.H. Luce is quoted here by F.K. Lehman in his book, *'The Structure of Chin Society",* Aizawl, 1980, p. 12.
25. *Ibid.*
26. *Ibid.*
27. G.E. Harvey: *History of Burma,* London, 1945, p. 4.
28. P.C. Choudhury: *The History of Civilization of the People of Assam to the 12th Century A.D.,* Guwahati (Reprint), Spectrum Publication, 1987, p. 75.
29. N.D. Chaudhury : *The Early inhabitants of North-East India with special reference to Mizoram, Paper presented in the International Seminar on 7-9 April, 1992 at Aizawl.*

30. S.K. Chatterji: Kirata-Jana-Krti, *The Asicatic Society*, Calcutta, 1994, p. 26.
31. *Ibid.*, p. 27.
32. *Ibid.*, p. 28.
33. N.D. Chaudhury: *Op.Cit.*, p. 1.
34. *The work is done by W. Vincent, W.H. Schoff also writes the Periplus.*
35. P.C. Choudhury: *Op. Cit.*, p. 28 (Foot Note).
36. *Ibid.*, pp. 31-35.
37. *Ibid.*, p. 34.
38. Edward Gait; A History of Assam, Guwahati, 1926, p. 10.
39. *Ibid.*, p. 34.
40. *For detailed discussion kindly refer to Kirata-Jana-Kirti.*
41. *Ibid.*, p. 34.
42. *Ibid.*, p. 35.
43. *Ibid.*, p. 16.
44. P.C. Choudhury: *Op. cit.*, p. 83.
45. G.A. Grierson; *Linguistic Survey of India*, Volo. I, Delhi (Reprint), 1967, pp. 41-48.
47. G.A. Soppitt : *A Short Account of the Lushai-Kuki Tribes*, etc. Aizawl (Riprint), 1976, p. 7.
48. E.T. Dalton, *Descriptive Ethnology of Bengal*, Calcutta, 1972, pp.110-111.

    G.A. Grierson; *Kuki-Chin Group*, "Linguistic Survey of India: *Op. cit.*, p.1.
49. A.C. Bhattacharya : *Progressive Tripura*, New Delhi, 1930, p.19.
50. R.N. Roychoudhury; *Tripura Through the Ages;* 1983, p. 17.
51. A.C. Bhattacharya : *Op. cit.*, p.19.
52. Rev. James Long; Analysis of the Rajamala or the Chronicles of Tripura (Reprint), 1955, p. 8.
53. *Ibid.*, p. 7.
54. Suhas Chatterjee; *"Early History of the Mizos" Proceedings of the North-East India, History Association (NEIIIA)*, Guwahati, 1988, p. 102.
55. Sangkima: *Some sources of the Early Mizos : "A Chronological Study"*, NEIHA Proceedings, Jorhat, 1993, p.91. A detailed discussion of the early history of the Mizos is given in this article.

56. *Ibid.*, p. 92.
57. A.G. McCall: *The Lushai District Cover*, p. 35.
58. Major General Sir James Johnstone : *Manipur and the Naga Hills;* 1971(Reprint), pp. 25-27; Published by Vivek Publishing House, 18-D, Kamala Nagar, Delhi – 7.
59. Col. W. McCulloch : *Valley of Manipur:* 1857, pp. 54-75, (Reprint 1980), Gian Publication, 11435, Shakti Nagar, Delhi.
60. *A description of the Burmese Empire,* p. 33, Chapter 6, compiled by Reverent Father, Sangermano, from Native Document and translated from his manuscript by Dr. D. William Tandy, Member of the Roman Sub-Committee, printed in Rome in 1833.
61. *Envoy Extraordinary and Minister Plenipotentiary of the Union of Burma, dated 15th May, 1960 addressed to Mr. Haokholet Ngailut, General Secretary, Kuki National Assembly,* Changoubung South, B.P.O. Kangpokpi, Manipur.
62. Sangkim, *Essays on the History of Mizos,* 2004, p. 27.
63. *Revolutionary leader siding with the British during the second World War.*
64. T. Gougin: *History of Zomis,* 1984, pp. 176-181.
65. B.B. Goswami, 1979: *The Mizo Unrest : A study of politicization of culture :* Jaipur; Aalekh Publishers.
66. Rev. Lalbiaktluanga, 1989, pp. 63 – 71: *Theological Trends in Mizoram. In Towards a Tribal Theology: The Mizo perspective.* K. Thanzauva (ed). Mizoram: Mizo Theological Conference, with the help of Eastern Theologies College, Jorhat, Assam.
67. *The Holy Bible* : Leviticus 26 : 12.
68. *Ibid.*, and Deuteronomy 4 : 27-28 and 28 : 64.
69. H.I. Marshall: *The Karen people of Burma; University of Columbia,* Ohio, 1929, p. 10.
70. Zaithanchhungi: Israel- Mizo Identity; J.R. Bros' Offset Printer, Aizawl, 1990, p.11.
71. *Letter dated February 3, 1984 from Lavy Benjamin, Gen. Secy of MPSNEIM (Manasseh People Shinlung-Israel North-East India, Mizoram) to the Chief Rabbinet (Read Rabbinical) Council, Israel.*
72. Rev. Lalbiaktluanga, 1989, pp. 63 – 71: *Theological Trends in Mizoram. In Towards a Tribal Theology: The Mizo*

perspective. K. Thanzauva (ed). Mizoram: Mizo Theological Conference, with the help of Eastern Theologies College, Jorhat, Assam.

73. M. Samra, 1991 : *The Tribe of Manasseh : Judaism in the Hills of Manipur and Mizoram: Man in India:* 71(1) : 183-202.
74. Ibid.
75. M. Samra, 1991 : Op. cit.
76. Dr. Khuplam Milui Linthang: *President, Manmasi Innpi, Manmasi Chate* (Kuki-Chin-Mizo), Thulhun Kidang Masa : 1967.
77. *Ibid.*
78. *Ibid.*
79. V.L. Benjamin and Y. Stephen, 1972, p. 2 : *Mongoloid Israels of Manipur State,* Bualzang: Manipur Jewish Organisation.
80. *Strong Indian tradition is available from the legendary myths of creation and the stories related with the prime ordeal Manu and those in the successive periods.*
81. Zauhangchhungi, 1990, p. 30 : *Israel – Mizo Identity, Aizawl, Mizoram : St. Joseph's Press.*
82. *"Conversion among the children of Menasseh" (unpublished paper school of Education, the Hebrew University).*
83. Sawngtinlam (n.d.): The Tuklemsom Tribe, Kangpokpi, Manipur : H. Seilal Press.
84. Myer Samra, 1991: pp. 183-202 : *The Tribe of Manasseh : Judaism in the Hills of Manipur and Mizoram Man in India 71(a). Prof. Myer Somra himself is a Jews, married to a Khongsai girl of Kuki (Miao) Tribe of Manipur and is now working in the Department of Anthropology, University of Sydney, New South Welsh, 2006, Australia.*
85. *E.B. Tylor: Primitive Culture* (2 Vols), 1874, New York, p. 1.
86. B. Malinawski: *Scientific Theory of Culture;* 1944, p. 67.
87. H.T. Mazumdar: *Grammar of Sociology,* 1966, p. 519.
88. T.S. Gangte: *The Kukis of Manipur,* 1993; p. 133; Gyan Publishing House, 5 Ansari Road, New Delhi-2.
89. *Ibid.*
90. B.K. Roy Burman : *Demographic and Socio-Economic Profile of the Hill Areas of the North-East India* (Census of India, 1961); 1970, p. 218.

91. T.S. Gangte, *Op. cit.*, p. 134.
92. T.S. Gangte, *Op. cit.*, p. 134.
93. T.S. Gangte, *Op. cit.*, p. 135.
94. *Ibid.*
95. *Ibid.*
96. *Ibid.*
97. *Ibid.*
98. T.S. Gangte, *Op. cit.*, p. 141.
99. *Ibid.*, p. 140.
100. T.S. Gangte, *Op. cit.*, p. 141.
101. T.S. Gangte, *Op. cit.*
102. *Ibid.*, p. 142.
103. Col. J. Shakespear: *The Lushai Kuki Clans,* 1712, p.1; Part I, Tribal Research Institute, Aizawl, Mizoram.
104. Sir Robert Reid : *History of Frontier Areas Bordering on Assam from 1883 - 1941;* 1942: p.105, Shillong.
105. T.S. Gangte : *Origin, Concept and Growth of Kut* : 1985, p. 8.
106. T.S. Gangte, *Op. cit.*, p. 8.
107. T.S. Gangte, *Op. cit.*, p. 9.
108. A.R. Radcliffe Brown : *African System of Kinship and Memago* : 1910, London.

3

Historical and Traditional Background of Customary Laws of the Meiteis

In early society, where the social organisation was simple, disputes were settled by the matriarch or the patriarch, or the council of elders, or elementary courts according to the prevailing social customs. There was no articulated system of law-making or law-dispensing power and conduct was regulated by practices that came into vogue spontaneously.[1] Thus the convention of passing attributes of custom from one generation to another which originally governed human conduct become customary and subsequently these acquire legalistic overtones. Violation of these becomes taboo and thus emerges customary laws which evolve in an intrinsic and inviolable ways.

Custom as One of the Sources of Law

Custom is not synonymous as customary laws. There may be various customs without legal authority as against which customary laws have sanction of the society, violation of which is punishable. It is regarded as one of the earliest sources of law. Normally, the common laws mainly consisting of customs developed into personal laws and the courts took due cognizance of it. Customs in our society still hold sway. Among the Hindus and the Muslims marriages are permitted according to procedure established by customs in their respective communities. Though the Hindu Marriage Act does not simplify the procedure, it does not abrogate traditional customs with regard to it. Similarly, traditional divorce by custom is also recognised.[2] The same is free of the many other institutionalized customary and personal laws. Laws were created to govern societies in a regulated manner and streamline chaos which had prevailed in unorganized society.

The history of Manipur before 33 A.D. remains vague and is presently under scrutiny and revaluation. In Manipur, between Nongda Lairen Pakhangba (33 A.D. – 154 A.D.) and Charairongba (1697 A.D. – 1709 A.D.) customs, both local and general, got established and were treated as the laws of the state. It prevailed, as it was marked by the Primary Council in an early case, Hurpurshad V, Shed Dyal[3] that a custom is a rule which in a particular family or a particular class or community or in a particular (Case) has from long usage, obtained the force of law. This rule is reestablished in Wahengbam Kokngang Singh Vs Wahengbam Ongbi Pishak Devi[4] that a custom is a rule which, in a particular family or particular class or community or in a particular district has long from usage, obtained the force of law. It must be old, certain and reasonable and being in derogation to the general rules of law, must be constructed strictly. Modern Jurisprudence has divided custom into legal and conventional. A legal custom is one whose legal authority is absolute as per and *proprio vigore* possesses the force of law. A conventional law, on the other hand, has no such absolute authority. Its authority is conditional on its acceptance and incorporation in agreements between the parties to be bound by it. The local custom may be either local or general while conventional custom is established practice, which is legally binding and has either expressly or impliedly been incorporated in a contract between the parties. Hence, it was held that in the absence of cogent evidence that alleged custom viz., the Sons on attaining majority became separate from their father during the latter's lifetime does not exist in Manipur. In those days both legal and conventional customs[5] were absolute.

The reign of Pamheiba alias Garib Niwaz (1709 AD – 1748 AD) is a landmark in this regard in the history of administration of justice in Manipur. Before that the king sat in the Cheirap, the highest court of justice. All cases were tried and disposed of in consultation with the Council of Ministers and the Sixty-four Phamdons. The king could not enforce his will against the social customs and conventions. In cases in which the king acted as a judge, he was expected to decide them impartially, and according to the customary laws of Meiteis which was considered to be the 'king of kings'. In the past any deviation from customary law was considered as a dereliction of duty.[6]

But when Garib Niwaz came to power a great change occurred in the nature of administering customary laws. Henceforth the laws *Strictu Sensu* had become imperative and as such the command of the king became operative. No one could violate it and any act contrary to the command of the king was considered as a dereliction of duty and therefore, punishable. This can be seen in case of O. Bhogeswar Singh's "Khagemba Langjee".[7] Meidingu Garib Niwaz tortured his subjects when he introduced religious reforms in Manipur.

Instances are galore, such as, firstly, one Pandit, Moirang Lalhamba by name was roped by the neck for his strong opposition against Ramandi religion. But he was saved by Louremba Khongnangthaba.

Secondly, as per Meitei Customary Law, deceased persons were buried. However, it was abandoned during the reign of Garib Newaz (1709 – 1948). Accordingly, as per his royal decree, dead bodies were, instead cremated since February (Pahirel), 1725, contended Gangmumei Kabui.[8]

Thirdly, though there was no such customary Law pertaining to construction of images of indigenous deities, as a religious binding law, during the reign of Bhagyachandra (1749 – 1798) installation of the image of Govindajee became legally binding since 1776. It was made from the trunk of Jackfruit tree.[9]

History has many records to show that whenever strict laws were allowed to stem, decaying wrong interpretations, the common people disliked it. Manipur's evidence shows implicitly that there was animosity between the king and his subjects during the reign of Garib Niwaz. With the introduction of Ramandi order of Vaisnavism through Shantidas Gosai the customs and conventions of Manipur changed. It had accelerated a pace of cultural integration of the state with the rest of the country. Many manuscripts of Manipuri Puyas were burnt and substituted by a number of fictitious Puyas which were later known "Shangai Phamang".[10]

From the above we infer that customs had the force of law in the administration of justice until the reign of Charairongba (1697 – 1709 A.D.) and some changes came over in it since the reign of Garib Niwaz (1709-1748 A.D.) It is not observable in Manipur only but all over rest of territories beyond our country. Indian customs and traditions have had great impact over Nepal, Burma, South East Asia and even East Asia – China and Japan. India's contributions to these countries, in the past, have been fundamental in character.

The loss of sovereignty of Manipur in 1891 A.D. had its immediate effect in that both the law-making and law dispensing powers were taken over by the British-India Government. The British, slowly but decisively wiped out the whole administrative system of the native state in order to give their laws through systemic governance. They re-established some of the many native courts, namely, the Cheirap, town Panchayat, Mohammedan Panchayat and Rural Panchayat Courts.[11] In addition to these courts, four other courts viz, Court of the Political Agent, Court of the Superintendent of the State, Court of the Assistant to the Political Agent and Court of the Assistant to the Superintendent of the State were also established. All cases both civil and criminal in which one of the parties was a British subject were tried in the Court of Political Agent. While deciding the cases they did not always follow the customary laws of Meitei but tried cases according to English Laws and procedures. During the period, 1891 A.D. – 1907 A.D. when Maharaja Churachand was a minor, Major Maxwell, in his capacity as the Superintendent of the State, tried cases that were not covered by the jurisdiction of the Panchayat Court and the Cheirap Court.[12] Thus the extension of British administration over the people of Manipur who were strongly averse to any domination or control was not without disturbance.[13] Nevertheless, when the State took up its function of administering justice, it could not totally abrogate the value of customs and customary laws of Meiteis. It accepted as valid some of the rules of rights already accepted by the society of which it was itself a product. No doubt, Maxwell could not easily abolish the evil practices of Lallup (forced labour) and slavery system in the Manipur's system of Governance. When Lallup was abolished in the case of the valley, it was retained in the form of 'forced coolies' in the case of hill people so that construction of roads could be speeded up.[14] Maxwell wrote : "Coolies for road making, for transport, for slavery, for police, for the military, have been supplied by the hill tribes. Tangkhuls were forced to serve in the Chin Hills in 1893. The Naga tribes who inhabit the hills traversed by the Cachar Road, work in the cold weather on the road repairs and provide postal runners throughout the year".[15] The main reason was that the customs of the hill people supported the use of unpaid labour for the common purpose of the tribe. The British thus misused the custom and enforced it limitlessly for their own advantages. The British interpreted laws in their favour and made a sham of native customs and laws. It reflected their mindset.

There had been a tremendous change during and after the British rule in the administration of the State. Even now custom has not wholly lost its law-making efficacy. Since customary laws are so deep-rooted, Sir James Carter significantly pointed out, "What has governed the conduct of man from the beginning of time will continue to govern it to the end of the time..."[16], but social change can be effected only through a wisely regulated legal stand in which the continuity of customary laws may not be mandatory but may play a significant role. We look into some of these concepts of customs.

Marriage

It has been very often repeatedly pointed out that marriage is not a mere union of sexes. It is a legally recognised union of man and woman. It is an act or ceremony by which man and woman become husband and wife.[17] In Gopal Kishan vs. Mithilesh Kumare[18] the Allahabad High Court observed:

> "... The institution of matrimony under the Hindu Law is a sacrament, and not a mere socio-legal contract. It is not performed for mere emotional gratification and is not a mere betrothal. Its content is religious. It is regarded as part of life of the soul. It is holy spiritual union corresponding to consortium omnium vitoe of Rome, a process by which the husband and wife become one."

Among the Hindus marriage is an institution. It is a sanskar. In Manipur, it is generally regarded as '*Luhongba*' or '*Yumpanba*' the social recognition of the practice by which man and woman live together as husband and wife to form a family. The etymological significance of *Luhongba* is derived from two 'Meitei-lon' terms 'Lu' which means 'Kok (head)' and 'Hongba' means to 'transfer' or 'change'. Here, *Kok* does not signify the organs of the human body. It may signify two things – first, the mental attitude of the bride, and secondly the heredity of the 'Yek' or 'Salai' of the bride's family. Etymologically, therefore, Luhongba means the transfer or change of the mental attitude of the bride from her natal life to the newly formed conjugal life. In other words, it may mean the transfer or change of heredity of the bride from her parents and clan to the bridegroom's. In the Meitei society, the importance of marriage lies mainly with the female side as the system of polygamy is followed and not polyandry and the society is also patriarchal.

The *Chatlam Lutin* of Meiteis favours monogamy. But it accords sanction to a man to marry any number of women provided he has the ability and confidence to support and maintain his large harem. '*Mou-Luhongba* divorcee-marriage' and '*Lukhra Luhongba* – widow marriage' were allowed but they could not marry their husband's brother and no proper rituals of marriage permitted to be performed. Only virgin could be married with proper rituals of marriage performed.[19] The marriage before puberty (child marriage) was not practiced.

Forms of Marriage

There are three forms of marriages among the Meiteis, two approved and one unapproved. In Hindu Law, the legal consequences of the approved and those of condemned forms of marriages were different but it was not so in the case of Meiteis. Even the child born of the unapproved forms of marriages could became the king of Manipur.[20] A woman married through any form of marriage became a 'Mou'.[21] The three forms of marriages are :-

(i) Marriage through proper engagement and negotiation among the guardians of the parties;

(ii) Marriage by elopement, also known as love-marriage; and

(iii) Marriage by force, that is, marriage without the consent from the bride herself or from her parents.

Out of the three forms of marriages, the first two were approved forms. It holds good even today in Manipur among the Meitei society. But the third one though was not an approved form; it presented a case of fete accompli which could not be ignored defacto. The parents of the girl had no other choice but to accept it and give it proper shape in society.

Polygamy

As mentioned, though the *Chatlam Lutin* of Meiteis favoured monogamy, the society permitted polygamy which was common among the well-do-do, polyandry was not permitted.[22] It was the ambition of most men of high rank and wealth to possess a large harem. Instances are many, such as, *Naothing-khong Phambal Kaba* (the coronation of Meidingu Naothingkhong (663 A.D. – 763 A.D.).[23] Chada Laihui also refers to the two wives of Lam Kyamba (1512 A.D. – 1523 A.D.), ten wives of Chingthangkhomba (1759 A.D. – 1762 A.D. and 1763 A.D. – 1798 A.D.) and twelve wives of Chandrakirti (1834 A.D. – 1844 A.D. and 1850 A.D. – 1886 A.D.).[24] Debendra in a short reign of three months, managed to amass ninety-six wives.[25]

The wives of the king have been classified as *Leimarel* (the first wife), *Apanbi* (the second wife), and *Leimakhubi* (the third wife) and *Leimakhubi Naha* (the fourth wife)[26]. The other wives had no titles but they were generally known as Leima.

Polygamy is also prevalent among the Chhothe tribe of the Mizo Society.[27]

Offer of the King's Wife to the Ministers

Another peculiar feature of marriage in Meitei society was that whenever the king was satisfied at the service of his minister or at his bravery he gave his wife to the minister concerned as the award of his service. Instances can be inferred from the legend of Moirang like '*Khamba-Thoibi*'[28] and *Tonu Laijinglembi*.[29] Such form of marriage was hardly practiced in other societies of the world. It had a propitiating character and an honour but in each case it showed that women did not have much rights and were used as property with alienable rights.

Conditions for a Valid Marriage

Under the customary law of Meiteis the following three conditions are necessary for a valid marriage:

(i) Identification of Yek or Salai between the parties;

(ii) Parties must be beyond the prohibited degree of relationship, that is they were not Yek-tinnaba (within the same gotra/exogamy), Shairuk-tinnaba (belonging to the same clan or lineage), Pen-dinnaba (persons belonging to different yek-salais from a common grandmother) and Pee-tinnaba (persons having a common maternal ancestor), Imungnaba (persons of common maternal grandfather) the law or rule of exogamy must on no account be abrogated or sidelined; and

(iii) Proper performance of ceremonies of marriage.

(i) Identification of Yek or Salai

(i) If the parties belonged to the same Yek or Salai, the marriage was void, unless it was sanctioned by the customs. T.C. Hudson writes, "The Meiteis are exogamous as regards the clans or salais into which they are divided but are endogamous as regards members of other tribes, though there are records of marriages between Brahmins and Meitei girls. The Angoms were not allowed to marry with Khaba-Nganbas, Moirangs or Luwangs.[30] Similarly, Bimola concluded that among the Meitei there are certain restrictions regarding marriage between the people belonging to the same clan called Yek.[31] The Luwangs were forbidden to take their wives from among the Khumans because they were the descendants of Poreiton;[32] and the Moirangs were not permitted to marry the Khaba-Nganbas etc.[33] because of their being four big exogamous kin groups as per Meitei kinship Puya; each group consists a number of Yumnaks (major lineages belong to different exogamous clan who are what the Meiteis refer to as Shailuk-Achouba (four big Shailuks)".[34] Likewise, the Ningthouja is restricted to marry with the Mungyanjam and Lairenjam.[35] Thus the main requisite of a valid marriage is that both the parties to the marriage should belong to the same tribe. At the same time they should not belong to the same Yek or Salai. These were clearly identified and recognised by the community of the ancient Meitei society. The main feature of the ancient Meitei custom was that both the parties to the marriage must belong to the same class or tribe was considered in the incident of Meidingu Paikhomba and the daughter of Maram Khullakpa (Ingallei). But the actual tragedy resulted in the fact that Ingallei belonged to the Khullakpa who happened to be an enemy of the king and as such Ingallei was treated as prisoner of war. A Prisoner of the war could not be the queen of the king.

(ii) Parties to be Beyond the Prohibited Degree of Relationship

As mentioned above, tradition maintains that one should not marry a woman of the same Yek or Salai. The parties should not be *Yek-tinnaba* or *Salai-tinnaba*, or *Pen-dinnaba* of each other. Custom, therefore, prohibited marriage between persons related to each other within certain degrees, probably for physiological, social and scientific reasons, so that a marriage was invalid if it was made between persons related to each other within the prohibited degrees unless such marriage is sanctioned by the custom.

A man, therefore, could not marry a girl of the same Yek or Salai as they were deemed to have descended from a common ancestor in the male line (patrilineal). Any union within the same Yek or Salai is deemed as *Yek-tinnaba* and is strictly prohibited by the Meitei custom. The child or children of such marriage illegitimate and the couple are liable to banishment.

Again, persons of different Yek or Salai who are the progeny of the same mother or grand-mother but of different fathers. or grandfathers are deemed to have descended from a common ancestor in the female line (matrilineal). People belonging to these Yeks or Salais are in no case permitted to marry each other in the Meitei society. Any union within these prohibited degrees is known as *Sairuk-tinnaba*. The prohibition is extended upto fifth generation.

Furthermore, a man cannot marry a lineal descendant of his mother or grand-mother. Any union of such prohibited degree is known as Pen-tinnaba. Such prohibition goes not further than one generation.[36] The Sanabam, the Salam, the Akoijam, the Nengoubam, the Laitonjam, the Huidrom,the Kasanam are for instance, Pen-tinnaba and as such marriage is forbidden among families with these surnames.[37]

In spite of the above prohibition the Chatlam Lutin permits the marriage system of the Mane-Matung Inba. The best illustration is provided by the story of matrimonial relationship between the royal family of the Meitei kings and that of Angom Ningthou.[38] Marriage system with mother's brother's daughter, known as 'preferential marriage', is very commonly practiced among many tribal groups, such as, Thadou, Paite, Gangte, Vaiphei, etc., except the Lushai, in Mizo Society.

(iii) Marriage Rituals

There are three stages in ritual ceremony of marriage in Manipur. The rituals are :-

(a) the betrothal;

(b) the formalities of Luhongba including Loukhatpa; and

(c) the Chengluk-Nungsang-Hangba and Mapam-Chak-kouba.

(a) The Betrothal

This is the first stage towards a marriage ceremony consisting of three major conditions. First, *Haija-Chatchaba* (engagement which is to be initiated by the bridegroom's parents) through elders of the clan to the bride's parents and the kinship relations is held twice or thrice. When parents go for *Haija-Chatchaba* they took with them vegetables and fruits. Secondly, after having proper agreement between the parents of both the parties *Yathang-thaba* (affiance and the like) is held with Waroipot (final decision before the members of the families). Thirdly, the engagement is completed with *Haijapot or Heijingpot Puba.*[39] During *Heijingpot*, the groom's party must bring in addition five seven or more baskets of fruits, of an odd number (*Chang-thokpa*) which are presented to the *Apokpa*, originator of the girls' sagei. These baskets must include *Heikru*[40] and *Heining.*[41] A phanek and Laiphi (garments) are offered to the household *Lai*, together with fruits, Kabok (puffed rice), Mana-Kwa (betel leaf and nut). Gift must be brought to the lam Lai (the deity of the area). These gifts of food are reserved for the Lai concerned, and may be distributed among the members and friends of the family. These are kept inside the house and only presented to the appropriate Lai when all the guests have departed. These may then be eaten by members of the household and outsiders. Some portions of the food are set aside for the girl and her immediate friends who remained within the house during the Haijapot ceremony. The rest of the food is distributed to the guests.[42] when the bride's parents are pleased with the imploration of the bridegroom's parents, the betrothal and noticed among the members of the clan and also to the village. Such a process is known as *Pumai-Urong-Khinba-Kakphei-Thaba.*[43] It is customary and is performed mandatorily. It is for the well being of the family and maintenance of social respectability.

If, after betrothal, the girl elopes with another man, the father of the original would-be-groom can claim the cost of the *Waroipot* or *Haijapot* or of both as the case may be.[44]

(b) The Formalities of Luhongba Including Loukhatpa

On the very day of marriage ceremony, there must be an occasion which is known as Lai-Tin-Thaba. For that purpose two Phiruks (baskets) containing of vegetables, fruits, flowers and sweets are brought by the party of the bridegroom. One Phiruk is reserved for Sagei Lai (the deities of the bride's particular Sagei) and the other for Lam Lai (the deities of the area where the bride resides). These two Phiruks are kept inside the house of the bride and offered only to the appropriate deities. Such offering signifies that the bride belongs to the family of the other sagei. After identifying and showing respect to the parents and guardian of the bride is gifted to the bridegroom.

The marriage ceremony, in ancient time was not accompanied by Kirtans nor did the bride put on Potloi.[45] The bride simply put on phanek and Innaphi (the local garments). On a fixed auspicious day which both the parties deemed fit, the parents of the bride with their kin relatives escorted the bride to the bridegroom's home with some dowry. After that the bride's parents offered them a good feast with which they concluded the marriage. But the prospects of the couple are determined by the rite of *Meitei-Nga-Thaba* (a special Manipuri rite) which is also known as *Ushin*.[46] Two fish of the same kind are set free in the pond and their movements are strictly observed which indicate the prosperity and longevity of the conjugal life of the bride and the bridegroom.[47]

An interesting feature of the marriage system in ancient Meitei Society was bride-price. There was a system of paying money, cow, etc to the bride. Such system is known as *Mangkat*.[48] Another similar case of marriage payment is in regard to the payment of a piece of gold or a simple item that may substitute the value of gold as per agreement between the parties of the bride and the groom, most preferably '*Sana Konyai*', in case the bride or the groom is Royal sibling married to a non-royal clan. This is called "*Sana Kwa-gok Hanba*".[49] This item is not returned on the demise of the bride or the groom whoever received the same. The phenomenon is evidenced in the story of '*Panthoibi Khongkul*' and '*Nongban Pombi Luwaoba*'. But when the husband dies, the parents of the widow had to pay back the *Mangkat* to the husband's family. If she is unable to do so she may even become the wife of her brother-in-law. This practice remained in use rather surreptitiously.

(c) The Chengluk-Nungshang-Hangba and Mapam-Chak-Kouba

Another important feature of marriage is the rite of *Chengluk-Nungshang Hangba*.[50] This rite is performed on the fifth day after the wedding by the bridegroom's party. Such *Chengluk-Nungshang-Hangba* is followed by *Mapam-Chak-Kouba*. This is the last rite of marriage which the parents of the bride provide and offer a good food to the couple. The rite is performed on the sixth day after the wedding at the residence of the bride's parents. On that day, the parents of the bride introduce the bridegroom to the near relatives and make him familiar with them to gain social respectability.

Here, it is pertinent to note that there is a peculiar feature in the system of marriage in Manipur about the girl who elopes, even for one night cannot be married with proper rituals of marriage. Nevertheless, if the parents of both the parties have mutual agreement on the elopement and special rite called *Loukhatpa* generally held at night could be performed. Such restrictions are no longer observed. Even for a woman who had eloped for more than one week the proper rituals are performed without any stigma. It has become an accepted form of marriage today and the Meitei society has compromised in the interest of the couple and for peace in society. The social turbulence gets settled gradually.

Awoonpot

The concept of *Awoonpot* (dowry) in Meitei society customary law has its source in archaic Manipuri literature Panthoibi Khongkul and Nongban Pombi Luwaoba, which mention the giving of *Awoonpot*. In Meitei society, the family of the bride gives dowry according to their means. Normally, a Lairum[51] cloth is included in the dowry. The other items consist of *Phanek* (female garment), *Innaphi* (female chaddar), gold ornaments and other suitable presents. If both the parties are of the same social rank they will also give clothes to the respective near relatives, but if they are not of the same rank then the party of the lower rank only gives to that of the higher.[52] An upward or downward social mobility is observed in such cases.

In the royal family of ancient Meitei society, twenty-five paris (62.5 acres approximately) of paddy fields were to be given in the marriage of every princess as dowry which was also a revenue-free estate. The paddy fields later on came to be known as *Kharpos* land.[53] One important feature in the dowry is that all gifts and presents to her, is owned by the bride throughout her life. She may sell, give or dispose it off at her will. Even after divorce, she retains her exclusive right over the property. This clearly refers to the tenets of the matriarchal system in which the stree-dhana remains with the lady for all times to come. It is normally handed down to women folk of the family only. It is a significant customary law.

Divorce and Child Maintenance

As in every society, divorce was recognised and permissible under the customary laws of the Meiteis. However, there is a little confusion as to the identification of the term in Manipuri equivalent. People commonly translate '*Khainaba*' into 'divorce'. Singh strongly opposed the identification of divorce as equivalent to Manipuri khainaba.[54] N. Ibobi was of the view that although '*khainaba*' and 'divorce' meant the same thing, they were different. If *khainaba* was initiated by a woman, her husband could claim *Nupi Mamal* (bride price), Rs. 50/- from her within a period of three years from the date of Khainaba. After three years the husband cannot claim it as it amounts to *lishang thaba* (setting free). If the man is unwilling to be reunited no '*mamal*' (price) is paid.[55] In Tonsija Vs Hera Singh,[56] it was held that the *Nupi* or *Nupa Mamal* is not payable if the *khainaba* is affected by mutual agreement of the parties.

The *Meitei Khainaba* became absolute after three years. A woman after Khainaba retained the Yek (clan) of her husband until her death or until she became concubine/ mistress of another person. Sons born of such union were prevented to be cooks of *Sagei-Chak-Chanaba* (Common feast of a clan) and *Lai-Chaklon-Katpa* (annual dedication of food to the deity of the clan). In later period when Vaishnavism came they could not take water from Shri Govindaji.

Meitei *Khainaba* was equal to divorce only in a restricted sense of physical separation of a wife from the husband.[57] An instance can be quoted from *Naothingkhong Phambal Kaba*. *Ura-konthouba* (568 A.D. - 658 A.D.), a Meitei King slaughtered the *Shelois* who intruded into the Meitei territory for invading *Haokap Chingsang* and *Khunpham Ngangjing*. The *Shelois* were extremely infuriated against *Ura/konthouba* and wanted to take revenge by killing his son Naothingkhong who was staying at his father-in-law's house (Wamei Lanthaba's house) But *Naothingkhong* was saved by the skill and presence of mind of his wife, *Pitanga*. The unhappy incident became a cause for physical separation between Naothingkhong and Pitanga.[58]

There might, therefore, be any controversy as to the identification of the Manipuri equivalent for English word 'divorce'. It, in any case, was permissible under Meitei custom also.

Procedure and Grounds for Divorce (*Khainaba*)

Divorce is permissible under Meitei custom as it is permissible under the Hindu Law, whether it comes from the husband's side or from the wife's. There is no condition attached to it, it can be obtained at pleasure on any of the following grounds:

(1) ***Adultery:*** Where the wife has, after the solemnization of the marriage had voluntary sexual intercourse with any person other than her husband it amounts to adultery. For instance, Nongpok Panthoibi was betrothed and got married to the son of Khaba but she had illicit relation with Nongpok Ningthou which became a cause for divorce later on.[59] A popular illustration was also available in the story of Luwang Nongban Yaithingkonu, when Konu, the daughter of Moirang Hongnemsumba, got

married to Khuman Kaoba, the former lover of Konu came in the guise of a Hillman and made self-introduction to Khuman Kaoba as the son of his wife's father's friend. Khuyon Haoba halted there for days and developed illicit relation with Konu. Sometime later two children were born to Konu – Thoinu Ahanbi (a daughter) and Haodigon Takol Louthiba (a son). It is noted that the relation between Haoba and Konu was unlawful and became a cause for divorce.[60] Such instances have had great impact upon the Meitei mind set which is reflected in several social practices prevalent among them. Judicial cognizance is taken in such practices.

(2) *Bigamy:* The Meitei custom does not recognise bigamy. Hence, a married woman can never have two husbands simultaneously. But she can be married to a second husband after Khainaba. The best and well known illustrations to this custom is found in the case of Panthoibi with Nongpok Ningthou,[61] and Luwang Nongban Yaithing Konu with Khuyon Haoba.[62] Both were married after separation from their respective husbands. Such social practices are found even today and form part of such social settlements.

(3) *Venereal Disease:* Where the other party has been suffering from a virulent and deadly disease like leprosy in a communicable form, divorce may be sought for. It was held during the reign of Meidingu Naokhomba (411 AD – 428 AD) that Thangyi Taopung Khomba got married to Toibileima, the daughter of Luwang Piba Punshiba. After having two sons viz., Sharan Ichen Ahanba and Yunaoroi Yaimaba, Toibileima was suffering from leprosy and then, she was divorced by Thangyi.[63] There are, however, certain exception to the rule which is substantiated even by the story of Thangyi and Toibileima that Meitei customary laws allow the re-union or restitution of conjugal rights of the spouse for the following reasons :

(a) where the incurable disease has been somehow cured through sufficient treatment; or

(b) when both the spouses have mutual consent and keen intention for re-union.

Illustration

Thangyi Taopung Komba and Toibileima got re-union when the latter was given treatment by Khoujim Chingu Ashiba and her disease was completely cured. After that a son called Kamutomba was born to them.[64]

(4) ***Disloyalty:*** When the wife ignores the advice of her husband and neglects the *Chatlam Lutin* of the family and the clan of her husband.

Illustration

Tampha, later known as Konthoujam Lairembi, neglecting the advice of her husband Lainingthou Sorarel and the Chatlam Lutin of his clan, took food from her parents with devorce. Her little son, Khoiriphaba was brought up by Lainingthou Sorarel.[65]

(5) ***Non-procreation of child:*** Divorce can take place where the spouses could not produce an offspring. In such cases the *Chatlam Lutin* allows the separation of the wife from her husband. However, exceptional by-laws are available through mutual consent of the parties against divorce, provided to the extent that the wife accepts the keeping of another wife by her husband and the husband desires polygamy. Here we see the justification of the saying – Men are by nature polygamous and they retained this privilege by keeping it as an honourable practice but socially it was looked down upon. Women who suffered

were neglected and down-stated for lack of economic means of livelihood. It was unjust.

(6) ***Non-Procreation of male child:*** If the wife has no male issue it amounted to cause for divorce. But the tradition among Meiteis allowed in such cases the practices of polygamy (*Nupi-lonba*). Sometimes, the wife who had no male child accepted another woman to be the wife of her husband to procreate and provide a son for the continuance of male line in the patriarchal mode of society.

Thus divorce could take place on any of the following grounds, that is, where the woman who was in proper wedlock but had no issue, or when the woman showed disloyalty to her husband or when the woman was immoral which was against the social behaviour or when the woman suffered from virulent and incurable diseases etc. If the wife was pregnant at the time of *Khainaba* (divorce) she was entitled to get pots of paddy per annum plus some amount of money meant for her maintenance for the period during which she was unable to work. The same could be given to a divorced wife with a sucking child. This was called *Angang Chakthak* (Maintenance of child). Such *Angang Chakthak* was allowed even to the concubine although she lived or did not live in the man's house.[66]

As regards the maintenance of Child (*Angang Chakthak* the child born of a wife, who is divorced is entitled 12 pots (weighing about 60-65 kg per pot) of paddy as *Angang Chakthak*. This customary practice is allowed even to the concubine, although she live or does not live in the man's house or to a wife even when she is living in her natal (parental) house. But the father is entitled to get his child back after the suckling period is over. Naturally, in the *Chatlam Lutin* of Meitei the maintenance of children is borne by the father or mother as the case may be in whose custody they remain.

Rights of a Divorced Woman

When separation takes place by way of *Khainaba* and becomes absolute and complete, a divorced wife can claim and take away her *awoonpot* (dowry).[67] However, there is an exception to the rule that if the divorce is initiated from the wife's side she cannot claim even the dowry, her real property.

Hanjinnaba (Restitution of Conjugal Rights)

The Literal meaning of '*Hanjinnaba*' is the re-union or reconciliation of the couple or the coming back of the divorced wife to her husband's house. It is customarily done before wa-loithoknaba.[68] However, this act of restitution is free from any binding because it is always at the choice of both, the estranged couple. They may re-establish their married life braving all stakes of their prestige and marital status. In the meantime, any divorced woman who is staying at her natal home is known as 'Mou-Hallakpi'.

There is no legal bar to the restitution of conjugal rights between husband and wife after Khainaba, however long it might be even after the wife had become the concubine of another man.

However according to the rules of chatlam Lutin, restitution of conjugal rights can be made on any of the following ground:

1. Whenever there is mutual consent or agreement between husband and wife and among guardian and relatives of both the parties;[69]
2. Where a son is born to them, the child has become

one of the main causes for their restitution of conjugal rights;[70]

3. When the virulent or venereal diseases has been cured by proper and well treatment. It was held between Thangyi Taopung Khomba and Toibileima during the reign of Naokhomba.[71]

In restitution of conjugal rights, the woman has more rights than the man, because the divorced wife even after having had a re-married life or having lived as a concubine of another person may again become his wife. However, the practice is regarded as social evil. In this regard the following rules may be noted:-

(i) The limitation of conjugal right is three years from the date of divorce.

(ii) The divorced wife belongs to the surname or family of her husband until re-marriage with another person is resumed.

(iii) There shall be no formal marriage ceremony for any re-marriage of married or divorced woman. Her second husband is always abhorred by the society.

(iv) The custom gives cognizance to a woman's formal marriage only once in her life. However, a woman without a husband, has a social stigma and therefore, re-marriage of such woman becomes permissible.

(v) There is no hard and fast rule in divorce, because it is complete when the wife has gone or has been escorted to her natal home, provided her husband had consented to it.

(vi) If the divorce is not confirmed within three years, then such divorce be presumed to have been confirmed automatically.

(vii) Any claim of either bride's or groom's price (if arises) shall be made within three years from the date of divorce and such claim shall be void if made after lapse of three years of divorce.

(viii) No claim of any type shall be made or given by the wife to her husband in case the latter is unwilling to the restitution of their conjugal life. If the divorce is caused due to negligence of the husband who dislikes to any restitution, then he is liable to pay claim or compensation to his wife. In such cases also the limitation is three years.[72]

Maintenance of Wife, Children and Parents

It is the natural and fundamental duty of a man to maintain his wife, children and parents so long as they are unable to maintain themselves. The Chatlam Lutin of Manipur is also bound by the natural and fundamental duties of man.

According to tradition, a father is under obligation to maintain his children till the time of their marriage. A son who marries at a very early age may be protected till he is able to earn his own livelihood.

Second, a father is under obligation to perform ceremonies of his children, such as Yupanthaba(Ipanthaba). It is a ceremony performed by the Maibi on the sixth day of delivery of the child. Chaumba is a ceremony of first rice or solid food eating generally performed in the sixth months after birth, but some persons does it on the third, seventh or ninth month. Nahutpa is a ceremony of piercing the ear. Lugunthangba is a ceremony of taking or wearing sacred thread, which is a Hindu tradition and the marriage ceremony of the child born of a divorced wife living with him or with his or her mother or any other relative. Hence the saying of Meitei tradition:

> *"Icha Poklabadi Icha Shemgadabani"*
> *"Macha Poklabadi Macha Shemgadabani"*[73]

Third, a married girl is always entitled to get proper attention of her husband by way of maintenance including food, shelter, clothing, etc. in every reasonable way.

Fourth, in the case of a divorced wife with infant child or children, living with a parental cousin of her, when she re-marries and goes to his house leaving the child or children with her cousin, the cousin may maintain them; when a divorced wife re-marries to another man, the father is liable for the maintenance of them. On the other hand parents unable to earn for their livelihood are to be maintained by their sons, or daughter in the absence of the former.

Fifth, a child living with a person who is under no obligation to maintain it and the father does not take the child to his house nor provides maintenance for it although the father gets notice that the mother is dead in that particular case, the person who is maintaining the child is entitled to have a claim against the father for the amount he had spent for the maintenance of the child.

Lastly, it is the legal obligation of a step-son to maintain his step-mother when the latter is old and unable to earn for her livelihood. In the absence of the step-son, a daughter or other near relatives, who are the rightful heirs after her death, generally support and look after her out of natural love and affection.

Adoption

Adoption was recognised in ancient Meitei Society. A person may take a son or a daughter in adoption. The kings and nobles maintained adoption as a customary practice whereunder even children of poor families belonging to different Yek-Salais were adopted. Instances as depicted in the Manipuri epic, 'Khamba Thoibi' exclude the adoption of two orphans viz., Khamba (the epic hero) and his sister, Khamnu by Salang Maiba (a person belonging to a hill tribe of Manipur). There are other instances of adoption in the so-called Moirang Kangleiron. Moirang Thoibi, the most beautiful princess and the epic heroine was brought up by the king of Moirang who had no issue. The existence shows that the Meitei custom admits the adoption of a female child also.

Meidingu Khunjaoba (1652 AD – 1666 AD), the forty-seventh king of Manipur had no issue. He adopted Paikhomba, the son of his younger brother, Tonaba. After the death of Khunjaoba, Paikhomba, being the son and successor of Khunjaoba, ascended the throne in 1666 AD.

A father can give for adoption the only son by one of his wives to another wife who has no male issue. For instance, Meidingu Churachand Singh gave his son Jai Singh by his third wife to his first Queen.

A father may give his son for adoption to his friend if the mother of the son dies. Khumu Lairijamba was the guardian of Khuchup Cheimiyang, the son of Kaklen Nongdam Athouba, when the latter gave him for adoption as his son.[74]

A widow can continue adoption even after the death of her husband Premomayee Maharani adopted Birchandra Singh after the death of Maharaj Surchandra.[75]

The adoptive parents, in the eye of Meitei law, are treated as natural parents. The status of adoptive children cannot be affected by the children of the adoptive parents born subsequent to their adoption. All enjoy the same rights and privileges in the matter of inheritance and succession to the property of adoptive parents.[76]

The system is still influential in the present system of Meitei adoption. The primary right of giving a child in adoption is that of the father. Nevertheless it is done in consultation with the mother.[77] The power of giving such adoption as it was practiced in Manipur could not be delegated. No single instance of delegation of power in adoption is available in Manipur till the present day.

Ritual of Adoption

Sagei Chak Khangba (a feast dedicated to the clan of the adoptive father) is performed as a customary ritual at the time of adoption. Sagei-Chak-Khangba could be performed at any time after the physical act of adoption. It appears to have a slight similarly with that of Datta Homam by the Hindus in adoption.

'Sagei-Chak-Khangba' is not necessary in case of an adoption in which the adopted child belongs to the same clan (Yek-Salai) of the adoptive father.

Right and Privileges of The Adopted Son

Naturally an adopted son loses all rights to his real father's property. His rights and privileges are equal to that of a natural born son. He inherits equality with his other brothers born of the adoptive parents after the adoption. Thus, in Manipur the adopted son could become the king in succession of the adoptive father. It was held in the reign of Meidingu Khunjaoba.

Minor and Guardianship

Chatlam Lutin does not specify any hard and fast rule to establish the age of major or minor persons. Cheitharol

Kimbaba, the Royal Chronicle and other Meitei Puyas do not clearly mention about it. However, Meitei custom codified by the Codification Committee consisted of seven persons viz., Mr. Lakshmi Narain, Chief Judge and Chairman of the Codification Committee, Shri L. M. Ibungohal Singh, Judge, Chief Court, Secretary of the Codification Committee, O. Thambal Singh, Member, Gourahari Sharma, Member, Moirangthem Ibungochouba Singh, Member, Sanajaoba, Member and Quasi Waliulla, Member brought out a new source on 'Minority'. It reads as follows:

> "It is now generally behaved that minority terminates at the completion of 18 years in the case of males.

In the case of females – 'Mou" is always taken to have attained Majority.

Ordinarily a girl is called a 'Mou" if she is married on when she has attained the age of 20 years.

In common parlance a young girl is 'Leisabi' if she is not married. There is no hard and fast rule according to custom to establish majority of your females who have not been married.[78]

Guardianship

A 'guardian' means a person having the care of the person of another or of his property or of both.[79] The Meitei tradition considers that when a couple remains in fact, the father, the male family member, is the natural guardian of the person and separates property of his minor children.[80]

After divorce, the father becomes the sole guardian of his children.[81] The mother is only entitled to keep a child during the period of suckling, because the father is entitled to get back after the suckling period. In the absence of father and mother, the eldest son or daughter becomes the guardian of the family.[82] In the absence of the father, mother (if she does not re-marry) is the natural guardian of her minor children. But if she gets married the sageis, the agnate of the father are the guardian of these children.

Nevertheless, as regards the guardianship of an adopted son, it passes on his adoption from his natural father and mother to his adoptive father and mother. For instance Meidingu Khunjaoba adopted Paikhomba, the son of Tonaba. When Meidingu Khunjaoba died he ascended the throne in 1666 AD. The instance shown lawful guardianship and succession by inheritance of the adopted son.

Inheritance and Partition

Although the Chronicle of Manipur does not say at length about the rules of inheritance and partition we know from the principles of Chatlam Lutin that the joint and undivided family is not the normal condition of Meitei society. Therefore, the Meitei society is characterized by the existence of (i) Patriarchal and (ii) divided family system. As a consequence, inheritance, succession and partition became the feature of the divided family as is elsewhere in the country.

Inheritance

A father is the absolute owner of all the property in his possession. He can alienate some of his properties to anyone he likes. But after his death, his sons inherit equally all the property left by him. In the absence of sons, their grandsons will get the property. However, in their normal practice, the son who is living together with the parents during their life time gets some more share than the other brother or brothers.

A widow, in the absence of sons and daughters, may inherit the property of her husband only for her lifetime. After her death, in case she has none, the agnate relatives of her husband inherit the property.

After the death of the father, the sons who inherit property bear all the expenses relating to the marriage ceremony etc. of the unmarried daughter.

Another important feature of laws of Meitei inheritance is that although a son inherits the property of his father all his dependents – the mother and sisters are entitled to resistance.

Thus a divorced daughter has got a right to live at her father's place so long as she does not re-marry. However, the right of residence of a divorced daughter in the homestead land of her maternal uncle was not recognized by the customary law of Meiteis.[83]

Partition

In the case of partition of family properties, all brothers take equal share among themselves. The share of a deceased brother is taken by his heir. But the father has got the absolute right to divide the property among his sons if partition is to be held during his lifetime.

Partition may be made during or after the lifetime of the father. But as T.C. Hudson says, "marriage is of course the cause of separation of the sons from the home",[84] it can be done after the marriage of his son or sons.

Often, there may be undivided family. In such cases also, the property left by the father can be partitioned, that is to say, each member knows his definite share. At the time of partition the eldest son gets, so far as the

Ingkhol (homestead land) is concerned the southern side, second son, next northern and so on and the youngest son the northernmost side so far lengthwise distribution is to take place.[85] But in the case of breadth-wise distribution, the eldest son gets the eastern side, second son next western and so on and the youngest son the westernmost side.

So far as the mother's right in the partition is concerned she cannot herself demand partition, but if a partition takes place between her sons, she is entitled to a share equal to that of a son after deducting the value of the "Nupi Maral" (woman's property) if any, which she might have received from her husband or father-in-law.

A wife is not entitled to any share in the property of her husband and cannot claim or demand for partition during the lifetime of her husband as he is the absolute owner of the property in his possession.

A sonless step-mother can demand partition as between herself and her step-sons after the death of her husband. And she is entitled to a share on partition between her step-sons, but her share is not determined by customary law. Share allotted to mother or step-mother on partition between her son or step-sons is given in lieu of, or by way of provision for, her maintenance.

Another important feature for both inheritance and partition is that if a daughter is to leave her husband's house by way of Khainaba (divorce) or by becoming a widow (Lukhra), if she chooses or is compelled to leave if she can claim residence in her paternal Ingkhol, as of right. It is an elementary custom. So no example or case law need be cited.[86]

The distribution of movable properties customarily done through the principles of 'Chakthung Phithungba'. It is the giving and taking of all permissible share for movable properties which are essential to a separate family. The immovable properties are distributed in accordance with the concept of "Sharuk-Tamba". In Manipur, sons are given a definite share of immovable property at the time of partition.

Succession and Law of Primogeniture

Another important feature of customary law of Meiteis was the rule of succession and the application of the law of primogeniture. From Nongda Lairen Pakhangba (33 AD – 154 AD) down to Meidingu Laitongba (1122 AD-1150 AD) the rule of succession was governed by the law of primogeniture. Atom Yoiremba (1155 AD – 1163 AD) the successor of Loitongba was succeeded by his younger brother Iwanthaba (1163 AD – 1159 AD). The succession of Atom Yoiremba appeared an irregular application of the rule of primogeniture.

After the death of Mungyamba, his son Khagemba succeeded him in 1597 AD. He ruled for 55 years in Manipur. After Mungyamba, three kings viz, Khagemba, Paikhomba and Charairongba ruled successively.[87] But Meidingu Khunjaoba died in 1666 A.D. without leaving any issue. His adopted son, Paikhomba ascended the throne. Paikhomba too died without leaving any male child. After him, Charairongba, a son of his younger brother, ascended the throne in 1696 A.D..

Garib Niwaz, the successor of Charairongba, was succeeded by his second son, Chitsai in 1748 A.D. By this, the old custom of allowing only the sons of the Chief Queen had been abolished. Garib Niwaz at the request of his younger queen Gomati nominated Chitsai as his successor superseding the eldest son Shyamsai.

Chitsai was succeeded by Bharatsai who was the half brother of the former and Goura Shyam, the eldest son of Shamsai became the king of Manipur in 1753 A.D. Goura Shyam and his brother, Chingthangkhomba reigned alternately for a period of five years and the latter was succeeded by his eldest son, Labeinya Chandra who was succeeded by his half brother Modhuchandra, who in turn, was succeeded by another half brother, Chourajit who was again driven out by another half brother, Marjit from whose hand the sovereignty of Manipur had been seized by the Burmese in 1819 A.D.

The Burmese forces, after occupying Manipur in 1819 A.D. placed one Jadu Singh, son-in-law of Garib Niwaz, on the throne of Manipur. But shortly he was replaced by Subol Singh, brother of Nar Singh.[88] On the conclusion of the Burmese war by the Treaty of Yandaboo in 1826 A.D. Manipur was declared independent, and Gambhir Singh, a half brother of Chourajit, ascended the tyhrone.[89] Gambhir Singh was succeeded by his son Chandrakirti. However, Nar Singh, an able and good natured prince acted as regent while he was a minor. Out of jealousy, the Queen Mother Kumudini attempted to assassinate him in consultation with one Nabin Singh. Being unsuccessful, the Queen Mother and Chandrakirti fled to Cachar.[90] Thus, Nar Singh, at the request of the people, formally ascended the throne in 1844 A.D.

Nar Singh, died in 1850 A.D. and was succeeded by his brother, Debendra. He was a weak man, quite unfit for the position.[91] Because of his weakness, Chandrakirti, could easily replace his position and again ruled over Manipur.

Chandrakirti died in 1886 A.D. after a reign of 35 years and was succeeded by his son, Surachandra, whose inability to control his more turbulent brothers led to the abdication and was the contributing cause of the disaster of 1891 A.D.[92]

Thus we see that during the period under-review the rule of succession was not uniform and the law of primogeniture was often broken since the time of Atom Yoiremba. Hence, it can be inferred that kingship in Manipur was not always hereditary. Sometimes the strongest man within the Ningthouja (Mangang) clan ascended the throne of Manipur. The people of Manipur also quietly accepted him as their king. Revolts were frequent and the Rajkumars often fell apart for they always wanted to have their say in governance.

Further, we have a peculiar feature of the rule of succession that females were never found to ascend the throne of Manipur. The chronicles of Manipur do not mention about female succession. Generally, the eldest son of the eldest wife stands first as the legal heir, in preference to any other sons of the wife or co-wives.[93] Viewed from this point of social and political condition it can also be concluded that Meitei society is patriarchal. In the case of property also, generally, it passes from father to son. However our research shows that the matriarchal traits are predominantly observable in the Meitei society.

Women's Property (Nupi Maral)

Nothing was mentioned in the archaic scripts and the Royal edicts of Manipur about women's property. However, the following are considered as women's property in the Meitei society as was held in the Hindu society.

First, awoonpot (dowry), which is given by the parents at the time of marriage.

Second, anything movable or immovable given by the parents or other relatives at the time or after the marriage.

Third, anything acquired by her own exertions (also known as self-acquired property).

Fourth, property given in lieu of maintenance of her minor child.

Fifth, property acquired by inheritance under the circumstances provided in the absence of her brothers (Mabung, Moupuwa), widow mother (Mama Lukhrabi), etc.

As regards the rights and liabilities of these properties, there is a peculiar nature of Chatlam Lutin of Meiteis that if the wife dies in the family of her husband the liability on her properties goes to the husband and not to her parents or relatives. This is strange but true.

It is interesting to give the customs prevailing among some societies whether, within the Meitei or other Mizo are similar.

The rituals of naming of a newly born child and its significance to the Pheiyeng Meiteis [94] and Mizos are similar.

Regarding the death rites and rituals the Meiteis[95] residing at places like Sekmai, Pheiyeng, Loitangkhunou, Khurkhul, Andro, Leimaram and Kwatha are more or less same as that of the Mizos. The Meiteis of Pheiyeng observed death rites exactly the same as are prevalent among the Thadou group of Mizo society. The female relatives of the deceased (Chanute of the Thadou), such as, aunts, daughters and grand-daughters are obliged to kill at least a pig of 5(five) *wais*[96] to serve exclusively the family members of the deceased in token expression of sorrow and grief. It includes persons who took part in digging the grave at the burial ground and those who are near and dear ones. The eldest son, though not the heir also has to perform in like manner to pay respect to the departed soul. Offering cooked rice to deceased is also one of the features performed in token expression of sympathy.

It will be pertinent to note that the Old Kuki group, such as, the Chothe follows the custom of adoring *Sanamahi* like the Meiteis.[97] It is one customary law other than they have such several similar customs and tradition with other fellow Mizo tribes. Its obligatory custom for a newly married daughter-in-law, as soon as she enters the house of her husband for the first time, to pay homage first to *Ima Leimaren* and then to *Sanamahi*. Secondly, the Chhothe is divided into 7(seven) clans[98] like the Meiteis and the Kabuis, such as also Mangang, Luwang, Khuman, Angom, Khaba-Nganba, Moirang and Sarang Leishangthem, marrying within the same clan is strictly prohibited. This customary law is practiced as per their prescribed code of clan exogamy, similar to that of the Meiteis.

Thus, we come to know that peoples of Manipur, at a particular point of time were of homogenous ethnic groups. However, in the long course of time different changes have taken place. We may conclude that these peoples are of common origin.

Conclusion

In early societies custom was the main vehicle of legal development. In India, while moulding the ancient Hindu law, the commentators and the text writers have by and large included the prevalent customs in their early writings. For example, the Srutis and Smritis have strongly recommended that customs be followed. Manu declared that it is the duty of the king to decide all cases according to principles drawn from local usages. When the Smrities fell out of date in relation to the needs of the contemporary society, the commentaries adopted the Smriti-law, by the process of interpretation, to bring it to accord with customs which had roots in the then society.[99]. Even today, the personal laws of the Meiteis have been recognised by judges and embodies in judicial decisions.

Nevertheless, with the advancement and development of society, coupled with the increasing mobility of the people, and maturity of the legal system, time has come when a uniformity of law become imperative. Some of the features of the traditional law are thus bound to be out of harmony with contemporary social conditions and facts of life. It had been felt to modify the laws in certain circles as to adopt them to meet modern exigencies and circumstances.[100]

REFERENCES

1. *G.C. Venkata Subharao,: Jurisprudence and Legal Theory, Lucknow, 1984;* p. 111.
2. A.K. Sarkar, (ed): Summary of Salmond's Juris Prudence, 1960; p. 75.
3. 1876, 3 Ind. App. 259.
4. A.I.R., 1954, Man, 9.
5. A.K. Sarkar(ed): Summary of Salmond's Juris Prudence, 1960, pp. 76-78
6. N. Ibobi Singh: *The Manipur Administration (1709-1907 AD),* 1968, p. 193.
8. Gangmumei Kabui : *History of Manipur,* Vol. I, Pre-Colonial period : 1991, p. 254.
9. *Ibid.,* p. 276.
10. M. Tombi: *Imphal, Cultural History of Kangleipak (Manipur),* 1975, pp. 90-91.
11. *Foreign Department Ext. A. Proceedings (Narrative of the State of Manipur) June 1903 No. 66 as cited by Lal Dena in his work 'British Policy towards Manipur;*1891-1919: 1984; p. 11.
12. N. Ibobi Singh, *Op. cit.,* p. 202.
13. Lal Dena, Op cit., p. 58.

14. *Ibid.*
15. *Ibid.*
16. James Carter: *Law, Its origin, Growth and function as cited by Monica David in her book, Legal Theory (Jurisprudence),* Allahabad, p. 77.
17. Editorial Advisory Board (ed) : New Standard Encyclopaedia, Vol. 8, p. 152.
18. A.I.R., 1979, All. 316.
19. There is a saying of the Manipuri tradition : "Nupigi Luhongbadi Amuktani; Nupadi Chamarak Hongba Yai." (A female can be married only once but a male can marry hundred times). In fact, a woman after suffering from khainaba from her former husband may remain with another as husband and wife but she could not get married with proper rituals. It is a kind of protection extended to women with dignity and honour who could be saved from exploitation and indignities of an evolving society.
20. N. Khelchandra Singh, : Chada Laihui, Fn 1966, p. 5-6, *"Meidingu Naothingkhomba forcibly took a pregnant woman, Yaoreiba chanu, wife of Thangyi Khongjromba of Chenglei. Their son Naophangba (428 A.D. – 518 A.D.) became the king of Manipur."*
21. *"Mou" means a "married or divorcee woman."*
22. R, Brown : *Statistical Account of Manipur,* 1874, p. 77.
23. Khelchandra Singh, N : Naothingkhong Phambalkaba :1967, pp.iii – iv(Introductory). Naothingkhong first married Pitanga, daughter of Wamei Lanthaba of Achong Yumlemba family of Sheloi Langmais. When he escaped from the Sheloi Langmais he took refuge from Punshi Yumoiba, king of the Khumans and got married to Khayoiron Keirunghanbi, daughter of Khuman king. Afterwards when he ascended the throne of Meiteis, the king of Moirang gave his daughter, Iwanglon Leima Namun Chaobi in marriage to him. Kingship knows no *Kinship. Concept was widely practiced in this region for the simple fact that every community wanted to be near the king through his consort who could belong to the community. Marriages were thus alliances for political expediency as well as a part of social legacy.
24. N. Khelchandra Singh : Chada Laihui :1966, pp. 110-111.

25. T.C. Hudson: The Meiteis; 1975 (Reprint), p. 76.
26. *Ibid.*
27. Thao Anita Chhothe, aged 21, Lamlanghupi Ward No. 2, Bishnupur. interviewed on 3.2.2006.
28. *Ngangkhaleima, the youngest wife of the king, Moirang Ningthou Puriklai, was awarded in honour of the service of Puremba when he killed nine tigers and saved the life of the king at Torbung.*
29. *Tonu Laijinglembi was also awarded to Kadeng Thangjahanba (a minister) in honour of her service to the people.*
30. N. Sanajaoba : *Manipur Past and Present,* Vol (I), 1988, p. 150.
31. Ksh. Bimola Devi : *Manipuri Women – A study in Manipuri – Past and present;* Vol-I edited by Naorem Sanajaoba:1988; p.165.Here it may be mentioned that there are some exceptional cases when marriage takes place between persons belonging to the same clan called 'yek' as for example, it is a fact that the mother and father of Bimola belong to the same yumnak called KSHETRIMAYUM as informed personally when I interviewed her aged 61 years, on 7-7-2006.
32. Poreiton's son Sintapung had two sons namely, Areng and Pamingnaba, of whose descendants were Khumans and Luwangs.
33. T.C. Hudson : The Meiteis; 1975, p. 75.
34. Ch. Budhi Singh : Marriage Systems in Meetei Society (15): Sources of the History of Manipur, Manipur University publication:1, edited by S.N. Pandey :1985; pp. 108-9.
35. While Pakhangba was as a refugee at Moirang, he had two sons (Mungyang Chaopa and Limiyipa) absorbed by Moirang Salai undr the sagies of Mungyanjam and Lairenjam.
36. T.C. Hudson : *Op. cit.,* p. 76.
37. Kalachand Singh (ed) : *Sagei Salarion.*
38. O. Bhogeswar Singh, (ed) : *Loina Shinlon,* 1967; p. A.
39. In modern age, *'Haijapot Puba' is also known as 'Heijing Puba'. It consists of basketfuls of sweets, fruits and the like to be offered to the would-be-bride's parents and their clan deities.*
40. *A small edible fruit (emblica officialis).*
41. *A large species of hog-plum, (spondias magnifera).*

42. Saroj Nalini Parratt : *The Religion of Manipur:* 1980; p. 82
43. M. Chandra Singh : *Meetei Luhongba, an essay in the cultural integration,* 3rd Issue, 10th October, 1974, p. 1
44. 1932, D.A.A. No. 48.
45. *Potloi means the garments put on by the Manipuri bride in modern system of marriage. It is a costume of Manipuri Rasa worn by the Gopis.*
46. *Meitei-Nga-Thaba", "Ushin" are sometimes known as"Mitam-nga Thaba".*
47. Saroj Nalini Parratt: *Op. cit.* p. 83. *There is a common belief in the Meitei society as to this rite that if the fish swim well and together then a happy and prosperous marriage will result. If the fish do not swim together the marriage will not be a success. This belief exists even today. This is a custom but not a customary law.*
48. *The paying of Mangkat holds good even today in the marriage of all tribals of Manipur.*
49. *Information collected from N. Nobinchandra Singh, aged 48 of Lairikyengbam Leikai, Imphal interviewed on 3.3.2006 and Th. Rampiyari of Kwakeithel, aged 60, interviewed on 6.5.2006.*
50. *The Chengluk Nungshang is a basket which contains rice, two discs of salt, three strands of cotton, tobacco leaf and ginger. These are covered with a cloth and tied with a bamboo string and placed at the Phunga Lairu, a place to the western side of the Phunga (fire place) which is regarded as sacred place by the Meiteis. The opening of such basket on the fifth day after the wedding is known as Chengluk Nungshang Hangba. It is the common belief of the Manipuris that the fortunes of the couple can be fixed through the rite. It is widely practiced even today.*
51. *The Leirum cloth is similar to that of the Tangkhul cloth. According to legend the Leirum cloth was put on by Nongpok Ningthou and Panthoibi.*
52. Saroj Nalini Parratt, : *Op. cit.*, pp. 82-83.
53. N. Khelchandra Singh, : *Lam : The Sahitya :* May-August, 1979; p. 19.
54. L. Ibungohal Singh : *Introduction to Manipur:* 1963; pp 89-

93. *"People commonly translate into divorce. As a matter of fact Khainaba is technical term, and has no synonym in English. It is not divorce in the true sense of the term"* But definitely has to do with the process of divorce.

55. S. Chauton Vs. Sanabam Lalit Singh, 1931, D.C.A. No. 146
56. 1938, D.C.A. No. 102.
57. N. Ibobi Singh, *Op. cit.,*1968; p. 199 (Fn).
58. N. Khelchandra Singh, *Naothingkhong Phambal Kaba* (Coronation of Naothingkhong), 1967, pp. 8-25.
59. M. Chandra Singh,(ed): *Panthoibi Khongkul:* 1963; pp. 39-80.
60. H. Angahal Singh, : *Yaithing Konu:* 1965; pp. 96-108.
61. M. Chandra Singh,(ed): *Op. cit.,* 1963, pp. 80-85
62. H. Angahal Singh, : *Op. cit.,* p. 117.
63. O. Bhogeshwar Singh,: *Ningthourol Sheirang; 1967;* pp. 236-237 and N. Khelchandra Singh, : Chada Lahou: 1966, pp. 12-16.
64. O. Bhogeshwar Singh : *Op. cit.,* pp. 238-240.
65. Konthoujam Nongkarol (MS): Manipuri Puya. N. Khelchandra Singh, : Parishadki Ariba Manipuri Wareng Lairik: 1972; pp. 14-19.
66. L. Ibungohal Singh, *Op. cit.,* pp. 92-93.
67. 1931, D.C.A.., No. 19.
68. *'Wa-loithokpa' is the social recognition or confirmation of divorce. In Meitei society, divorce acquires a binding force only after the formality. In this formality both the parents, the Sagei Pibas and elderly localmen together orally enquires from the Souses. They decide whether the divorce is proper or not. If any divorce has been confirmed by Wa-Loithoknaba then there is restriction as to restitution of married life or the coming back of the wife to her husband's house.*

69&70. *These are accepted by the custom and have been retained since long. Therefore, no illustration or instance needs to be cited.*

71. O. Bhogeswar Singh, (ed). *Op. cit.,* pp. 238-240.
72. M. Kirti Singh, : Meitei Customary Law: *"The Lanmei Thanbee"*, November, 1983, pp. 3-4.
73. *The saying implies that a father is liable for his children at*

any cost. If one has children one has to see that they properly grow up into men.

74. M. Ibotombi Singh : *Khuchup Cheimiyang:* 1976; p. 31.
75. L. Ibungohal Singh, *Op. cit.*, p. 96.
76. S. Raghumani : *Jurisprudential Study of the interaction of Meitei Customary Law and Hindu Law. (Thesis submitted to Kurukshetra University, 1985)*, p. 188 (MS).
77. N. Manijao : *Chingda Satpa Ingallei: 1969; pp. 11-19. Tonaba gave his son Lainingkhomba, later known as Paikhomba to his brother Khunjaoba in consultation with his wife, Tangja Kombi.*
78. Codification Committee : *Manipuri Customs*, 1960; pp. 29-30.
79. R.K. Agrawala, *Hindu Law, Allahabad*, 1982; p. 172.
80. *As regards the separate property of the minor children, there is a common practice in Manipur which holds sway even at present that the parents reserved some paddies or money separately in favour of their children especially for female children known as "Marannai Touba"*
81. H. Angahal Singh, : Yaithing Konu, 1965; p. 107. *When Luwang Nongban Yaithingkonu was divorced by Khuman Kaoba Hingamba the latter was the sole guardian of the two children, Thoinu Ahanbi and Haodigon Takol Louthiba.*
82. *The tradition of Moirang Kangleiron considers Khuman Chanu Khamnu as the guardian of Khamba when their parents died. Kuwanglon the sister of Khuyon Haoba was also considered as the guardian of the latter.*
83. H. Angoubi Vs. Nongmaijing Sharma, A.I.R., 1953, B.
84. T.C. Hudson : *The Meiteis*, 1975, p. 77.
85. L. Ibungohal Singh : *Introduction to Manipur*, 1963, p. 95.
86. *Ibid.*
87. Ray, L. : *History of Manipur*, Calcutta: 1958; p. 29.
88. R., Brown, *op. cit.*, p. 63.
89. Major Snodgrass : *Narrative of the Burmese War*, Appendix No. VI :1826; p. 365.
90. L. Ibungohal Singh, and N. Khelchandra Singh, (ed.), *op. cit.*, p. 261.
91. J. Johnstone : *My Experience in Manipur and Naga Hills*, Delhi, p. 84.

92. Robert Reid : *History of the Frontier Area Bordering on Assam, 1883-1941:* 1983; p. 53.
93. Roy, J., *op. cit.*, p. 39.
94. *As narrated by Ningthoujam Ningol Nungleppam Ongbi Tombi, aged 51 years, Pheiyeng, Singda Dam, Manipur (Interviewed on 5-10-2005)*
95. *Ningthoujam Memcha, aged 35 years, Leimaram.*
96. *Meaning - 1(one) Wai is equal to 1 (one) fist.*
97. Source Person - *Thao Anita Chhothe, Lamlanghupi Ward* No. 2, Bishnupur.
98. Rev. Renghang, aged 65 years, *Pallel, interviewed on 17.7.2006.*
99. M.P. Jain, : Outlines of Indian Legal History, Bombay, 1972, p. 597.
100. *Ibid.*, p. 601.

4

Historical Traditions on Social Institutions of the Mizos

MacIver said,[1] Social Institution is the established form or condition of procedure characteristic of group activity. So said, Sutherland and Maxwell[2] that it is a set or web of interrelated folkways, mores and laws which enter in some function or functions. Likewise, Green,[3] contended that Social Institution is the organisation of several folkways and mores into a unit which serves a number of social functions. And Ginsberg[4] was convinced to attribute it as definite and sanctioned form or mode of relationship between social beings in regard to one another or to some external object. Similarly, Gillin and Gillin[5] said that it is a functional configuration of culture pattern including actions, ideas, attitudes and cultural equipment which possesses a certain permanence and which is intended to satisfy felt social needs. Yet, Horton and Hunt[6] said that it is an organized system of relationship which embodies certain common rules and procedures and meets certain basic needs of the society.

It is clear that Institutions are forms of procedure. Every organisation is dependent upon certain recognised and established set of rules, traditions customs and usages which may be given names of institutions. They are the forms of procedure which are recognised and accepted by society and govern the relations between individuals and groups. Thus, marriage, education, property, religion, etc. are some of the main institutions.

Characteristics of concept of institution may therefore be attributed to the means of controlling individuals, collective activities of men, proceedings which are based on customs and dogmas, means of social control that must be compulsorily obeyed by individuals which has symbols of material or non-material values that receive social recognition.

Marriage

Aspects of marriage as an institution are strong social indicators the dynamics of which bring about intensive changes in many fields of interactions of the couple in particular, and the family in general. So marriage emerges as a social arrangement by which a couple is legitimized in their physical relationship and their child is given a legitimate position in the society which is often determined by parenthood in the social sense.[7] The Mizos do not think of marriage necessarily, as a union, based on romantic love although beauty as well as character and health are always sought in choice of a wife.

Secondly, in Mizo society, a marriage involves making of payment by the bridegroom or his kin to the father or close relative of the would-be bride in case the father had expired. Such system of understanding of the nature of marriage alliance was also prevalent in a great number of societies in ancient and modern times in all parts of the world. Making of payment of marriage by the bridegroom either in the form of kind or service to the bride's kin is an essential part of establishment of legality.[8] Marriage payment was held officially in South Africa as per native custom with payment of Mithun in general.

Here Hindu marriage customs, traditions and rituals are of interest because they not only have bearings on tribal forms of marriages but also have cross-cultural evidence all across the country. For details see Manu's Dharmashastra, Kautalya's Arthasastra, and other relevant literature and secondary sources.

Among some Mizo tribes, practice of marriage payment is prevalent and is known as 'bride-price', which is paid in cash, kind and 'mithun'. Some people believe that 'bride-price' is a completed word of marriage payment, alleged to have been coined by British administrators during the colonial British period in India. To avoid redundance, the term 'marriage payment' will be consistently used to mean 'marriage price' or 'bride-price' in this work.

There exists many systems of marriage forms in Mizo society of which the following selected ones are significantly practiced even today:

(i) Nularim

The word '*Nularim*'[9] stands for formal courting of girls by young boys and not vice-versa. It has become an institution exclusively for the purpose of formal mixing of young boys and girls as it happen in many tribal and ethnic communities, e.g. among the Gonds, Bhils and Oraons of Chotanagpur. Courtage naturally and normally begins in the mid-adulthood when boys and girls are about to attain their puberty. This institution is called 'Nularim' by the Dulian (Lushai) speaking Mizos which is now known as Mizo language and '*Nungak Hel* or *Nangek Hel*' by other Mizo tribes, who speak Thadou, Paite, Vaiphei, Simte, Zou dialects etc. in Manipur and adjoining areas.

Likewise, such practice exists among the *Lakhers* called '*Laisacharei*'[10] which is said to be more humanely refined than '*Nularim*' in its etiquettes and mannerisms. Out of such courtship institutions many love-affairs between boys and girls grew which resulted in their nuptial relationship in due course. Such marriages were considered legitimate and desirable for it brought about social integration, mutual cooperation, familiarity and respect in society. It also stabilized the relationships between the couple among themselves and in their families.

(ii) Makpa Chung Khung or Makpasungkhum

This type of marriage is resorted to when there is no son or heir to the parents of the girls. A couple who has one or more daughters without a son to look after them in their old age, the father in the girl's family, in consideration of their future life in the absence of a son may admit a prospective son-in-law to his family. Customarily he may not take usual marriage payment from him. Mizo society has a very strong patrilineal system, wherein the question of prestige arises for the prospective son-in-law. So, such marriage practice is seldom acceptable. This type of marriage is also practiced among the Hmars and is called '*Makpasungkhum*'.[11] Prevalence of this system of marriage is mentioned by Hrangthiauva and Lal Chungnunga[12] in their joint work on Mizo Chanchin.

(iii) Zawn (Dawn) Puan Phah

This system of marriage is also resorted to when a situation arises in which after an agreement has been reached upon for a marriage but could not be solemnized for unavoidable circumstances. Under a situation like this, the boy and the girl are allowed to be married in the girl's house signifying that they are permitted to make love in conjugal relationship at that stage, and for any reason whatsoever, after *Zawnpuanphah*, if the marriage did not take place the boy is compelled to pay a fine of four mithuns[13] which is to be cleared at once and that there could be no excuse to defer the marriage.

(iv) Manbo

In marriage of this form, 'marriage-payment' is not considered.[14] When a woman leaves her husband *sumchchuah* (divorce of husband by wife) the whole '*man*' (bride-price) is refunded to her relative. Traditionally, it may so happen that the divorced wife longing for her children may repent after sometime and approach her ex-husband for a compromise so that she may be accepted again as his wife. In case she is accepted the husband is not obliged to pay the '*man*'. The relatives of the wife also have no right to claim the same from her husband. All that can be done by the relatives of his wife is to seize her entire personal belongings and properties and sever their relationship with her for life.[15] This is known as '*intuithlar*'. Despite this, sometimes they may stake a claim for Rs. 40/ - which is known as '*banman*'. Yet, customarily, they are not entitled to get it. The only person who can claim a '*banman*' is the *Pu*, grandfather of the woman. Such kind of strained relationship occurs rarely. However, time being best healer, the tense relationship between the husband and his in-laws subsides and normally a working relationship returns and consequently the '*man*' is paid.[16]

(v) Sazumeidawh

In this form of marriage, the payment of bride-price is not made or is necessary. The contracting parties agree that they will get married and that the woman shall not claim her usual marriage payment and the man shall be at liberty to leave her and divorce her at any time without incurring any penalties. Marriage of this sort is very **rare**.

These are more common with daughters of widows than with girls whose either parents are alive, A father is generally sufficiently wide awake to prevent an arrangement which would be so disadvantageous to the daughter and her family. For a marriage of this sort, no '*palai*'[17] is necessary, a mere agreement between the parties is sufficient.

(vi) Luk Khung

This type of marriage is resorted to under compelling circumstances. When the boy and the girl, on their own accord, had sexual relationship, resulting in the pregnancy of the girl. In order to avoid social and familial embarrassment they get married on their own without observing any marriage formalities but taking consent of their respective parents. However, as per the custom, the boy can not skip[18] the binding force of customary law which ensure payment of marriage-payment.[19]

(vii) Marriage by Elopement

This form of marriage takes place normally when the boy and the girl have fallen in love and formal procedure for arranged marriage or any other sort of negotiated marriage settlement can not be fulfilled for any of the following reasons:

(a) When the boy and the girl or either of their parents are in abject poverty[20] and are unable to bear the expenditure to be involved in a properly arranged marriage, elopement is resorted to.

or, (b) When a boy and a girl fall in love and either of their parents are strongly against their marriage for some reasons the boy and the girl take their own decision and without consulting or taking consent of their parents they get married despite social objections.[21] Such marriages are common both among the tribes and civilized people.[22]

or, (c) The third type of marriage by elopement may be done on account of impregnation of the girl. They may be compelled under the circumstances to elope to avoid criticism, etc.[23]

(viii) Fan

Fan marriage breaks the normal marriage systems Since it is akin to the system of marriage of *Sambandham* (Here the marriage results from the relationship between a woman and her lover) practiced by the Nayars.[24] In a 'fan' marriage, a man who is a lover of the girl goes to live in the house of the girl without observing any formality[25] including whatever little '*man*' is due to be paid. This type of marriage inflicts the prestige of the man and therefore, is not common. The disgrace that the man thus imposes upon himself is indirectly compensated with exemption of payment of normal 'man' to the family of the woman. In case, he is compelled to pay 'man' he has to do so at a reduced '*man*' or Tlai or Rs. 20/-. This reduced '*man*' is granted to the man as a compensation to the disgraced situation he is placed in. In case, the man dies before regularization of the marriage and the woman is '*Thisen Pailo*' (a woman who has no issue by the husband) her people will get no price at all.[26] If the woman is *Thisen Pai* (a woman who has issues by the husband) posthumously, then the child by the married '*man*', can be claimed by his relatives and the '*man*'- the ordinary marriage-price from her deceased husband's relatives can be claimed less '*Tlai Fanman*'. If the woman dies before the marriage is regularized her relative can claim nothing. If a man is Fan and subsequently the girl refuses to marry him she must give him a *zawlphun*.[27] How this custom emerged, we have no idea but certainly it was not in good taste. It was in a way to rationalize a disgraced union causing stigma to a family-tradition.

(ix) Child Marriage

It is practised among the Lakhers,[28] Thadous and other tribes in Manipur. It is prevalent only in the society where the practice of cross-cousin marriage exists. Cross-cousin marriage is the marriage between a man with the daughter of his mother's brother's daughter (MBD). The marriage of this kind within relation is much favoured. The preliminary negotiations are settled by verbal agreement and no marriage payment is made till the girl is of marriageable age. It is only a prelude to emphasize the fact that the child is more often than not the product of mother's brother's daughter marriage systgem. This marriage in other words is better known as 'preferential marriage'.[29] This was practiced in early societies all over India and neighbouring regions.

(x) Mother's Brother's Daughter Marriage or Neila or Cross-cousin

"A part of every kinship is a system of set of regulations concerning marriage between persons related by kinship or through marriage".[30]

There are rules, which prohibit marriage between persons who stand in certain relationships. The rules vary greatly from one system to another. In many societies there is what is called a rule of exogamy by which a man is forbidden to take a wife from amongst the women of his own group (lineage, sub-clan, clan or moiety) or the Sapinda, a person descended patrilineally from one of his patrilineal ancestors, within seven generations, of the Hindu Law. On the other hand, in some systems there are certain relations between whom marriage is not merely permitted, but is regarded as desirable. The term 'preferential marriage' is commonly applied to customs of this kind. The commonest example of cross-cousin marriage is marriage with the daughter of the mother's brother or wife's brother's daughter.

Many theories on the origin of cross-cousin marriage have been propounded. Tylor[31] considered that cross-cousin marriage is the direct result of the simplest form of initial exogamy. Fraser[32] thought that the preference of the cross-cousin marriage was the outcome from dual organisation with which traces of the same are associated everywhere. He suggested that marriage with the daughter of mother's brother or the father's sister was due to their cheapness for a man to claim the hands of such cousins and getting as wives either without price or at a lower rate than he would have to pay for a girl with whom he was not related to her. It may also be in consideration that the marriage with cross-cousin as preferential marriage in consequence of direct practice earlier of interchanging sisters. But Westermarck[33] opined that practice of mother's brother's daughter or father's sister's daughter marriages originated from similar relatives, there is no reason why one of them should be regarded as preceding cause of the other. Rivers[34] on the other hand believes that in Melanesia this institution arose out of gerontocracy. In India and elsewhere cross-cousin marriage is derived from the bisection of the community into two exogamous moieties or classes such as is found in some Australian tribes. And Crawly[35] believed that cross-cousin marriage is a well-known mark of dual exogamy. However, according to Lowie[36], while consistent with the moiety system, cross-cousin marriage does not directly follow from it. Therefore, he was convinced to say that cross-cousin marriage in all probability is not a prohibitory phenomenon that had evolved from a single cause but one that had inadequately arisen in several centres from diverse motives. Rattray and Buxstone view that cross-cousin marriage is found on the co-existence of two forms of descent in one social system. But Seligman[37] contradicted this view and suggested that cross-cousin marriage had arisen from the inheritance of wives from the mother's brother. Swamton[38] was of the view that possession of the property played a dominant role in the tribal consciousness as in British Columbia, the motive of keeping desirable belongings within the family circle may lead to marriage with the father's own sister's daughter or the mother's own brothers' daughter.

Tout[39] propounded that the concept of property laid at the bottom of this type of marriages that though descent were counted exclusively on the mother's side, authority of the father was recognized to a considerable extent for he had voice in the disposal of his daughters in marriage and frequently to arranged matters that his legal inheritor and successor; the sister's son should marry one or more of his daughters. This might allow share in his property and not be wholly deprived under the clan rule of his possessions as under their laws nor hereditary property or rights would be alienated or passed over to the members of another man even though the recipients were the donor owned children.

Ghurye[40] has shown the probable connection between dual organisation and cross-cousin marriage, following the foot-steps of Rivers[41], after a careful analysis of hypothetical forms of marriage arising out of another contact between different groups of patriarchal and matriarchal societies. Chatttopadhyay showed that dual organisation and cross-cousin marriage could not go hand in hand, though under certain conditions the latter might arise out of the disintegration of the former. He also stressed on the term, house-hold exogamy in determining avoidance in marriage and origin of dual organisation with a superior and inferior moiety.

Though the tribes under study are of patrilineal society

yet, an earlier striation of matriliny cannot be overlooked because in some of the tribes matrilineal traits are still dominant. These people came in contact with the latter patrilineal immigrants or superior culture and marriage between them were frequent. During this period the immigrant people in order to secure their sister's family with better economy situation introduced the marriage of the sister's son to their own daughters. The contact in some area led to the formation of dual group and both types of cross-cousin marriage were permitted. But when the domination of patrilineal people was complete, the avoidance of father's sister's daughter came from the idea that father and father's sister inherited the same blood to her daughter who also inherited the same blood to her daughter who also inherit through her mother was not marriageable and was forbidden. This idea is still prevalent among the Chothe, Mantaks, etc. In some cases, patrilineal dominance is so strong that in the absence of mother's brother, the claim to the bride price accrues to his son i.e. mother's brother's son gets the payments for his father's sister's daughter as is found among the Mantak.

In many tribal societies in the north east of India including Mizos, cross-cousin marriage is very popular. The same is true with the Nayars of Kerala, the Brahmins of Tamil Nadu and among the Tribal belts of Northern Indian States. In such cross-cousin marriage, the most common one is the marriage of mother's brother's daughter 'Neinu'[42] or 'Neihnu'[43]. It is considered as – Preferred marriage. The marriage bond, uniting the two families is not allowed to be broken by the death of partners. Thus the unity of family is continued by marrying even into 3(three) generations – his own, the one above and the one below.[44] The 'Neila'[45] marriage is favoured in most of the Mizo tribes including Lakhers,[46] Thadous, Zous[47] (Zomi) except the Lushai who can marry any woman other than his own mother and sister. This is similar to the practice among the Hamites.[48] Hamite is the descendant of Ham's second son of Noah (Gen 10:6), member of Egyptian or other Noah African people now known as Hameties, of group of African languages including ancient Egyptian, Berber and Cushitie. However, Lal Biak Thanga[49] says that even parallel cousin marriage of the first generation is practiced though not encouraged. Contrary to this, other Mizo tribes, notably, the Thadous, Gangtes, Paites, Vaipheis, etc. it is considered incestuous and, therefore, strongly prohibited. In the case of the Sailo family/clan,[50] the marriage of first cousin is also allowed for the advantages secured during the days when inter-village feuds were practices.

(xi) Marriage by Engagement

This system of marriage is arranged in such a way that the parents of both with the consent of the boy and the girl agree resulting to a settlement. This is known as Dan Thieng Inneih[51] and this type is seldom resorted to.

Before going into details it is pertinent to know first the Chongmou[52] marriage, it means marriage with royal like dignity grandeur and pomp, studded with elaborate rites and rituals to the minutest extent possible.

Dan Thieng Innei is known as 'Chongmou: va: pui[53] among Thadous and their cognates, Paite, Gangte, Vaiphei, Simte, Zou", etc. which has a very detailed elaborate ritual ceremony. In this form of marriage the bridegroom's parents send '*Palai*' (go-between or representative) among Dulian speaking people or '*Becha*' and '*Tucha*'[54] among the non-Dulian speaking people to the parents of the prospective or *would be bride*, asking for the hands of their daughter in marriage with their son. In case, the girl's parents are agreeable to the proposal they kill a pig for the '*palai*' of the boy's parents in token expression of their positive response. Traditionally, such a feast is accompanied with heavy bouts of Zu[55] (yu). The method of taking '*Zu*' is not done in cups or glass as is normally the way of drinking any liquid substance. The drinking bout is done directly from the jar of '*Zu*' sipping it through a bamboo inserted therein alternately by the boy's group and the girl's group. The feast offered to the *palai* or *becha* of the boy is known as '*Sumtansha*'[56] (similar to modern usage of memorandum of agreement). Under this agreement certain settlements are agreed upon such as the amount to be paid as marriage-price and how much thereof to be brought on the day of finalization of marriage negotiation. If afterwards the question of return of the 'man' (marriage payment) should arise for some reason, leading to divorce then this '*sumtansha*' expenditure is returnable.[57]

On this occasion, the date for taking away the bride from her natal home is also fixed and the Palai of the boy would inform the boy's parents accordingly on their return.[58] There may arise a problem regarding the marriage payment but it has to be settled finally before the date is fixed for taking the bride away from her home. After marriage, the husband's home is all that matters for the bride.

In the meantime, preparation for the occasion is made on both sides. '*Zu*' items of marriage-payment, number of *palais*, young men for wrestling purpose at the girl's residence all are pre-arranged. In this connection slight variations in the procedure can be observed. While, the Mizo speaking Thadou-Kuki, Paite, Zou, etc rely on reciprocal verbal assurances of both the parties for fulfilment of their agreement in regard to the mode of marriage payment; the Dulian speaking Mizos who appear to have become more advanced resorting to putting the whole transaction of marriage payment in writing by a village writer known as '*Khowchhiar*'. In doing so the '*Khawchhiar*' takes particular care to record[59] the exact items including cash of the marriage payment handed over to the bride's family showing at the same time balance to be paid in the presence of two witnesses with a copy each thereof to both the parties.[60]

It may so happen that the father of the girl would like to charge extra 'man', '*Mankang*' for his daughter. This is done when the father of the girl wishes to show his exceeding affection for his daughter so that she might have two natal homes[61] for her so that when ever she is in need she can have two homes called 'Nunglam'[62] to fall back upon.

For this purpose, father of the girl assigns a man close to him to receive the 'Mankang' [63]

> "...... so that they be in obligation. The man thus given the privilege considers the girl as his own daughter. In the same way the girl also regards the man taking the additional bride-price (Mankang) as her own foster father. Thus, when the bride-price is paid, the boy's father has necessarily to pay two Mithuns instead of one as lead-bride-price known as 'Man – Lamkai"

Now, as the formal negotiations are settled, the girl is obliged to throw a farewell party to her friends of the village at the residence of the man who receives the 'Mankang'. Meantime, it is customary that the boy's party assumes responsibility to take care of the girl so as to avoid any untoward incident to happen to her. The following day in the afternoon boys of the girl's village come to the residence of the girl and start challenging the boys of the groom's party for a wrestling competition.[64]

> "This challenge is in token expression of their uncompromising attitude for winning the hands of the girl of their village, and as also a last attempt to enact revenge for such insult meted to them. Then starts wrestling, and with the wrestling is over, the villagers along with their guests, drink, sing and dance together the whole night to bid farewell to the bride-to-be."

Incidentally the first wrestling bout takes place on the arrival of the boy's party to the village of the girl. In this wrestling the boy's party usually allow the girl's party to win on the belief that if the girl's party wins she has a bright family life and a happy future with many children. The next day the boy's party is given a feast and a send-off to the girl. On this day also in the evening wrestling for the second time takes place. The feast of this day is given in honour of the girl which in other words is a farewell-feast to her. This is called '*Chanu lhah na*'. The sacrificial meat for the feast is divided into two halves. The second half comprising of the waist portion including the two hind legs is set apart to be taken home by the boys party while the first half is cooked for the feast. The portion given to the boy's party is called '*Chanu sa*' meaning meat share of the daughter. It may also be noted that in all the three wrestling-bouts the girl's party has to be the winner compulsorily.[65]

It may also be added that the young men who take part in the wrestling must be perfect with no disabilities. Customarily, none of them must lack a limb or an organ or even a little finger joint. This condition also applies rightly to the *Thempu* (priest) who officiates at the wedding.[66] Such beliefs are considered auspicious and harbinger of good fortune.

On the day of feasting, drums and gongs are played and songs sung in the evening by all together. The next day is the day for the bridegroom's party to depart triumphantly with the bride and the marriage is complete except for the wrench of paying up the balance of 'man' by degrees on instalments.[67] Herein it may be added that after the bridegroom has taken his bride to his house marriage is not consummated till she has revisited her father's house on a subsequent date previously agreed on, when a further instalment of the *Manpi* or *Manpui* (marriage-payment) is paid. This date may be a few days, month, or even three month later.[68] Soppitt also gives an interesting example of *changsan*[69] (Jansen) marriage on similar situation.[70]

It is pertinent to mention the manner in which the bride is sent-off, involving elaborate rites and rituals as discussed by Gangte[71]:

(i) The girl is made up to dress with her hair plaited on the left hand side or upside down into three coils;

(ii) Her petticoat called 'Poner' is worn left hand side and is pinned together at the ends by split of a kind of bamboos called 'Gopi Keh'.[72]

(iii) Her bangles and bracelet are removed as a symbol of the end of her spinsterhood;

(iv) She leaves her parent's house necessarily before sunrise.

(v) The priest gives the last rite of farewell to the girl by letting her sit in the middle of the house where the main pillar of the house stands. This is called 'Sutlai'. He utters farewell rituals prohibiting the gods and goddesses for her health and prosperity and thereafter let her drink a cup of 'Zu'.

(vi) As she comes out of her parent's house she does holding one gourd in her left hand called 'Hailam Dowm'.

(vii) When she is about to come out of the door of her parent's house she crosses the door out her left leg first.

The above rites are symbolic of the rituals observed when a woman of status is given a funeral rite. It signifies therefore a girl given to a boy in marriage is considered expired in her natal home so far as her activities are concerned. Together with this it is an expression of the value attached to married woman that when she is to devote her entire life towards bringing up her children and welfare of her family without a divided mind mixed up with her natal home. This is known as '*Malang Khot*'. Interestingly the same rituals are performed in the communities belonging to the Big Tradition on the mainland.

(xii) Konglo

This form of marriage is very seldom practiced. By '*Kanglo*' it means 'waist earning' and therefore, it implies that as the marriage-price the man or the boy has to earn favour of the parents by placing himself and his services at the disposal of the parents of the girl for whose hand he was aspiring in marriage. For this purpose, the boy has to work for the family of girl for specific number of years on completion of which he is entitled to marry the girl for whom he has laboured. In this regard Shakespear, said that it is only natural that the actual ceremony was of little importance for the couple have been living as man and wife during the service period.[73] This system was prevalent in the olden days among the Thadou,[74] Aimol, Vaiphei, Cherei, Kom, Chothe, etc. Interestingly, it is also found having been practiced by the ancient Hebrew as quite evident in the book of Genesis of the Holy Bible[75] which said that Jacob met Rachel at the well of a village where they came to know their relationship, on the self-introduction of Jacob as Rachel's father's sisters son. On hearing this, Rachel, left the well, went to inform her father of her meeting with Jacob. Laban, Rachel's father immediately came to the well to meet his nephew, Jacob, where they embraced each other. With these greeting formalities Laban claimed that Jacob was his bone and flesh, meaning thereby that Jacob was his nephew. Thereafter, Laban asked Jacob to work for him enquiring at the same time as to what would be his wage for the same. Jacob replied saying that he was prepared to work for him for seven years for which he would receive the hand of the younger of the two daughters, Leah and Rachel in marriage. Laban accepted it. Accordingly Jacob served his uncle, Laban. On completion of seven years of service, Jacob requested his uncle to give Rachel. As marriage ceremony or feast was hosted, Jacob was permitted to consummate his nuptial relationship. Jacob was under the assumption that his marriage was with Rachel. However, to his surprise, he found the next morning that it was not with Rachel but with Leah. So he complained to his maternal uncle, Laban, as to how it could happen. Laban explained to Jacob as per the custom the younger sister should not supersede the elder sister and so he gave Leah in marriage to him. And further said he would give Rachel as well, provided, Jacob was ready to serve him for another seven years for her. And so, Jacob did the same and married Rachel[76] on the completion of another seven years.

This short story shows that the marriage of mother's

brother's daughter', 'waist earning' marriage system and the restriction not allowing supersession by younger to the elder sister as prevalent among the Jewish tradition are also prevalent among some of the Mizo tribes such as Thadou, Zou, Aimol, Purum, Kom, Chiru, Anal, Lamgang, Chothe, Mantak, Tarao, Wainem, Paite, Lakher, Maring, etc.

The Meitei also practiced the same custom of marriage with cross-cousin before adopting various Hindu customs and becoming Hinduised.[77] Bose on careful analysis of the terms of relationship suggested that cross-cousin marriage which might have been practiced among them in early ancient period appears to have been presently discarded. He further sought the genealogical table that could be proof of cross-cousin marriage. Even now, Bose maintains that a notional fee is paid to the mother's brother at the time of marriage. This custom of payment to the mother's brother, probably as compensation for not taking his daughter, may be suggested as a remnant of the earlier prevalence of this type of marriage.[78] It may also be added that the relationship terminologies used in respect of mother's brother's son and daughter as '*Ibai*', '*Itei*' and '*Inama*' respectively if they are elder to the ego are similar to the terminologies used in addressing ones brother-in-law and sister-in-law as are prevalent presently. The Phonetic representation 'ei' denotes blood relationship.

(xiii) Levirate

According to Deys, the term "levirate" is a French word meaning frother-in-law which again means husband's brother.[79] This is a form of marriage in which a man marries the widow of his deceased brother. There are two types of such marriage – the senior levirate and the junior levirate. While the senior levirate enjoins the younger brother to marry the widow of the elder brother, the junior levirate requires the elder brother to marry the widow of the younger brother. Of the two, the former is more common.

In ancient Hebrew system when a man died without son, his brother was required to marry the widow and got a son by her who was counted as the son of the deceased brother so that he kept the male line of the lineage alive.[80] Since the Vedic times, the system of Niyoga[81] prevailed. Niyoga means a custom practised by farmers in Punjab, Haryana and some north Indian states at the time when a husband dies without male issue living behind, the society considers it obligatory to let the widow marry the younger brother of her deceased husband to perpetuate continuity of the family through the male line, according to Brara,[82] so that the property of the family might remain in tact with the late husband's family. It is evidenced from burial ritual of the Rig Veda that states that the brother-in-law of the deceased should marry the widow, may be only in cases where the deceased man had left no son. [83] It was, therefore, considered necessary that arrangement should be made to secure him an offspring, for the *Rigveda* recognises the keen desire of Vedic Indian for a child to perform funeral rites. [84] It is considered as an institution by its nature to the effect that law of succession of sons to father is so firmly established that even a fictitious or adopted son was preferred to a real brother.[85] In both, the Hindu and the Hebrew, there are lots of Thibetan polyandry and they are same in both.[86] The appointment of a brother to perform such a duty as the heirs would be no wise abhorrent to a people who had recently experienced of a practice of Thibetan polyandry. Moreover, among a people who had such experiences, it would not be surprising to find the fiction that a child begotten by one brother was truly the child of a deceased's elder brother. It will, at least, be conceded that the origin of so strange an arrangement must have been the same as similar to the Hebrew one and in India. Whatever it is, generally accepted levirate wherever it exists is considered as reminder of Thibetan polyandry opined Mc Lennan. [87]

On the other hand, Maine,[88] in his work, Early Law and Custom, explained that Hindu levirate by their desire for offspring, and connecting it to other customs which are still in existence that enable a sonless man to claim sons without having begotten them. It is also claimed that Niyoga is later than levirate, though Mayne[89] was convinced to say that levirate is only an enlargement form of Niyoga, which came into an effect after the death of a man or in case of his being chronically impotent. The case of Pandava in the Mahabharata is a point. Spencer[90] explained that the levirate is simply a prevailing custom that entitled the brother to inherit the wife of his brother (widow) and that she might be an entitled part of the property to be inherited. A woman's primary role to be a provider of sons to keep the family continues the lineage was a striking factor but Niyoga enjoined it as sacred.

Starke,[91] however, complained that Spencer did not contribute towards explanation of this duty and accept that it was only a statement that it was always the duty of the brother to contribute to his elder brothers well being and maintain the dignity and integrity of the woman while providing her the much needed protection against exploitation of widows.

Tylor[92] was of the view that levirate is accounted for a customary of substitution belonging to the period when marriage is a contract not so much between two individuals as between two families, often made, when the couple are infants unable to understand it in fact sometimes even before their birth. There are many instances where the parents have settled the marriage of their Children even before their birth. Though it may seem ridiculous but they are true. Even today some communities practice them.

Similarly Fraser,[93] said that the custom of sorarate and levirate indicate prevalence of forms of marriage between a group of husbands who were known to each other and a group of wives who were sisters to each other. Ramayana effectively demonstrates sorarate practice when we find that the four brothers get married to four sisters respectively – Ram to Sita, Laxman to Urmila, and so on. We may conjecture that the cause of divergence between the two customs was the greatest strength of the passion of jealousy in man than in woman, sisters being more willing to share a husband between than brothers to share a wife. Social customs often tended to get distorted and abused. But in societies such practices often created more stability in family than distability.

Westermarck[94] observed that Fraser attached much importance to the fact that the levirate and sorarate were often found among the same people but this is only to be impacted in the case of two customs which are evidently more or less akin to each other. They may both be a consequence of marriage emerging as an institution by considering as a woman for whom a price has been paid may be in the family after the death of her first husband, so she may also have to be replaced if she dies herself. Moreover, as the children of a widow are best cared for if the step-father is their uncle, so the children of widower are best cared for if their step mother is their aunt. And above all, both the levirate and sovarate practices preserved the union between the two families. Marriages among the communities on the mainland often still are between families rather than among two individuals.

Chattopadhyay[95], shows the wide-spread prevalence of this custom in Northern India and Dasgupta[96] illustrates decisively the prevalence of levirate in Ramayana, which is also of great importance as to antiquity of this institution.

Hence we would like to maintain that our research and field survey has thrown up interesting facts to be examined about the prevalence of this institution in Manipur among the different tribes & Chin-Kuki-Mizo ethnicity. Some facts are discussed below; tribe wise:

(i) The Aimol

Among the Aimol this type of marriage is very rare though junior levirate is more common and is practiced in case where the widow is still young.[97] The main consideration among them is that if the levirate marriage is accepted the requirement for the man to serve for three years in the house of the bride before marriage is avoided. He is also saved from the trouble of marriage payment.

(ii) The Mantak

Levirate is widely practiced in the society of Mantak.[98] Though senior levirate is permissible, junior levirate is more common. The reason for the prevalence of this custom is mainly on account of economic consideration.

(iii) The Anal

The two forms of levirate prevail in the Anal customs and traditions though the junior levirate is more common.[99]

(iv) The Lamgang

The Lamgangs, [100] in consideration of the economic

condition and the burden of marriage payment too adopt the two types of levirate. Here too, the junior is more preferred.

(v) The Tarao

Among the Tarao,[101] polygamous marriage is prevalent, in addition to this, the marriage payment system is a must at the time of marriage. Along with that, the performing of marriage cannot be escaped. So in order to avoid all these formalities, the levirate marriage is prevalent.

(vi) The Kom

The Kom,[102] like the Zou can marry the younger or elder deceased brother's widow if he is unmarried and claims this right within three years of burial or herning of the corpse. There was at one time fine fixed by the village elder if the man or the woman disagreed to levirate in the Kom customs. But this had been gradually discarded which ultimately led to the assent in particular of the girl was needed.

(vii) The Wainem

Among the Wainems[103] the junior levirate is prevalent but the senior levirate is a social offence. The Wainems, influenced by the social norms and customs of the Meitei led to the extinction of levirate system of marriage.

(viii) The Thadou

It is customary for a brother to take wife of the deceased brother although he be already married. So among the Thadous, the two forms i.e. senior and junior levirate are prevalent.[104]

(ix) The Chiru

The Chiru society also has the levirate system of marriage but the senior one is totally forbidden. Though, the junior levirate system is in prevalence, it is not favoured by the general mass.[105]

(x) The Purum

The levirate system, though rare in practice is still found. It is to avoid service[106] and the marriage payment. The junior levirate has developed into a custom but not the senior levirate. [107]

(xi) The Rangkhol

Among the Rangkhols levirate type of marriage occurs only when the circumstance arises, such as availability of eligible unmarried brother. Some exceptions are also there. In this regard Bhattacharjee's[108] name deserves special mention. He was very specific to say, "An interesting custom among the Rangkhols was to render service to the father-in-law for three years before the marriage and two years after".

(xii) The Lakhers

Among the Lakhers, custom of marrying the deceased man's widow by the brother is very common. Here, the prevalence of the same is mainly due to economic factor. The marriage payment would be out of question, since the levirate marriage does not require payment of much amount than the usual.

(xiii) The Marings

We notice the prevalence of junior levirate among the Marings.[109] In this connection, if the widow is young the unmarried brother is preferred. In this system, the man who is getting married to the widow of the deceased brother, the service to be given to the bride's father and the marriage-payment are altogether waived off. Thus, the brother who marries his deceased brother's wife is relieved from fulfilling those formalities.

While dealing with the subject matter, it has been observed by us that levirate marriage is very much a living tradition and has developed into an institution especially among the Aimol, Anal, Mantak, etc. However, we found that among the Wainems and the Chirus who are found to have been greatly influenced by the Meiteis have discarded the system from being practiced especially in respect of senior levirate, which is mainly due to dislike for polygamy because of the fact of the widow being the elder brother's wife. Therefore, the practice of senior levirate would automatically lead to polygamy. Secondly, economic factor also played a very important role. The high bride-price and service in the house of the prospective in-law for several years put a great hardship on the people. In order to avoid this burden levirate marriage provided a solution of the exigencies demanded.

Marriage Payment or Bride Price

As case studies, we have tried to look into this practice among the Lushais, the Lakhers, the Thadous, the Zomis, the Old Kukis and some minor groups. Our research has revealed that it was indeed a wide spread phenomenon and quite deep custodian every such community which dotted this region. It was a common practice among them and had significant sociological dimensions.

The Lushai

Marriage payment or bride-price or marriage price is the most important factor in a Mizo marriage. No marriage can be performed unless part of marriage-payment is made in advance by the bridegroom to the bride's family. It was paid in terms of mithuns when barter system was practice of the time. A mithun used to cost rupees forty as fixed by the British India administration in 18th Century when currency system was first introduced in this part of the

North East. Some clans had fixed the prices for their maids in the past.[110] It varied from four to ten mithuns depending upon the antecedents, blood and beauty of the bride. Marriage-payment for a chief's daughter was as many as ten mithuns or more[111] for the Dulien (Lushai) speaking Mizos. Minor concessions could be given during the time of payment. In this connection, marriage payment were practically never paid up in full at once at the time of wedding for the reason that hardly anybody had enough money to pay the same at once.[112] Generally there was the custom of marriage-payment only in instalments and the remaining to be paid after some time i.e. twenty years or more.[113] The customary laws of Thadou, Gangte, Vaiphei, Paite, etc. in this regard are quite widely different from the ones described hereinabove.

Marriage-payment is a sacred institution prevalent in Mizo society. It is however not to be understood as a sale-price.[114] It is not a commercial transaction. Marriage payment was sometimes used as a weapon for a clever parent to reject a suitor[115]. If it is really felt that the usual payment of any part of the same was unduly delayed or was not intentionally paid, the aggrieved party could seek the chief's permission to seize any of the property of the debtor against the claim.[116]

The marriage payment consisted of two parts (i) the *Manpui*[117] and the *Mantang*. The *Manpui* is the price that has to go direct to the girl's father or in his absence, to her brother. If she has none of them, it has to be received by her nearest male relative. The general rate of *Manpui* is five mithuns or Rs.100/- if the girl had dowry or '*Thuam*' in the Dulien language but in case she does not carry, the rate of it was four mithuns each Mithun being fixed at Rs. 80/- by the British administrators. The custom of increasing Rs. 20/- was prevalent if the girl was provided with *Thuam*.

It is pertinent to mention that the Lushai (Dulien speaking Mizos) custom is slightly different from others in dealing with matters relating to marriage payment. It happened in circumstances where the girl was adopted by a man since childhood then the price went to him. In cases where male relatives failed to receive the marriage payment, the mother of the bride did not marry again and had taken all the responsibilities for her daughter (bride) she would let her mother receive the payment or she could select anyone to receive her marriage payment. In case her mother remarried and had gone to live with her husband under whose care the girl was brought up could be entitled to receive the marriage payment.[118] In case she is a '*Talak*' or illegitimate child, her mother could receive the marriage payment.[119]

During the course of our survey, we found that Parry was right about the '*Mantang*' or the subsidiary price of the bride, which was normally distributed to different categories of persons. [120]

(a) Sumhmahruai, Rs. 20/-, this price is payable to the bride's father or brother.

(b) Sumfang, Rs. 8/- is payable to the bride's father or brother.

(c) Pusum, Rs. 6/- goes to the bride's 'Pu' (the maternal uncle of the bride).

(d) Palal, Rs. 5/- is to be received by any person, selected by the bride as adopted father. The Palal in reciprocal has to give the bride a fowl and Zubel (pot with rice beer) as Lawichal (wedding feast given by recipients of Mantang).

(e) Ni-ar, Rs. 2/- has to be received by the parental aunt.

(f) Naupuakpuan, Rs. 2/- is entitled by the bride's elder sister in consideration of her having carried the bride about in her cloth when the child was a baby.

The above-mentioned subsidiary price or '*Mantang*' are the integral parts of marriage payment. In addition to this, there are also two optional 'mans'- they are *Thianwan* and *Lawichal*.

(i) *Thianman* Rs. 2/- or Rs. 3/- is payable to a friend of the bride, it is from the *Manpui*. *Thianman* is refunded in case the bride left her husband *sumchchuah* (divorce of husband by wife) or *Uire* (adultery).

(ii) *Lawichal* Rs. 2/- is a payment (not compulsory) payable only when the bride and the bridegroom are from different villages. When the bride is escorted by a group of friends and a man, who leads them to the bridegroom's residence. This man is known as '*Lawichal*' in the language of Dulien speakers. He is sometimes rewarded Rs. 2/- which is also to be refunded in case the bride later leaves her husband '*Sumchchuah*' or '*Uire*'.

Moreover, the following rates of marriage payment are realized:

(i) Tlai means head of one mithun's price Rs. 20/-.
(ii) 'Tlai Sial' means half mithun Rs. 20/-.
(iii) 'Sepui' means a full grown mithun Rs. 40/-.
(iv) 'Seding' means a full grown mithun or Rs. 40/-.
(v) 'Senufa' means a mithun and calf or Rs. 60/-.
(vi) 'Puikhat' means Rs. 20/-.
(vii) 'Puisawnsial' means Rs. 20/-.

The Lakher

Marriage payment among the Lakhers was quite high and this worked as a deterrent to easy divorce and fortified the position of the wife. Like the Lushais, marriage payment in the Lakher-customs was shared by a long line of relatives even aunts of the bride have to receive part of it. Sometimes, sharing of the same was so complicated that litigations continued endlessly.[121] The main price was called '*angkia*'. Higher clan Lakhers also adopted the custom of taking higher rate of '*angkia*', which varied from 10 to 70 rupees. The different parts of the marriage payment, are the '*angkia*', the '*puma*', the '*nongcheu*', the '*nangcheu*', etc. All these prices have their own subsidiary prices.[122]

The '*angkia*'[123] as the main price is taken by the father of the bride. In some Lakher society, the '*angkia*' is received by the eldest son (brother) for the eldest daughter. Likewise the youngest daughter's *angkia* goes to the youngest brother.

The next payment is the '*Puma*'[124] which is payable only to the bride '*pupa*' who is her maternal uncle. The rate at which 'puma' is payable depends on the rate of the *angkia* and if it is 60 rupees the rate of the '*pumapi*' or 'puma' payment is also 60 rupees and is generally claimed when the couple settles down as man and wife.

The third marriage payment is the '*Nongchue*'.[125] which means 'the mother's price'. If the mother and father of the bride have been divorced, it is payable to the bride's mother. If they are still married, it is payable to the bride's mother's sister.

The fourth marriage payment is the '*Nangchue*'[126], which means the aunt's price and is payable to the bride's eldest paternal aunt.

Here it would be significant to note that among the mainland communities, instead of cash, goods are sent across to every member of the bridegroom by the bride's party and vice versa.

The Thadou

Among the Thadous, the marriage payment has an interesting legend.[127]

Chongthu was the younger brother of Nongmangpa, the Chief of the underworld. As per Thadou custom, in the presence of the elder brother called '*Upa*', the younger brother called '*Naopa*' cannot become a chief. So, Noimangpa, being the elder, was the chief, Chongthu also intended to become the Chief. Therefore, he went out in search of a suitable land where he could establish himself separately as a Chief.[128] He found one. On his plan to become a chief, he wanted to go with his own closed friends whom he could trust. Thus, he arranged for the marriage of each of his selected men. In doing so he made the marriage payments of each bride to their parents. In those days, no valuable property or cash was available. All the valuable items that one could think of was a '*Paigen*'. This was a belt made of leather and decorated with a kind of beads, called '*Longchang*', in seven lines[129]. This was then considered to be a very rare and valuable item of property. This could only be afforded by the chief alone. So, traditionally it became associated with the sole property, the right of which was vested only in the chief and was venerated very much being associated with a certain amount of superstition.[130]

Chongthu being the younger brother of *Noimangpa*, the chief, had access to it and when he arranged for the brides of his friends with whom he planned to go to his newly found land, he paid the '*Paigen*' to the parents of the girls as marriage payment. It so happened that though the commoners dared not refuse to accept the '*Paigen*' when offered to them as marriage payment subsequently, they could neither dare keep it with them owing to their superstitions attached to it nor could they dare refuse the bride in marriage[131]. Thus, along with the bride, the parents returned the '*Paigen*' to *Chongthu* saying that being a valuable property associated with the Chief exclusively, they dare not keep it or else, the wrath of the unseen supernatural power visit them and bring misfortune to them[132]. This process went on and on until *Chongthu* was able to arrange 30 of his best and closest friends with the payment of '*Paigen*' as the marriage payment.

Hereafter, marriage payment of every clan was paid in terms of seven mithuns based on the seven lines of '*Longchung*' on the '*Paigen*'. This however needs further investigation and confirmation, the prevailing different versions on the matter among the Thadou tribes needs specific enquiries..

Our research into ethnicity and folk lores reveal that since then marriage payment came to exist though in actual practice there are variations among the clans in terms of kind and number of mithuns. However, assuming that the following structure is the broad base for marriage payment as propounded by Crawford.[133]

Bride-Price Structure of Thadous

	Clan		*Price*
1.	Doungel	i)	selsom (10 mithuns)
		ii)	dahpi ni (2 big copper gongs)
2.	Sitlhou	iii)	dahbu ni (2 sets of three different small sizes of copper gongs)

		iv)	Khichang ni (2 ear beads)
		v)	Khichong ni (2 bead necklaces)
3.	Singson	i)	Selsomlanga (15 mithuns)
4.	Kipgen	i)	selsom (10 mithuns)
		ii)	dahpi ni (2 big copper gongs)
5.	Haokip	iii)	Khichong ni (2 bead necklaces)
		iv)	Khichang ni (2 ear beads)
6.	Chongloi	i)	Selsagee (7 mithuns)
		ii)	dahpi khat (1 big copper gong)
		iii)	dahbu khat (1 set of three different small sizes of copper gongs)
7.	Hangshing	iv)	Khichang khat (1 ear bead)
		v)	Khichong khat (1 bead necklace)

Crawford is the first and only person so far to work on the customary laws of the Thadou ever-undertaken by an authority. The work did not pretend to be exhaustive and was printed in such a form as to enable officers to make their own additions. Examples of then existing court practice in the matter of loans and oaths were inserted even though they were not strictly speaking customs. Therefore, the book is not intended to be a legal code. He was sincerely assisted in his enquiries by William Shaw, B.C. Gasper, L.L. Peter, the Sub-Divisional Officers of Tamenglong, Churachandpur and Ukhrul respectively and by J. H. Hutton, Director of Ethnology and J.C. Higgins, Political Agent in Manipur. In his work he rendered valuable suggestions and advice. Today in high sight we feel though the work is not comprehensive as it could have been, it is however, worth while to be used as the basis on which Thadou customary law could be built up for more detailed study. It provides the base for analyzing the customary laws of the Thadous.[134]

Shaw[135] in his study on the Thadou observed several

deviations from what Crawford had specified in his work. He contended that the question of amount of marriage payment among the Thadous was not definite and commented that the chiefs and wealthy persons usually claimed and paid the equivalent of ten mithuns, Rs. 200/- in cash, 23 dahpi (large gongs), 2 dahpu (set of two gongs), 2 khichang (ear beads), 2 khichong (necklaces). He did not name any specific clan of the Thadous. He further opined that ordinary person often actually pay a couple of mithun, khichang and khichong. As in an instance, he said that a pig in some cases may be taken as one mithun and that as per his personal experience he had come across cases where Rs. 40 had stood for 4 mithuns, a jar of 'ju' for a khichang or khichong. Thus in actual practice the parent of the bride hardly ever received the marriage-payment in full but in the form of more or less fictitious substitutes. He was emphatic in this regard to the effect that the parents loved to name large amounts as the 'man' not with any idea of getting it, but to be able to boast that their daughter was married for so much. Often when enquired as to what precisely they had received, it was found that actually a much smaller amount had been accepted in full satisfaction by a system of fictitious values. This is very similar to the practices among the Lushais, Zomis, etc. Fictitious values have more often created false pretensions of wealth and richness, which became bones of contentions later and led to unhappy marriages.

It must also be mentioned that Hutton[136] was convinced to have observed the fact that the first and last number of the marriage payment by mithun must necessarily be paid in mithun (selkeng-liding by this it means that marriage payment has to be by live-mithun). The first and the last marriage payment must in no case be substituted in any form of cash or kind.

Gangte[137] another authority working on the marriage payment of the Thadous maintains that the marriage payment of the Singson Thadou is 30 mithuns without any other items added to it unlike the other Thadou clans. The higher rate of marriage payment among the Singsons has no origin according to him. It is said, the Singsons are the direct junior collaterals of the Sitlhous. So when their senior collateral (Sitlhous) increased the marriage payment the junior also deemed it proper to follow suit. [138]

During the course of our research we found that one common conspicuous missing fact is that of '*Lutom Laisui*', a very important and compulsory item in the marriage payment. It signifies the importance of father and mother of the bride. '*Lutom*' is given to the father of the bride in token expression of gratitude. Likewise, '*Laisui*' is an exclusive item to be given to the mother of the bride for having given birth to her daughter from her naval. Here, it must be said that, while the father is shown respect for his paternal masculinity, the mother too is highly respected for giving birth to the child.

In this regard, it is interesting to state that there cropped up differences between William Shaw and J.H. Hutton, who out of confusion literally dealt with the two terms out of ignorance of the language and meaning provided to the two items. Shaw[139] attributed 'Lutom' as a gift given to the mother and 'Laisui' to the father. Hutton[140] contended otherwise and explained that Shaw got it the wrong way round. In doing so, he explained saying that *Laisui* means a woman's waist-band, while *Lutom* is a man's loincloth. They were cloths for bride's parent and further contended that it could be accounted for a money payment of Re. 1/- and Rs. 2/- respectively, that a woman can claim for property and that a Thadou woman can make in her own account.

Similarly, we found another feature that has not been dealt with by the several authorities in regard to *Manpi* which stands for principal marriage-payment that consists of one mithun on the tail of which one piece of big bead '*khichang*' through the ear of which the tail of the mithun can be made to pass through as a decorative piece[141]. This bead is counted as equivalent to one mithun. Therefore, the *Manpi* or the principal mithun is counted as to bear the price of two mithuns. The principal mithun is expected to have given birth to as many calves as possible. It is believed that with such principal mithun included in the marriage payment similar number of many children are in return given birth by the bride. Therefore it is insisted that such principal mithun should necessarily reveal calf bearing[142].

We also observed that the broad based marriage payment as shown above is not totally followed by different clans. As for an instance, the Haokips of Chassad lineage known as the seniormost (*piba*) of the Haokip take ten mithuns inclusive of the principal mithun[143]. However, as for other junior lineages of the Haokip clan of the Thadou, the marriage payment is fixed at eight mithuns.

Another pertinent point we have observed i.e. the fact that though the marriage-payments of different clans are fixed it is customarily not paid in full throughout the life time of the bride. The practice of marriage payment is that provided the principal mithun accompanied by one or more subsidiary mithun can be paid, the remaining marriage payment be not necessarily in terms of mithuns. They can be substituted in kind. Symbolically the counting could represent mithun depending on the agreement between the groom's and bride's parties.

We have also observed that in some societies such as that of Sumatra and Malay Archipelago, marriage payment in full[144] had to be made compulsorily so as to be eligible for father-right. By this, it implies that the children of father-right marriage payment system, the children are of exclusive possession of the father. Similarly if no payment is made at all, the children belong to mother and her kin. These South East Asian social traits could have entered the Thadou social customs during their period of origination and intermingling of their culture with tribes in Manipur.

The Zomi

Among the Zomis the payment of marriage price also forms an integral part which has a high social value. In their custom, it is also called 'Manpi' (principal price). In every society of Zomi (chin) or Kuki or Mizo tribes, unlike the Meitei's, marriage ceremony process takes two days, one for sending off the bride by the parents, and another day for wedding, which is to be performed at the bridegroom's place. A would-be bride cannot be send-off unless and until the question of 'Manpi' is settled as mentioned earlier. This is paid by the bridegroom side to the bride's parents and has to be received by the father of the bride. In case he is dead, the price goes to the nearest male relative on his side, preferably, to the eldest or the youngest male member who is the heir-apparent.

In general, among the average Zomi, marriage payment 'Manpi' or principal price is fixed normally on the following four factors:[145]

(i) the clan to which the bride belongs,

(ii) the amount of dowry the bride carries,

(iii) the beauty of her, and

and (iv) mutual understanding.

Chief's Family or Aristocratic Family

If the bride belongs to chief's clan or aristocratic family, the normal price of such bride is ten mithuns or equivalent value of ten mithuns in terms of rupees but only in name. Once the principal marriage payment i.e. one life-mithun is paid, the rest of the price can be substituted in kind like gong, even valuable household utensils made of copper, silver, alluminium, etc.[146] When marriage is solemnized the parents of the bride offer a sumptuous feast in bidding fare-well to their daughter by sacrificing a pig or a cow or two pigs or two cows depending on their capacity and quantum of guests. This is a normal standard followed by an average Zomi. In symbolic significance of final settlement of marriage negotiation all the elders from both the sides gather with a mug of rice bear each in their hands would partake specific portions of the sacrificial meat together. This is known as 'witness supper' of the marriage. This 'witness supper' is preceded with formal handing over of the marriage payment. After deliberation they have to agree finally by accepting the marriage payment or totally refunding the same in good faith, which occur rarely.

The following is the generally accepted agrteement by Zou or Zoumi or 'Chin' as far as the marriage-payment is concerned.. It is practiced even today.

Sialsuam (ten mithuns)	—	Chief or Aristocratic clan.
Sialthum (three Mithuns)	—	Commoners.

Though virtually covered under the Zomi Customary Law as described hereinabove, marriage payment of the Paites is a bit different. The marriage-payment among them is normally one mithun and a calf, 'Sial Nuta'. As per fixation of the British administration, one full grown Mithun costs Rs. 40/- and Rs. 20/- for a Mithun calf called 'Tai' or '*Tlai*' which means half. Zomi clans like Zou takes only

'*Sialnga*' (five mithuns) only. The Zous stick to maintaining their customs since time immemorial. The obligation of the bridegroom towards the bride's party is significant in their social and cultural life. Any relationship between two clans who are involved can also play a role in determining marriage. Thus we find that sometimes the marriage payment can only be symbolic which means the expense of the wedding ceremony are counted as marriage payment. If a poor boy is not in a position to pay he may be allowed to pay later. A boy may also be exempted from paying the same if he causes elopement of the girl and also if he simply moves to the house of the girl and waits until the girl is ready to marry him.[147]

In addition to '*Manpi*', there are also the other subsidiary marriage-payments. They are as follows:

(i) *Puchum* Rs. 4/- goes to the maternal uncle of the bride.

(ii) *Niman* is equal to that of *Pusum*, which is to be accepted by the paternal aunt.

(iii) *Thaman* or *Palal* equal to that of *Pusum* is the labour or service price to be reciprocated for taking the charge of the parents of the bride and is usually given for the head of the family. It is prevalent among the Gangte, the Paite, the Simte, the Thadou, the Vaiphei also.

(iv) *Thallouh* '*sum*' (price goes also to the nearest relative of the head of the family.

(v) *Lamman* or *Thiansum* is a small amount of money that goes to a bride's friend as a token of love.

(vi) *Nuapuan puak* 'man' is the price for the cloth used for carrying the bride when she was a child by her mother or elder sister. It varies from Rs. 4/- to Rs.

20/- as the class of the clan she belongs to. These payments in cash or kind suggest complete cessation of ties of the girl who is getting married with her family as she has to start her own family with full devotion and understanding.

The Old Kukis: Among the Aimol, Anal, Chiru, Chothe, Kolhen, Kom and Purum,[148] etc, the marriage payment is also divided into several parts. To mention a few of them is that, among the Aimol, the bride's eldest brother gets Rs. 6/- and each of the other one rupee less than his immediate senior. The paternal and maternal uncles receive Rs. 2/- each, the aunt and the elder sister also receive Rs. 1/- each as *niman*. Among the Anal and Purum the marriage payment must not be less than a pig and a piece of iron a cubit in length but the girl's relatives try to get as much as they can. The bridegroom has also to feast the family of his bride three times on pork, fowls and rice washed down of course with plenty of Zu. But a Chiru girl has a marriage payment of only one gong. A Chothe girl's marriage payment comprises of a spear, a dao and a fowl and the same is sealed by the consumption of much Zu. The marriage payment of a Kolhen girl is a gong and Rs. 7/- to her mother and Rs. 7/- each to the elder and younger brother and the maternal uncle.

The marriage payment of the Kom girl is very high, the father receiving one gong, four buffaloes, fifteen cloths, a hoe, and a spear, the aunt taking a black and white cloth. The Lamgang bridegroom has to pay his father-in-law three pigs or buffaloes or cows, one sting of conch-shell beads, one lead bracelet and one black or blue petticoat. A Tikhup father of the bride receives a gong, ten hoes, one dao and one spear and also Rs. 7/- by maternal grandfather.

Apart from paying all items of marriage payments such as mithun, cow, pig, gong, bead, necklace, spears, dao, money and whatever ought to be paid by the bridegroom, three years service is to be served to the bride's family. This practice is prevalent among the Aimol, Anal, Chiru and Purum. During this period of service he works with dedication as if he were a son of the house.[149]

Our survey has shown that the low rates mentioned as marriage-payments are certainly due to the sluggish economic wealth generation and poor economic condition of the tribes. Even today the plight of the many tribes is not better off. These monetary gifts became rational but the responsibilities that the marriage entailed for both the bride and the bridegroom was enormous. Responsibilities were indeed domineering over both the parties. The spirit of sharing responsibilities was reflected in the methods of gift exchange and their acceptance.

Similarly the aspects of inheritance draw our attention which indeed is an inseparable part of Mizo society. A close look, like the concept of inheritance reveals that Customary Laws are very clear as far as the similarities among the distinct groups are concerned.

Inheritance

Inheritance is a kinship institution the dominant pattern in family organizations in any society.[150] Natural as this may seem it nevertheless creates a troublesome social environment as a source of conflicts. Each individual in a family can procreate several offsprings, and thereby a problem of inheritance created. This necessity constantly arises because of 'dividing the property' of the family among the members History tells us that no scheme of division has ever done full justice to all the parties concerned.

Morgan[151] defined 'inheritance' as the distribution of property among the cognate kindred. With descent in the male line, the children of a deceased person would stand at the head of the cognates and very naturally receive the portion of the heritance. To Lowie,[152] rule of inheritance is like the whole of property law reflects the total ideology of a society. 'Laws of inheritance indeed gives an unprecedented insight into the socio-economic and political formulations of any society.

Real or personal property, which is inherited by heirs according to law the process of succession to a property; the devolution of the property to the heir on the death of a owner are precisely opined by Hari Mohan Sinha and Dheeraj Narula[153] as the right to succeed to the state of an intestate. Sometimes it is loosely applied to the right of devises or legates in a 'will' made in their favour if the persons who might have taken on intestacy. The estate goes itself to which the right attaches.

Inheritance is not only intended where a man has land or tenements by descent or heritage but also every fee simple or fee tall which a person has by purchase may be said to be inheritance, because his heirs may inherit it after him. One may inherit by creation, as in the case of the kings grant of peerage, by letter patent, etc. Corporeal or handled; incorporeal inheritances are rights issuing out of annexed to, or exercised with, corporeal inheritances, as advowsoms, tithes, annuities, offices, commons, franchises, privileges, services, etc. There is also several inheritance, which is where two or more hold lands severally; if two men have lands given to them and the heirs of their bodies, these have a joint estate during their lives, but their heirs have several inheritances. Goods and chattels cannot be turned into an inheritance.

Cannons of inheritance are the rules directing the descent of real property throughout the lineal and collateral consanguinity of the owner dying intestate, who is technically called the purchaser.

Lowie[154] observed that since 1715, the English law has recognized the power of the property owner to disinherit his wife and children. The French Civil Code aiming at protection of the family units, limits the testation power to will his property according to the number of offspring; he may dispose freely of half his property if there is a single child, one third if there are two children and so forth, the denomination of the fractions he may assign at will exceeding by one unit the number of his progeny. In the United States of America, Louisiana stands out from all the other states in recognizing the legitim (right of the widow and children) irrespective of testamentary disposition. The growth of American Inheritance Laws out of English law of inheritance is an example of evolution – descent with modification; colonial conditions were unfavourable to a rule of primogeniture, which had been abolished everywhere by 1798. The general adoption of inheritance taxes in western civilization is another sign of the influence of ethical conceptions on property rights. In short, nature of complex and simple societies alike has inheritance rules that mirror the social ideology of the people.[155]

And according to Rivers, the distinction between transmission of property (inheritance) and transmission of office (succession) is hardly justified.[156] As the scholar admits, it is contrary to legal usage but what is more significant if "property" denotes not wealth but the title to it, then office is simply one of the privileges, which potentially involve inheritance. In Australia, artifacts are few and are bound to remain such as long as the natives rove about means of transportation. On the other hand, a Murngin inherits from his father the right to perform certain dances and also his magical power in some localities.[157] The different ways of inheritance varies in the manifestation in prevailing societies like Russia is also pertinent that in 1927 the Government made a limitation on the subject matter which is ten thousand gold roubles and the remainder is taken as the State's property.

Regarding the position of a testator is peculiar says Davis[158], he would like to control the property even after his death. It signifies the power of the testator. Such control indeed, gives threatening to the youngsters with disinheritance if they contravene his wishes. While processing the testator's wish, the community has also to think of not injuring the interest of the others. It looks with suspicion upon whims barn of petty quarrels upon peak will and upon efforts to bovine the perpetuity. He further claims that for the protection of State, Church and family, the standardization of inheritance custom should be maintained so that embarrassing situations to close relatives and competitors may not be created. And these ties on the community, for standardized inheritance customs will avoid unseemly conflicts.

In most civilized societies testation is neither completely free not completely automatic. The testator is permitted to exercise a choice with respect to a part of his wealth but the other part must be divided according to definite rules among prescribed relatives. There is usually, for example, a legitim, a legally enforceable claims of widow (as mentioned earlier) and children to at least a part of the dead husband's or father's estate.[159]

Among the laws of the Latin American states, the

Spanish Code (old) is prevalent which is divided into three unequal parts;

(i) the first and the largest (legitima) is for legitimate children or other near relatives and cannot be willed to any one else;

(ii) the second (mejora) is an extra portion to be given to certain children, often one or more sons, sometimes the elder; and

(iii) the third is available for free testation – often for the benefits of church.[160]

The extra portion usually represents the land and buildings from which the family derives its sustenance.

Cole[161] has maintained that in all peasant countries there is still a strong tendency to think of real property at least as belonging to the family rather than the individual. It is the family's means of life from which no member can be shut out except for positive misconduct. The family in the next generation will be several, they may find impossible all to live on the family- holding and yet when the holding is divided it may lose its efficiency. The heirs may, however, keep the holding in common and seek to enlarge it. This custom approximates a joint family system, popular in our country and some Islamic countries. In the individualistic cultures, however, equal inheritance quickly leads to division of property. An alternative to this is the custom of 'impartible inheritance' whereby only one son is given the family holdings. This type of inheritance is precisely the prominent one prevalent among the tribes. This son may be oldest (primogeniture) or the youngest (ultimo geniture or Borough English) or he may be chosen by the father according to ability. Each custom found in various localities has had its advantages and disadvantages. Inheritance by the eldest son means that 'he must take all the responsibilities for everything'.

Sometimes inheritance among the offspring reaches its most serious situation, when the physical nature of property is small in size, and cannot be divisible or shared among sons or inheritors. This system ultimately results to the shortage of economic security of a family. It is vividly reflected in many Indian family and ethnic societies. Moreover, Garratt[162] confirms "in India the subdivision of agricultural land by heirs has reached an extreme degree, so that the average holding is too small not only for efficient cultivation but also for the adequate support of a family".

It can be seen that in both industrial and landed economics when instruments of production are privately owned, inheritance are privately owned, inheritance becomes an important basis of class distinction especially if it is of the impartible type. But as family holdings in urbanized industrial societies of modern nations have grown more fluid, consisting of money, stocks, saleable capital, it has become easier to divide the inheritance. Chester[163] opines that, "In the United States today, in case of intestacy, the children, both male and female, share equally in the inheritance.

Lushai – Dulian speaking people: When we look into our own societies in the North East we find that the Mizos are patriarchal and their laws of inheritance are based on descent through the father's lineage. The law of inheritance of the Lushai is called '*Rokhawm*'. It is simple and without any complications.[164] But this concept is contradicted by Parry.[165] He considers it complicated. The youngest son who is called the '*fatlum*' inherits the property. He is the formal heir. The legitimate son has the priority over the son of a secondary wife or of a concubine '*hmeifa*'.

In actual practice, however, a man's property is divided among all his sons unless anyone of them quarrells with and gets separated entirely from him in which case he would have no claim.[166] A *'sawm'* or an illegitimate son also can claim his father's property and in which he has no step brother or brothers, he is entitled to inherit his father's property. The system of inheriting property of father is known as *'DAROKHAWM'* in the Lushai custom. If there is no male issue, the property goes to the next of kin on a male side and that the inheritor is normally the deceased man's brother or his son, then this type of inheritance is known as *'PAMI ROKHAWM'*[167] Daughters or females in the family are in no circumstance entitled to do so.[168] But inheritance by women *'hmeibhia in ro-a khawm'* is there only in case no other male heirs are available. A woman, she may be the widow or the daughter, may inherit property in which case the daughter should not have become a widow.[169] Another type of inheritance by widow is prevalent among the Lushais. Though the law does not permit woman to inherit property, sometimes, it happens, a man dies leaving his wife with small children including son, then she on behalf of the rightful claimant for his deceased husband's property may inherit. In this connection, the widow can take a male heir from the husband's side to be her guide. There is also one case of this type, where a mother continues to occupy the *'khumpui'* or the big bed without dividing the deceased husband's estate among sons.[170] It rarely occurs and a mother often thinks fit for managing the administration of household, etc.

The logic of the youngest son inheriting the father's property is that he is considered to be the fittest person to look after his parents in their old age when the elder brothers would be freely grown up and able to stand on their own legs. But this custom does not apply to a chief (who is succeeded by the eldest son). A chief sometimes has more than one village and he may distribute to the ones he may think fit but would invariably retain the chieftainship of the main (ancestral) village with the eldest son.

Moreover, as the society of these Dulien speaking people are segmentary, there are also another different types of inheritance law;[171] such as (i) Unau Ro-Khawm, (ii) Unau-Bul Tak Tak Lo Rokhawm and Laichin Rokhawm, (iii) Chawmhlum Rokhawm, (iv) Zawnchawp Rokhawm, (v) Pu Rokhawm, (vi) Ni Rokhawm, (vii) Fa Rokhawm And Una Fate Rokhawm, (viii) Ramhrangami Rokhawm, (ix) Michuan Rokhawm, and (x) Rokhawm Duhlo, which draw our attention. These forms are subtle but quite significant. During research we found that:

i) **Unau Rokhawm** is a type of inheritance by which a brother of the deceased person, who has very small children, may inherit the estate. The inheritor has to take care of the widow and all the responsibility of the children. It is a socially responsive system.

ii) **Unau-Bul Tak Tak Lo Rokhawm and Laichin Rokhawm:** In case this system is prevalent only when the deceased man does not have any male heir thus, falling to his clan or distant relatives for providing a successor or inheritor of his property. It is an accepted form.

iii) **Chawmhlum Rokhawm:** Such type of inheritance occur only a man who goes to help a man who does not have anyone to look after him or refuse to so by his relative. The helper inherits the man's property. A sense of obligation demands a right in inheritance and the individual who intends help gets the property.

iv) **Zawnchawp Rokhawm:** A man during his lifetime may dispose of his property. He may even disown his own son on valid grounds e.g. if the son unduly neglects to look after him or runs away from him.[172] A man without any relations at all to him is appointed as his heir by 'Will' for he is approaching death in near future. The appointed heir must arrange for the funeral of the man and he inherits the property of the deceased person.

v) **Pu Rokhawm:** A man inherits from his paternal grandfather and great uncles provided that there are no heirs.

vi) **Ni Rokhawm:** A person can inherit from his paternal aunt if she has no issue.

vii) **Fa Rokhawm And Una Fate Rokhawm:** If a man dies childless during his father's life time, his father will inherit his property and a father will inherit before the deceased's brothers. If a nephew dies, his property is inherited by the uncle.

viii) **Ramhrangami Rọkhawm:** This type of inheritance is practised when circumstances arise where a person whose son stays far away and both do not have the chance to live together particularly at the time of his father's death. Before the deceased person's death, he usually nominates his heir a man whom could be trusted. The inheritor buries and performs whatever necessary for death rituals and so automatically he inherits the property of the deceased.

ix) **Michuan Rokhawm:** A person, who is not related

to anybody, wanders from place to place without a definite certainty, and in case he dies at hosts house, the customary laws ensure that the owner however inherits his property. But the place where he dies is *Zawlbuk* or the *thirdengi* forge, then the chief will inherit his property. Since these cases rarely happened so the custom fell into disuse.

x) **Rokhawm Duhlo:** Though a man cannot refuse to accept an inheritance which has descended to him as the nearest direct heir, sometimes he tries to inherit on the ground that acceptance would mean that he would have to pay up the deceased's debts. Such individuals were helped by the society.

The Lakher

Inheritance or 'Reutang' among the Lakhers is interesting. It is the eldest son who takes all the property and also takes the responsibility for his father's including his father's '*ru*' or death due. The paying of mother's '*ru*' is compulsory for the youngest but he has no share in inheritance at all. In this regard, the eldest son, though it is at his discretion, shares a portion with him. This is similar to the inheritance law of the Gurkhas as described by Vansittart[173] in his work on the Gurkhas. If the deceased man was one of the two brothers the estate goes to the survivor. If the deceased was the eldest of the three the estate goes to the youngest brother. If the youngest or middle brother dies childless, the estate goes to the eldest brother or his heir. In the case of four or more brothers, the eldest and youngest brother inherit from each other if either dies childless and if a middle brother dies childless his estate goes to one of the other middle brothers or his heirs.[174]

If a young man dies without children his father inherits

his estate or may allow one of the deceased's brother to take it. The heir whoever he is, must pay the deceased's *ru* or *death due*[175] The brother and nephew also inherit the deceased's estate before the sons by concubines or mistresses and bastards, before a mere fellow-clansman.

Unlike the Lushai, the Lakhers do not make "will", they are all intestate, all property must descent to the customary heirs. And regarding '*reutang*' by women, it is only in the cases of two:

(i) if the deceased person had no son except daughter or daughters, here articles usually recognised as women's property like clothes or ornament left by the deceased were to be identified which custom is also prevalent among the Rangkhols.[176]

(ii) in case a man dies leaving minor child or children, then his wife on behalf of his eldest son, is entitled to the custody of his estate and may continue to occupy her late husband's house and bring up his family provided she does not marry again.[177]

The Zomi

In Zomi society, all the children – sons and daughters are equally entitled to inherit properties of the parents, equally, with the exception of the youngest son, who would inherit two or more shares than the others as the shares of the parents whom he shall duty bound look after them in their old age including the responsibility to bury them with requisite death rituals and ceremonies thereof. In case a parent does not have male issue the youngest daughter will take the entire responsibilities to look after the parents as should have been taken up by the youngest son.[178]

The source of this information is taken from the work of Maung Tet Pyo on the customary laws of the Chin Tribe that existed in 1884, translated by Maung Shwe Eik Myook: Assistant Government Translator, British Burma, with general remarks by Dr. E. Farchhanser, Professor of Pali and Government Archaeologist British Burma, the Chin Hills Regulation (received the assent of the Governor General on the 13th August, 1896, published in the Gazette of India, 1896, Part.I, p. 609 and *Burma Gazette*, 1896 Part.II, p.261); the Pau Cin Hau Religious and Script Movement in the Chin Hills as recorded in the Census of India, 1931; the Panglong Agreement signed between the Members of Executive Council of the Governor of Burma and the Representatives of Burmese Frontier Areas on the 12th February, 1947 the Report of Frontier Areas Committee of Enquiry (Evidence of Witnesses) from Chin Hills and Arakan Hill Tracts), 1947; the provision of Chin Special Division in the Constitution of the Union of Burma, 1948, and off-quoted notes and remarks made on the generic term Lushai-Kuki-Chin by eminent historians and writers, like Henry Yule, Father Sangermano, G.H. Luce, etc

The contention of Khup Za Go appears ideal and is a new thing so far as the Mizos, the Kukis, and the Zomis in Manipur are concerned. In this connection, Gougin[179] said that these people being of very strong patrilineal society, inheritance law has given heavy weightage to the eldest son, if not the exclusive heir. This law in general is similar to the inheritance laws of the Thadou, Paite, Gangte, Vaiphei, Zou, Simte, Lakher, Pawi (Lai), Kom, Chiru, Rangkhols except in the case of Lushai, Hmar etc. in whose case the inheritance is given to the youngest son which is similar to the practice in respect of other neighbouring non Mizo group such as Meitei, Kabui, Tangkhuls, etc. It may also be added that these Mizo groups mentioned, being too strong of patriarchy the daughters have no place in the laws of inheritance. This group of Mizo tribes called the daughters as '*Chanu*' or '*tanu*' or '*fanu*'. These daughters are not regarded as full members of the clan or lineage to which they are born. They are considered merely as 'daughters' supposed to have come to the lineage or clans as 'temporary guest' assuming that they would be given in marriage to their future husbands where they would be placed in a significant position even on their death, dead price, 'longman' is to be given by their husbands or eldest sons to their natal homes provided they give birth to son or sons in recognition of procreating the male lineage of their husbands.

Contrary to this, extreme system of inheritence where daughters are not counted as members of the clan or lineage in which they are born, it can be observed that there are societies where daughters are given a place of dominance in all aspects of life over the sons. Such societies are known as Garos, Khasis, and Jantias who are of strong matrilineal societies in the North East India. This group of matrilineal people have a very similar system with that of the Nayars in the South India mainly in Kerala.

In due course of our investigation we found that some interesting but contradictory laws of inheritance also prevail; e.g. some of the old Kuki tribes such as Anal, Purum and Lamgang, divide the deceased father's property into shares according to the number of sons. The youngest son inherits the ancestral house and supports the widow; thus it is akin to the Lushai custom.[180]

The Thadou

The laws of inheritance of the Thadous from father to eldest son exclusively irrespective of the number of sons born to the family persists. To share, or otherwise, of his ancestral inheritance with his younger brothers is entirely left at the discretion of the eldest son. Even his father cannot stop inheritance of his eldest son over his property under normal circumstances.

In case a deceased man does not have male issue, the property cannot be inherited by daughter. It has to go necessarily to his male senior lineage closed to him by relationship. Herein, the contention of Crowford[181] may be mentioned in that if a Thadou has no male issue of his own, his property including his right to claim marriage price, dead-price (longman) etc. and his debts go to his eldest brother or his eldest brother's son, if the eldest brother is dead or a failing brother, to the eldest of the nearest male line. A younger branch cannot do so until all the senior branches are extinct 'ingam' in Thadou male line.[182] Customary Laws prohibit such things in order to streamline social responsibilities and sensibilities.

Woman Law of Succession and Inheritance

In none of the above Major tribes of Mizo, such as, Lushai, Lakher, Zomi and Thadou, not a trace of customary law relating to women succession and inheritance was found to have been mentioned whatsoever. The customary laws of the said tribes in this regard appear lopsided. Herein, the work of Aleaz[183] on the issue is relevant to be taken note of.

Joking Relationship

During the field work and after interviewing several chiefs and families we found that in terms of inter-personal relationships customary laws provided an escape value for relieving the stresses generated among the family members through a systemic relationship which are popularly known as Joking relationships. Herein individual members cut jokes with each other and address each other with funny names, meaningful yet harmless and make statements or express words which have double meanings. This practice makes the stressful moments lighter and enjoyable. Members of the family do not take such expressions to heart but enjoy it by sharing them wit and humour. It ultimately leads to bonding of individuals and strengthens it.

The term "Joking relationships" first appeared from the writings of Labouret[184] and Paulme.[185] They were followed by Pedler's[186] note on what are called 'Joking Relationships' with the suggestion that some general theoretical discussion of the nature of these relationships might be of interest to readers as prevalent among the Mizos. Marcel Mauss has published a brief theoretical discussion of the subject in the 'Anmuaire de l'Ecole Pratique des Hautes Etudes, Section des Sciences religieuses, 1927-28. It was also dealt with by F. Eggan in Social Anthropology of North American Tribes, 1937, pp.(75-81). A.R. Radcliff-Brown[187] has defined the term 'Joking Relationships' as a relationship between two persons in which one is by custom permitted and in some instances required, to tease or make fun of the other, who in turn is required to take no offence. It is important to distinguish two varieties. In one, the relation is symmetrical, each of the two persons tease or make fun of the other. In the other variety, the relation is asymmetrical but in every case it acts as a safety valve in interpersonal relationships.

There are also many varieties of the same practices in different societies. In some instances often the joking or teasing is only verbal, in others sometimes it includes horse-play; in some the joking may include elements of obscenity, in others not.

Social relationships of such institution are vastly scattered, such as the inhabitants of Fiji and Tongo.[188] At the level of psyche the joking relationship is a peculiar combination of friendliness and antagonism. The behaviour is such that in any other social context it would express and arouse hostility, but it is not meant seriously and must not be taken otherwise. There is pretence of hostility and a real friendliness. To put it in another way, the relationship is one of 'permitted disrespect'. Thus any complete theory of it must be part of, or consistent with, a theory of the place of respect in social relations and social life generally. But this is a very wide and significant sociological problem, for it is evident that the whole maintenance of a social order depends upon the appropriate kind and degree of respect being shown towards certain persons, things and ideas or symbols.

Examples of joking relationships between relatives by marriage are very commonly found in Africa and Mizo society[189]. In the Mizo society it is noticed that the joking relationship is prevalent between a man and his wife's sisters and brothers. But in some instances there is joking terms with his wife's younger brothers and sisters but not with those who are older than she is. This joking with the wife's brothers and sisters is usually associated with a custom requiring extreme respect often partial or complete avoidance between a son-in-law and his wife's parents. This relationship is most intimate, affectionate, free and frequently made manifest between 'grandparents' and 'grandchildren' among most of the Mizo tribes who have the custom of 'alternate generation' naming system as an indispensable social institution. Such cordial relationship without inhibition is called 'Pu-Tu' relationship.

The joking relationship is clearly only appropriate

between persons who in the general social structure can treat each other as equals and this generally means persons of the same generation or those related as 'grandparent' and 'grandchild'. For the wife's parents and other relatives of that generation and sometimes for the wife's elder sister, an attitude of respect is required.[190]

'Alternate-generation' naming system is yet another form of strengthening interpersonal relationships.

In this connection, the naming system among the Mizos such as Thadous, Zous, Paites, Vaipheis, Gangtes, etc. is relevant by which these Mizo tribes take the name of one's father's father by male-child or father's mother's by girl-child. This is called 'alternate generation' naming system. By this, a boy child is given the first syllable of his name after the last syllable of his grandfather. Likewise, a girl child is given the first syllable of her name after the last syllable of her grandmother. A model of such name system is given below:

A man named Lienchungnung has a grandchild by his son, Mangzahau. When his grandson is to be given a name it has to begin with the first syllable 'nung', the last syllable of his grandfather. In order to construct a name, the first syllable taken from his grandfather has to be added with two or three more syllables for a complete name. Now, therefore, the name starting with the Syllable 'nung' is to be joined either 'kho thang' or 'ja thang' or whatever syllables one may choose. Similar is the case with the baby girl. Thus the replacement of grandparents by their grandchildren is in a way recognized in the wide spread custom of giving a child the name of a grandparent.[191]

Therefore, it is said that the son of a man is father of his father. Hence a joking relationship gets originated from the naming system called 'Alternate generation'. This system is prevalent among most of the Mizo tribes except Lushais and some others. Its peculiar system is singularly conspicuous among, perhaps all the communities the world over, and is 'unique' as a living social institution. By the name of a man or a woman, his or her pedigree is easily established and the family genealogical tree systematically constructed with more or less correct precision. The practice signifies ancestor worship and recognition of elders in society. It also reflects the partial existence of genetic characteristics of a grandfather in the grandchild, whereby the familial ties and bending between members of the family become far stronger and also brings about unity. The ties are irreducible.

Divorce

Another important area wherein Customary Laws plays a significant role is in the practice of divorce. In Mizo society divorce is becoming rampart. So we looked deeper in this segment and found that the role of divorce was becoming increasingly rampart. Perhaps it is the bane of modern civilization.

A study of divorce could not be undertaken in isolation. It has to be necessarily linked with marriage. In fact it is the outcome of negative aspect of marriage. For this it will be in the fitness of things that the concept of marriage and the certain religious beliefs need to be given as the background as to how divorce is looked upon by societies. For this purpose the concept of marriage as an institution according to Christianity and Hinduism was briefly looked in to understand the issue of divorce. According to Christian concept of marriage, it is accepted as sacramental and indissoluble except through special dispensation or for the grievous causes for it is said, the Gospel according to Saint Mathew,[192]

> "... But I say unto you, that whosoever shall put away his wife, saving for the cause of fornication(Chaste), causeth her to commit adultery and whosoever shall marry her that is divorced committeth adultery"

Similarly, the Gospel according to Saint Mark [193] says,

> "And he said unto them whosoever shall put away his wife and marry another, committeth adultery against her and if a woman shall put away her husband, and be married to another she committeth adultery".

According to Bhushan and Sachdeva,[194] the Hindu Shastra regarded marriage a bond of indissoluble in life, the wife was to worship her husband as a god and that there was no such thing as divorce in the Hindu law. However, there existed the custom of divorce among the lower castes.

Westermarck defined marriage as the "more or less durable connection between male and female, lasting beyond the mere act of propagation till after the birth of offspring". Groves defined it as "a public confession and legal registration of an adventure in fellowship". Lowie defined it as a relationship permanent bond between permissible mates." Malinowski defined marriage is a contract for the production and maintenance of children." According to Lunberg, marriage consists of the rules and regulations which define the rights, duties and privileges of husband and wife, with respect to each other.[195] According to Horton and Hunt, "marriage is the approved social pattern whereby two or more persons establish a family".[196] Mazumdar defines marriage as a socially sanctioned union of male and female for the purpose of (a) establishing a household, (b) entering into sex relations, (b) procreating and (d) providing care for the offspring.[197] According to Anderson and Parker, "marriage is the sanctioning by a society of a durable bond between one or more males and one or more females established to permit sexual intercourse for the implied purpose of parenthood".[198] According to John Lary and Ruth Monroe people get married because of the feeling that being in a family is the only proper way indeed the only possible way to live. People do marry because it is their social duty to perpetuate the institution of the family or because the scriptures recommend matrimony or because they have fallen in love with each other but they live in a family as children and cannot get over the feeling that being in family is the only proper way to live in society. In almost all the societies one or the other form of marriage exists.

Despite such contentions of the eminent scholars that supported the ideal concept of marriage as found in the religious belief of Christianity and Hinduism, the deviant human behaviour cannot adhere to such idealism. Hence the indissoluble concept of marriage as sacramental has to be abrogated for which circumstances through special dispensation or the gravest causes as to be provided either as a legislation or mechanism to meet the exigency of situation. This, therefore, necessitated several national courts, though differed in details treated marriage as variable institution, not as a private contract between two persons that did not concern governmental authorities. This has given way to the legislation of divorce in the courts of law in modern society. Divorce as such is indeed a calamity and designed even for those who rejected the sacramental views. It was therefore found indispensable to enact legislation to legalize divorce in western countries in the late nineteenth century. As for instance Germany, France and Switzerland introduced civil marriage asserting that divorce as such, might be accorded acknowledgement of the society whether or not there was, to be an ecclesiastical ceremony also. This saved the way for the erring husband or wife to be condoned before and after separation from each other. In England[199] it also took a measure for cognizance of divorce in English law so as to legalize equal right to both, the wife and the husband. Davis attributed the United States as the largest country where incidence of divorce took place after the Second World War estimating approximately one in every three marriages. Yet, he was convinced that the rate in Egypt was higher than in United States. He further expressed the view that the reason for divorce was not necessarily on the emphasis of marriage and marital happiness based on a culture. Instead, it was due to the urge for individual happiness that explained the high rate of divorce. The second reason he attributed was due to practice of free and open courtship. These two factors together give way to the romantic complex in which the force of suppressed sex desire and whims of personal feelings combine to induce a maximum amount of irrationality.[200]

The Hindu Marriage Act, 1955 has recognized the right of a Hindu[2010] woman to divorce her husband. Under Section 13 of the Act[202] any marriage solemnized whether before or after the commencement of this Act may on a petition presented by either the husband or the wife be dissolved by a decree of divorce on the ground that the other party:

(i) has committed adultery; or

(ii) has ceased to be a Hindu by conversion to another religion; or

(iii) has been incurably of unsound mind for a continuous period not less than three years immediately preceding the presentation of the petition; or

(iv) has, for a period of not less than three years immediately preceding the presentation of the petition been suffering from a virulent and an incurable form of leprosy; or

(v) has, for a period of not less than three years immediately preceding the presentation of the petition been suffering from venereal disease in communicable form; or

(vi) has renounced the world by entering any religious order; or

(vii) has not been heard of as being alive for a period of seven years or by those persons who would naturally have heard of it, had that party been alive; or

(viii) has not resume cohabitation for a period of two years or upwards after passing of a decree for judicial separation against, the party; or

(ix) has failed to comply with a decree for restitution of conjugal rights for a period of two years or upwards after the passing of the decree.

Besides the above grounds, a wife may present a petition for the dissolution of her marriage on the ground:

(i) in the case of any marriage solemnized before the commencement of this Act, that the husband had married again before such commencement or that any other wife of the husband married before such commencement was alive at the time of the solemnization of the marriage of the petitioner;

Provided that in either case the other wife is alive at the time of presentation of petition, or

(ii) that the husband has, since the solemnization of the marriage, been guilty of rape, sodomy or bestially.

A petition for divorce cannot be presented before a period of three years of marriage. The Act also provides for judicial separation on the ground that the other party:

(i) has deserted the petitioner for a continuous period of not less than two years immediately preceding the presentation of the petition; or

(ii) has treated the petitioner with such cruelty as to cause a reasonable apprehensive in the mind of the petitioner that it will be harmful or injurious for the petitioner to live with the other party; or

(iii) has for a period of not less than one academic year immediately from a virulent form of leprosy; or

(iv) has, for a period of not less than three years immediately preceding the presentation of the petition been suffering from venereal disease in communicable form, the disease not having been contacted from the petitioner; or

(v) has been continuously of unsound mind for a period of not less than two years immediately preceding the presentation of the petition; or

(vi) has, after the solemnization of marriage had sexual intercourse with any person other than his or her spouse.

Divorce may give more independence to the wife, yet,

it is not ideal situation, Divorce has got many minus points, which are detrimental in the first instance to the children and parents in particular, and the society at large. Therefore, the Hindu Marriage Act, 1955 gave provisions for divorce, it must not be taken as a convenient lot for either of the two partners to resort to divorce course of action.

In contrast backward tribal people, including primitive societies as a rule do not have such elaborate legislation of law both in religion and governmental sanction for wedlock and divorce which may be provided with little formality said Lowie.[203] In giving easy instances of divorce, he gave example of divorce as were collected in his field study "by Schebesta ... from Greenland Holm found a young Eskimo woman who had just left her sixth husband, a contemporary Hapi woman is known to have had eight official husbands. In this latter instance, strictly monogamous tribe, Titiev discovered marked instability; 34% of 826 men and women investigated had been divorced at least once, and the same tendency is substantiated by historical evidence for earlier periods.

All the same, Dey and Dey[204] were convinced to say that divorce is universal among the primitive society and that dissolution of marriage might be obtained by one of the two parties. As an example they give the Khasi instance of divorce for reasons of adultery, barrenness and incompatibility of temper. The party either the wife or the husband desiring dissolution of the marriage may have to pay compensation to the other party.

Among the Lushais(Mizo) dissolution is a simple affair If a husband turns out a wife he must pay compensation to his wife. Similarly, if a wife deserts her husband or is caught in adultery, she must pay back the marriage payment to her husband. We know that even Gonds allow divorce freely on grounds of infidelity, carelessness in household work, barrenness or quarrelsomeness nature. Dissolution is also easy among the Khasis. A wife may be divorced on ground of infidelity, barrenness of wife, laziness, refusal for living together and the habit of stealing.

In addition for the purpose of fuller study on marriage and divorce, few cases of polyandrous tribes might prove richer dividend on the subject. Mazumdar[205] in his study on the polyandrous societies of the Himalayan region among Jaunsar Bawar, High caste Hindu Brahmin and Rajputs (Khasas) that women as well as men are free to divorce their spouses and they can remarry without much difficulty. As an instance he found that a woman could change several husbands without losing her prestige provided her prospective husband was ready to pay compensation known as 'Chhoot' or 'Kheet' to her divorced husband. The amount which was Rs. 1500/- as prevalent in 40s subject to fluctuation in rupee value.

It is interesting to note that Lushais among the Mizo, it may be recalled that in as much liberal as a man can marry any girl except his own mother and sister, divorce is easy and liberal as possible to the extent that a man can do so at his will with the simple word, "I divorce you".[206] This contention is very closed to the divorce system of the Muslim when a man can divorce his wife at his will with the utterance of '*Talak*' three times. The bonds of matrimony are extremely loose and are very easily ripped off.[207] The divorce system of the Lushais as *Barkataki* attributed, appears in confirmation of the contention of Parry[208] who stipulated the prevalence of several ways of divorce as the man simply says "I Mak You" (I divorce you) and the woman is divorced. The divorced wife, if she is *Thisenpal* (with child or children dead or alive) is entitled to get her remaining marriage payment including the *thutphah* but nothing if she is *Thisenpallo* or barren. A woman who has been Mak can take with her all her property and her *Thuam* or dowry.

The second way of divorce is that a woman may willingly leave her husband and is known a *Sumchchuah*. In this case, the marriage payment made earlier has to be refunded[209] to the husband's side. Her personal belongings as well as her *Thuam* are also to be taken by the girl.

There is yet another system of divorce prevalent in the Lushai society known as *'Fanghmano Ei'*, if a man after divorcing his wife, Mak, by using his *palais*, calls his wife, if she agrees, reconciliation takes place, a sum of Rs. 20/- is paid as *Fanghmano Ei*.[210] Sometimes, it so happens that the wife divorces her husband, *sumchchuah*, he needs not pay the fine i.e. *Fanghmano Ei*.

Our field work has revealed that in such a society like Lushai, the custom of sharing the divorce fine is also noticed. Such a custom is called *'Sumlaitan'* which takes place by agreement between the husband and wife.

There is also the prevalence of divorce known as *Peksachang* by agreement. If husband and wife agree to separate, they can agree that the amount of the payment already paid up will suffice that is to say the man will not claim the return of any part of marriage payment he had already paid and also the woman on her side will not claim for the outstanding payment that is still in due.[211]

The prevalence of divorce, called *Pasal Awmloh Hlana Chhuak* is also found among the Lushais. It is occurred only in circumstances, that the couple after getting married, separates owing to the husband having left the country or being confined in jail or for any other cause, being away from home for a long period.[212] The wife patiently waits for her husband's return is the normal obligation. On the contrary if she leaves for her natal home, *Lumchchuah* or she dies while longing for her husband, the returning of whatever necessary due to custom is out of question in the former but in the latter, the relatives of her may claim.

Divorce on account of insanity is not without experience. Instances are galore. If the husband or the wife goes insane, either of them may claim for divorce. However, a probationary period of three years is given for recovery before actual divorce takes place. This is called as divorce due to insanity (*Atna Vanga Inthen*).

Another type of divorce, *Nuipui Thansan* is that of abandonment of the wife by the husband. In such case a peculiar situation emerges. As mentioned earlier in the case of inheritance among the Lushais no female is entitled to inherit any property, whatsoever, as is the case among the Thadous and the Zomis. But in the present case, the abandoned wife has the right to inherit all the properties earned before divorce such properties include movable and immovable properties, including landed properties. Subsequently, it may so happen that the husband may like to return to his abandoned wife. Under such circumstances, the abandoned wife has got the absolute discretion either to accept or reject him.

The next type of divorce is called *Kwangkasula Mak*. By this, it means that the husband wishes to bring in a new wife in place of his wife. In this case their properties are divided between the wife and the husband with the wife getting items, such as paddy and rice, maize, millet and also the earthen ware pots. The children are also given the liberty to choose either to stay with the mother or the father. Notwithstanding, the husband has the exclusive right to receive the marriage payment of all his daughters even if they happen to choose to stay with their mother. Likewise, the ancestral bed or main bed of the wife and husband called '*Khumpui*' (Khunpi in Thadou and Zomi) necessarily remains with the husband. This is true in the case of Thadous and Zomis.

In addition, Lal Biak Thanga[213] emphatically maintains that divorce takes place even on flimsy grounds because of incompatibility of the partners in their sexual relationship. If such incompatibility is due to the husband, it is called "*Zang Zaw*" (Male impotency), and "*Chhuping*", if the wife is unable to perform wife's duty to her husband according to Parry.[214]

Adultery among the Mizos

They are of two types. One that is committed during the lifetime of both the husband and the wife, and the other one committed after the demise of the husband by the widow. In case of adultery committed during her husband's life-time, the entire marriage payment is to be returned by her relatives. She is also to forfeit her dowry or *Thuam*, and other property such as cloths, beads etc.[215] If she commits adultery after the death of her husband while being in his house, it is also equally treated as adultery committed during his lifetime. Adultery as such is called *Uire*. It is taken as a crime.

In this regard the contention of Barkataki[216] that divorce often takes place at the instance of the members of the husband's family, if they are not pleased with the bride is often true. Although it may be initiated by either party, divorce usually takes place at the instance of the husband. The status enjoyed by men in this respect can be easily appreciated from the old saying that "A wife and a bad fencing can be changed at any time". Divorce can also be effected by the wife by refunding the marriage payment. This is resorted to only when the wife finds her situation intolerable. If the wife leaves her husband in this manner, it lowers the prestige not only of the unwanted husband but also of the husband's family. And therefore, this process is rather unwanted and avoided as far as practicable.

Before a separation or divorce is considered final, due allowance is made for the frailties of human nature and time is allowed for the husband to reconsider/repent and call back his wife. Several broken marriages are mended in this manner. The cooling period is thus understandable for it is a safety valve, which lets the steam go, and helps mend the interpersonal relationships. In some cases the relatives of the wife make some demands of the husband who wishes to recall the wife as evidence of good faith and a guarantee of good behaviour in future.

Thus, a wife has to keep the home warm and be on best of terms with the husband for getting divorce is easy.[217]

Divorce is possible in the Lakher Society and a man who wants to divorce his wife can do so at any time. Likewise, a woman may divorce her husband.[218] The Lakhers unlike the Lushai wife, do not divorce, for the higher rate of marriage payment to be refunded. This has strengthened the hold of affection in the family particularly between the husband and wife who ultimately bring stability in their marriage. It has also been observed that the Lakhers do not take the course of divorce so easily on flimsy grounds. It is also a fact that Lakher husbands resort to seeking divorce in larger number than their wives It is mainly because of the fact that the womenfolk pay high regard to the feminine qualities by remaining virtuous and by building stable family rather than taking the liberty of resorting to divorce, and ruining their future.[219] Women understand that they are home-makers and not home-destroyers.

However, there are several forms of divorce which are similar to that of the Lushais except divorces due to insanity of either the wife or the husband called *Hrupathlie hasala* and adultery known as *Aphei* committed by the wife.

It is to be noted that in case of divorce due to insanity of the husband, the wife is given the choice to marry her brother-in-law if her husband does not recover from the illness within an agreeable period of time provided she is willing to do so. In the case of *Aphei*, the wife is at once turned out by her husband. The adulterer is liable to pay fine as per customs of the clan of husband or the village[220] to which they belong. This system prevails among the Thadous and Zomis.

Thadou Divorce

Soppitt in his work on the Kuki Lushai tribes in 1893, observed[221] that the traditional system of divorce practiced among the Thadous since eighteenth century till the period he undertook the study was definite to say, "Once married, no divorce is allowed except for adultery and even in these cases, if there be children, it is resorted to. The adulterer is heavily fined but he/she does not otherwise suffer punishment.

It is a masterpiece of contention, which can be observed as being prevalent even today. Yet, Crawford observed[222] that when a married woman did not behave as a virtuous woman should, the entire *mankat* (marriage payment) plus one mithun as a fine for causing disgrace (*maithi*) or *migepman* as adultery price by the adulterer to the aggrieved husband has to be paid.

In case a widow living in her deceased husband's house has a liaison with a stranger *maithi* is payable even if no pregnancy follows.[223] This is exactly similar to the Lushai system called *Uire*.

Divorce may also occur due to cruelty of husband toward his wife. Under such atmosphere in the family, the wife not being able to stand cruelty of her husband may ultimately ask for divorce. The Thadous belonging to strong patrilineal society give no right whatsoever to women to whom may be attributed the main cause of cruelty of husband rather than to the wife.[224]

In such kind of divorce the initiative often comes from the side of the wife leaving her husband's place. The guilt presumed to have originated from the wife due to her inability to bear or to encounter her husband. Therefore, though, in point of fact, husband is the root cause of divorce the wife is implicitly alleged to have taken the step towards divorce for which she was found with fault. The husband, therefore, is exempted from any fine imposed under the normal dispute cases. Hence, the wife is penalized to return to the aggrieved husband the entire marriage-payments except the *sumtansha*[225] (a pig killed by the girl's parents for fixation of the girl marriage-payment).

Zomi Divorce

Divorce system among the Zomis has more or less similar customary laws with the Thadous, Lushais and Lakhers except that they have their peculiarities. If a man commits adultery with a married woman belonging to someone else, in such a case, the adulterer is liable to be punished by refunding the whole marriage payment to the husband of the adulteress. In addition he is to compensate the man with a fine of one mithun and to perform a salam rite which stands for condonation of his act of adultery by killing a pig in the house of the man.[226]

In our research we have found that a similar system is being practiced among the Anals whom Gougin "preferred" to call Anal Zomi[227] who charged a sum of Rs. 2000/- and a jar of rice beer in token restitution of the disgrace inflicted to the husband of the adulteress.

Old Kuki Divorce

Divorce among the old Kuki though not frequent is also easily obtained. Despite slight variations in the details of governing the process of divorce the system as such on the whole is the same among all the tribes of *Lushais*, *Lakher*, *Thadou*, *Zomi* and *Old Kuki*. But in the case of *Tikhup*, an old Kuki tribe, if a woman goes astray the fine imposed against the seducer is the double the marriage payment, maintained Shakespear.[228] Likewise, he found that in the case of Anals the fine imposed on the seducer was a sum of Rs. 50/- to be paid to the aggrieved husband or in lieu of it he had to host a feast to the village. It is interestingly observed by us in this regard that there is a big difference in the fine imposed on the seducer between what Shakespeare and Gougin found. This may be attributed to the time gap between the two authorities. While Shakespeare observed the fine imposed on the seducer as Rs. 50/- at the time he studied on the subject in 1912,[229] Gougin found it Rs. 2000/- as fine imposed in the year 1984,[230] after a gap of 72 years.

Birth Rite

We are aware of the fact that in any society, modern or primitive, the birth of a child is welcome. It is an addition of a living human soul that adds to the population of the society in which the child is born. It is considered that birth of a child ensures perpetuation of the family lineage. This act of procreation is considered indispensable for a living society lest it becomes extinct.

As an inseparable and significant aspect of Mizo society the customary laws and its traditionally accepted norms with respect to both rites and rituals were investigated. Some of our inferences are highlighted which reveal a deeper sense of social responsibility. Here the tradition which has been built over the past generations has indeed become socially appreciative.

We researched into the tribal groups under our study and found that they have certain birth rites which are significant and when analyzed deeply show some common traits which throw light upon their common origin.

There is no elaborate birth rite performed in the case of Lushais and Zomis, but they have some simple ceremonies at the time of birth and soon thereafter. It is most probable that in the ancient days such birth-rites must have existed. The brief account given by Gougin[231] mentions that the Zomi in general maintained a high tradition in regard to birth, a natural reverence for those who by virtue of birth become the chief of the village or a clan or a family that is to say the elders get a respectable place in a society. This is an universal practice but in the case of Zomi, we found this was exceptional.

Lakher

With the birth of a child the mother is made to confine herself within the house for nine days if the child is a girl and for ten days for a male child. This confinement period is called *Nawkhutlong*.[232] While the mother is confined in the house, the father whenever he goes for work; makes a bamboo pin, and place it in the hand of the child telling it not to follow him. This is to protect the child from having misfortune, e.g. getting quashed with stone or cut with a dao or an axe. On the fourth day the child is taken to the street of the village with a hoe and a small pot of cooked rice. While the baby is held by its mother, another woman pierce its ears with a thorn from a lemon tree or porcupine's quill. The ceremony of ear piercing called *Radeido*[233] is celebrated on the ninth day for a girl child and tenth day for a boy child.

Every new born Lakher child has two names.[234] Unless the child is given two names it is believed that misfortune may fall on the child because it is feared that the God, called *'Khazanpa'* may forget the child. This system is also practiced by the Tibetans.[235] Normally a male child is given the name of his grandfather or anyone of the ancestors who had been a great warrior or hunter. Likewise a girl child is given the name after her grandmother or ancestress. However, it is generally preferred to give the name of a rich, wise, great warrior or famous hunter in the hope that attributes of person after whom the child is named may descend upon the child. It is also a fact that naming of a child after a friend or fellow villager is considered an insult and is imposed fine on the parents of the child by the chief and elder.[236] On the *Radeido* day, the baby's hair is cropped and is kept short regularly until the child is eight or nine years old after which it is allowed to grow until it is long enough to be tied in a top knot or a bun according to the sex. On the final cropping called '*Sarang*' the child's name is given.[237] On this day a fowl-propitiation is performed as part of the naming rite. And when the child is of two or three months old, another rite is performed called '*Nawhri*' to protect him from all kinds of disease called '*hri*' and 'misfortunes'.[238]

Thadou

Similar to the Lakher belief in the ceremonies of birth and naming of a child the Thadou also has an interesting legend. On such legendary belief the practice of the Thadou at the childbirth is that a provisional name is immediately given to the new born child as soon as the child comes out of the mother's womb simultaneously with the cutting of naval cord by a split of bamboo.[239] This provisional name is associated with the superstitious belief that unless it is done so, the '*Thilhas*' (evil spirit) may overtake the person attending to the mother and the child. It is believed that if the *Thilhas* give name of the child ahead of the attending mid wives the life span of the child is under the discretion of the *Thilhas*. It is faith among the Thadous.

One interesting thing is the process of delivery of the child among the Thadou group. A jar of *ju* is kept prepared with full maturity of fermentation for eight to nine months. It is distilled to be offered to the mother of the child as medicinal potion. It is a fact that with the offer of the *ju* to the mother her entire bowel contaminated by the pregnancy and child-birth gets completely cleansed. This process gives immediate strength to the mother and good health is ensured. In this regard there appears slight difference from the contention of Shaw who maintained that the naval cord was cut with a knife or bamboo split.[240] However Hutton[241] differed from this contention and his views have been convincingly proved. He maintained that the use of knife or any metal on occasions, such as, child birth is considered as taboo among the Thadous. He gave similar belief prevalent among Nagas as well as many other tribes e.g. the Moi of Annan, the Kayan of Barneo and Tinguian of Luzon.[242]

After delivery of the child and immediate offer of ju to

the mother, the real name of the child is given by elders and closed relatives of the family. At this stage though provisionally the name of a boy is selected after his grandfather and grandmother lends her part name in the case of girl child. Thus, in most cases this provisional name is confirmed on this occasion.

The restriction to the mothers not to leave the house for some days among the Lakhers is also prevalent among the Thadous which is called *Naolaichan*. It is done after three days after birth in the case of girl baby and five days for the boy child. On this very day commences feeding of the child. The mother gives food to the child from her own mouth as birds feed their young. It is called *Nao-an-mop*.[243]

This is followed by another rite called *Kilhalho*. It is performed after the birth and naming of the child. In the process, the part of '*Thempu*' (priest) comes into the picture. A twisted cotton thread is prepared in the middle of which feathers of a cock is tied. Holding the two ends of the twisted thread around the neck of the child the *Thempu* will perform propitiation, which includes begging for the health and future prosperity of the child to God. After doing so the *Thempu* will tie the thread around the neck of the child with his blessings spraying a mouthful of ju around the child symbolizing purification of the child including the surroundings.

The next stage of birth rite is '*Naopui*' (Christening of the child) performed at the residence of the maternal grandparents or uncle. According to Gangte,[244] on this occasion the parents of the child take the following items with them.

(i) One jar of rice-beer called '*jubel*' and

(ii) One cloth called *puondum* (a black coloured with two lines of white colour on the border, lengthwise).

The christening party comprises *'Tuchas'* (representatives drawn from female relatives of the family such as aunts, sisters, etc.) and *Bechas* (representatives and closed friends of the family such as uncles, brother, good friends, etc.) leave for the maternal grandparents or uncle of the child early in the morning. On their arrival at the maternal grandparents or uncle's house, the party is not allowed to enter instantly. They are stopped at the *'Haungcha'* (verandah). The *Becha* of the maternal side cuts ginger into pieces and *'Thempu'* (priest) performs purification rite on completion of which they are allowed in the house. This signifies that the child is spotless and is not impure when they take him or her to the house of the maternal grandparent or uncle. All kinds of evil influences and bad things that may befall the child are then warded off by the performance of the purifying rite at the door with ginger. This ritual has only changed forms but is found in every ethnic community. Among the meiteis, it is by burning fires.

This follows all the ritual formalities on completion of which the visiting individuals are given a feast together with some presentation including the half portion of the sacrificial meat. Thereafter, they leave the maternal grandparents or uncle of the child's residence with the blessings from the *'Thempu'* of maternal side.

Old Kukis

Among the tribes of the Old Kuki, the birth ceremonies are much alike. In every clan there is a period during which the mother's movements are restricted in some ways.[245]

Among the Aimol, like the Thadou, the period is also five days in case of a boy, and three days for a girl. Among the Anal and Purum, three days in both cases. The Chothe, Kom and Vaiphei, the restriction is for five days for both boy and girl. Among the Kolhen and the Chiru the period is extended to ten days. As for the Tikhup restriction on the mother's movements lasts only till disposal of the remnants of afterbirth by special persons who clean up the house. It is observed that unless this is done no one may take fire flame from the fire place or remove any article from the house. And on the conclusion of such period sacrificial rites and rituals are performed.

Among the Aimol, the 'Thempu' (priest) pours out a libation of Ju and herbs in front of the house and invoke the child's spirit to take up its residence within the inborn infant.[246] The name of the child is also given on this day which is similar to the Thadou system of naming. On the birth of a child, the Anal system of performing the birth rite is slightly different from others, in that the 'Khulpu' (priest) utters incantations, 'ju' and fish are distributed to the whole village to invoke the house hold gods (sakhua) so that the soul of the child is summoned.[247] For a new born Chothe, the *Thempu* sacrifices a fowl and sip ju and incantates over a piece of turmeric which is then thrown out of the house. Again, on the fifth day, a fowl is killed then the name of the child is given. In the process of naming of child, the *Thempu* drops three grains of rice into a cup of water, if the grains sink, it is an indicative of approval of the name given but if they float, another name is to be selected.

Among the Chiru, the *Thempu*, on the tenth day, performs the sacrifice. In this process, first it starts by planting a *rakeng* tree in front of the house, then the

Thempu kills for the mother a cock or a hen according to the sex of the baby. Now the parents of the child eat the cooked meat, only the flesh, the bones are not thrown or eaten by anybody, and they are buried in the house. Then two or three jars of Ju, which have been kept readied for this day, are consumed by married persons. The Thempu sips some ju and sprays it out from his mouth onto the walls inside the house muttering charms. The name giving ceremony '*Keng-puna*' or '*mingpuna*' follows immediately by killing two cocks or hens according to the sex of the child. The *Thempu* smears the blood on the infant's forehead and navel, some of the feathers being tied with the hair of the child.[248]

The ear piercing ceremony is identical with slight variation among the old Kuki tribes as observed by Shakespeare.[249]

Among the Kolhen, the ear piercing ceremony is held on the tenth day and like the Chiru, name giving is also performed on this day. The maternal grandfather is obliged to give the child a pair of brass-earrings, bracelets, leg ornaments and a string of glass beads. In this connection, the name to be given is different from that of Aimol and Chiru. The Kolhen practices the custom of taking the name of maternal grandfather in the case of a boy child. This custom is also prevalent among the Koms, giving a feast for the purpose on the expiration of the five days' 'Sherh' [250]. The paternal aunt performs the ear piercing ceremony. The Lamgang ceremonies are the same as those of Anal but the father is prohibited from eating the flesh of fowls during the '*Sherh*' period and no other animal is sacrificed during such period.[251]

While comparing with other Kuki tribal groups, we are convinced to say that the Purum customs are simple.

The Thempu comes and mutters charms on the day of birth and returns on the third day for confirmation of the name of the child with a libation of Ju. No sacrifices are allowed. On the second day, the midwife gives the name of the child without performing ceremony and on the seventh day the piercing of ears is observed, this too, without ceremony.

The Tikhup, usually celebrates the child naming ceremony in a feast on which the elders of the community are invited. A cock is killed for the child's ritual part and ju also is served. In a poor family, where the parents cannot afford for such feast, it could be postponed till the child attains the age of two years old.

These small ceremonies which are performed among the several groups point towards a common origin and common belief system. While some ceremonies keep the individuals involved forget the pain and sufferings that arising out of the moments of delivery some others performed on account of make-belief systems for invoking longevity for the mother and child. These observations on ceremonies can be observed as common phenomenon in context of world civilizations in general and cutting across all cultural lines in India in particular.

Death Rites

Like birth of child every society has its own funeral rites as well.[252] When a member of a society dies, a group of people usually including close kinsfolk of the dead, assemble round the corpse, mourn for it, and arrange for its disposal.[253] The assembly is not merely a matter of choice, but it is dictated by obligation of a strong sanction. Likewise, the mourning is also usually not left to the discretion of the mourner's own emotions.[254] He is expected to mourn in prescribed forms, the intensity of his grief is almost codified according to the kinship status and not infrequently he receives some material acknowledgement of these services. It may be thought that the funeral rites would be concerned primarily with the fate of the soul of the dead man to facilitate his continuity and well-being in the next world. This is often the case, but frequently this aspect receives only small attention. There may be a little talk about the afterworld and of the soul, which has departed and few rites to ensure its safe passage and preservation. Most of the time may be occupied with feasting and exchange of goods and future arrangement for the members of his family. There is much truth in the view that the essential function of the ritual is to deal with the survivors rather than with the dead. As Radcliff-Brown has shown for the 'Andaman Islander' the death of an individual leaves a gap in the social group and disturbs the emotions of those who still live. The funeral ritual provides a channel for the expression of these emotions, and enforces consideration of the role that the individual has played in the social life.

Firth[255] contended that closely connected with the religion of any society is the mode in which the bodies of the dead are disposed of. Burial in the earth is the simplest and most natural mode of disposing of a dead body, and this mode is prevalent among the Mizos. There are slight variations in the method of burial and the choice of a grave but the general system prevails throughout Mizo societies. Even the Meiteis not so long ago had practised burial of their dead. It is after the second coming of the Hindu cultural influence that cremation was accepted as the form of disposal of the dead. This becomes more popular mode as it was considered to be more hygienic than burial.

Lushai

Davis[256] in his study on the North Lushai Hills published

in 1915 observed that among the 'Sailo' and other elite clans, the body of a dead man was never buried, that after death the body was placed in a coffin, hewn out of a large log and that the coffin was placed on the floor of the deceased's house, near the fire place and was connected through a hole in the bottom with the ground below the house by a bamboo tube through which fluid of the body got deposited. The body was then placed in the coffin, which was hermetically sealed with clay and left in front of the fire for a period of four or five months. By the end of this period, the body was fully decomposed and decayed. When only the bones remained, they were then collected and placed in an ordinary wicket-basket and subsequently kept in the house.[257]

As for ordinary man, the custom was to place the corpse on the floor in a sitting posture. He was dressed up in all his best clothes. So dressed, the corpse held a levee as it were, of all its friends and relatives came together to mourn the death for one day at least. Thereafter, the dead body was placed in a coffin and buried near the house.

So we can see two different trends. However, one thing that was common was the ritual of collecting bones and burying them for posterity.

Lakher

Among the Lakhers, immediately after the death of a person a gun is fired[258] so that the spirit of the dead man reach the '*Athiki*' (dead person's place) and also to signal the villagers that the sick person is no more alive. The body is washed with warm water, the hair is greased and properly tied and also properly dressed with a loin cloth, a cloth and a puggree[259] in case of a man and with all her best clothes for a woman.[260] Two bamboos are placed diagonally against the wall at the back of the house, and a mat is placed across these bamboo and the body is laid on the mat in a reclining position with its feet on the floor. Just above the dead man's head, against the wall a shelf is erected for placing rice and cooked eggs for the soul of the dead man. And it is disgraceful if flies are found sitting on the corpse, thus special attention is taken. '*Rikia*' or '*wake*' is held by all friends of the deceased who bring '*sahma*' (rice beer) known as '*Bupa*'. To accompany the spirit to '*Athiki*', mithun, pig or whatever is available is sacrificed. Throughout this wake (*Rikia*) dancing with the beats of drums and gongs everyday, rice, meat and *Sahma* (rice beer) are placed in the deceased's mouth. The Pupa stands on the verandah facing towards the dead body telling to go to *Athikhi* happily and not to worry about his relatives.[261] After this the Pupa cuts the beam and doorway of the house with a dao. After completing these, he dances round inside the house three times, and is followed by another man dancing at a time with two more men. At the end of each round one has to stamp his feet to show that the dance is over. The dancing in this process is called '*Rakhatla*' and the object of the same is to please the soul. '*Rikia*' is observed for two or three days.

Lakhers burry their dead bodies in the evening near the house. The Pupa leads the burial party followed by young men carrying the corpse and the relatives, he lays down the corpse, pushes the feet first into cove at one end of the grave. And before pushing down to the grave, the wife or husband of the deceased taps the body gently with his or her hand biding farewell by telling not to worry about him or her and also to go happily to *Athikhi*[262]. Then the priest closes the grave with a stone and also covers it with a flat stone on the grave to place meal every morning until memorial stone is erected. In this connection, the

Pupa after performing all his duties, before returning home, accepts 'ru' (dead man's price), which is paid by the relatives of the deceased. Prior to this, Pupa is obliged to kill a pig. A death due consists of a main price called '*rupi*' and the following subsidiary prices shown below[263]:

(i) *Phavaw* (a pumtek bead);

(ii) *Raibong* (a sahma pot);

(iii) *Bongta* (a small sahma pot);

(iv) *Sietla* (The payment to be made because a mithun was killed for riha. This was prevalent in the olden days, but it is hardly killed , however, rice is still claimed);

(v) *Pangbu* (a cloth);

(vi) *Atu* (a hoe) and

(vii) *Thuasang* (dao)

The above discussions of the death ritual is only for the chief, rich man and important persons. However, the normal death of commoner and that which occurred due to unnatural circumstances are totally different as far as the formalities are performed.

Unnatural deaths[264] are regarded as unlucky, and anyone who dies unnatural death as a result of being killed by a wild animal, drowned, falling from tree, in a war or in a shooting accident is known as '*Sawvaw*'. The dead is normally kept outside the village where it is closely watched by lighting fires by the relatives and friends. The next day, the corpse is brought to the village, and is kept at the verandah of the deceased's house[265]. After performing the *rikia* (wakes) it is buried before dawn outside the village in the west so the evil spirit may carry away. The grave is also different from the ordinary ones. No memorial post or stones are erected for a '*sawvaw*' or is 'any food for his spirit placed in the grave'. However, if *reha* is observed then the head of the animal is deposited along with the corpse. The Lakhers never use coffin like Lushai and other Mizo tribes.

As per Lakher custom, death ritual regarding the place where the person dies if it is a friend's house then, the sacrifice of a pig and fowl[266] is a must by the deceased's relatives for the purification of the profanity that takes place. In addition, giving of 10 rupees as a fine to the Pupa is prevalent. These people who take part in the funeral service are as per the list of books approved by the Committee at 15% discount to cross over the kindled fire already arranged at the entrances of their respective house lest they carry the *hri* of the spirit.

The death rites and rituals of the Lakhers, in one way, are very similar with the Meiteis. It is the practice of quenching the old fire used till the funeral ceremony is completed and the kindling of new one is commonly prevalent. And all persons who have touched the corpse have to cleanse themselves by washing their bodies with water and rice[267]. Rice is a symbolic item for it is taken as the purest form of all things, which removes the evil smell of the corpse and other defilements.

It is pertinent to mention that while performing blessing-rituals and opening of grave women play a dominant role–

First, the wife of pupa performs the blessing-giving programme in the evening of the burial day. She brings a fowl and some '*sahmahei*' (*anthawm* in Thadou), sacrifices the fowl to console the souls of the surviving members of the deceased's family[268] and with the blood of the fowl she anoints each of their big toe and offers them a little *sahmahei*.

This ceremony is called *Thlathleu*. It is an important rite performed for bringing peace to the souls of the deceased's family and also to protect them from evils. It is believed that a dead person must not visit in the dream of survivors while they are asleep.

Secondly, the aunt, who is the sister of the deceased opens the grave and she is therefore, to inherit whatever items are inside the same. This is called 'Thupahma' which is the price of touching the evil smelling remains. It was the common custom of a Lakher or a Thadou or even any Mizo before the advent of Christianity. So a common customary law can be seen existing among all Mizo tribes. Valuable articles such as beads, gongs etc., which have been owned by the family are deposited along with the corpse. It is very curious to understand that 'articles of value' buried in vaults should ultimately descend in the female line in the law of inheritance.[269]

Zomi

The Zomis also practiced the formalities like the other Mizo tribes. They had, however, slight variations. Of course, the formalities are dependent on the status of the individual as well as nature of the death. Like the Thadous and their cognate tribes, the process that has to be followed is practically the same with stringent ritual ceremony and practices.

Gougin[270] contends that whenever a person dies, all the villagers throng to the house of the ill-fated family, and they inform all the family relatives who are far and near. The death rituals are arranged for higher status men such as the chief and his family members, and wealthy and rich men and men of fame. The corpse is placed on the floor, dressed up properly with hair well-combed. On a bamboo frame, the corpse is made to recline in a sitting position. All the relatives, women in particular sit beside the corpse. Like the Lakhers, they also carefully watch that flies do not jump upon or sitting on it. Sometimes the dead body is kept for months together in case of man of the status and fame. However, the dead body is kept only for one day for ordinary man. A feast is hosted by killing a mithun, or pig or cow or goat whatever is available. In the meantime, the village women bring 'ju' which is sipped by all who throng to the ceremony.

Before the dead body is buried, dance is performed by elders, guns are fired and people chant while elders encircle the corpse. And they also sing the traditional song of the family.[271] Then the dead body is clothed with all his dresses and decorations. When all the formalities for burial is completed, the corpse is deposited in a wooden coffin prepared for this purpose. In this context, we found that in early days the idea of coffin was totally absent according to most of the works of eminent authorities. We can agree with Gougin's assumption that a coffin is of recent innovation, an outcome of adherence to Christianity.[272] The Meiteis too keep the dead body in an open coffin just before burial.

The Zomi in general believe in life after death.[273] It is also contended by Sing Khaw Khai[274] that dead is treated like the living one. At his funeral, the dead is offered everything that he might need in his next life. Thus the dead body is adorned with ornaments, all personal belongings of value like gun, etc. On the top of the grave, '*zuthawl*' and skulls of animals killed by the deceased during his life time are hoisted on the trunk of a tree with selected branches thereof erected over the graveyard. In addition, one bamboo is inserted into earth of the graveyard to mark the same so that they are not trampled upon.

There are also different types of death rituals performed depending the nature of death. The first type is the '*Lanjiuh*'. In this case, an infant who dies after living for three or four or a week, is buried under the house. Its rituals are very simple. Then, among the Zomis, the payment of two to twenty rupees to the '*pu*' of the deceased is prevalent. This system is called '*Lukawng*'. The *Lukawng* of the '*Boi*' (slave) is expected by the chief. The death rituals of the unnatural death are known as *Sarthi* or *Saa-si*. In case of such death, the burial takes place outside the village after completing the formalities.

Our survey and research shows that the Lushai, Lakher, Zomi, Thadou, etc. believe in the concept of transmigration of soul after death. It can be observed from the death rituals as practiced and as described above.

Thadou

Dalton found the Thadous and their cognate tribes bury their dead but even amongst the poor the bodies are first allowed to lie in estate for several days.[275] And the corpse of great men are placed before slow fire till the flesh is effectively smoke dried and then laid out dressed and equipped for a month or two. Before the process is started, the corpse is washed and is wrapped in a cloth. [276] If the death occurs in the morning or during the night, the corpse is buried in the (next day's) evening. The burial takes place outside the house.

According to Gangte, deaths are divided into three broad divisions,[277] namely:

(i) '*Thi-pha*' (Natural death);

(ii) '*Senhut*' (child-hood death upto the age of three); and

(iii) *'Thi-sie'* (unnatural death).

(i) 'Thi-pha' (Natural Death): As soon as the death takes place, it is informed to all the relatives of the deceased by sending messengers to their respective places. It is believed that the messengers, on their return and after they have reached the deceased's house, *'Kitom'*[278] (brandishing whatever in the hands as a weapon, either scythe, gun, axe, etc.) is performed and who does not do *kitom* he will be sick or any misfortune may happen upon him. In the meantime, the dead body is kept for burial and the people await the works of digging of grave, funeral ceremony, etc. to be completed. As for the location for the grave, the village *'Thempu'* (priest) selects the same accompanied by *Tubul* (highest *Tucha*) female relatives. The digging work is first started by the *Tubul*, by digging at least one or two strokes with a spade symbolizing the commencement of the work,[279] then the others follow. Right from this work gets started, the *Tubul* is not allowed to go to the spot nor is he allowed to enter the house till the corpse is buried. This is called *Lhan chan*. A separate *jubel* is arranged for him to be sipped exclusively by him. However he may invite others to join him. When all necessary formalities including the *Phui Sam*,[280] are done with and a dedication rite by torching the well-framed corners of the grave is completed, the *Tuchabul* announces that 'the grave is ready'. The *Thempu* leads the funeral party, followed by others crying and *kitoming* proceeding towards the graveyard[281]. The *Thempu* also performs *kitom* at intervals on way to the burial ground in the midst of others. Gunshot or blank fire is done in case the man is of fame or status. Then the corpse is laid down in the grave. It is a new dimension in the funeral rites.

Immediately after burial service, a large pot or brass with beads and silver dipped in water is arranged for the *Lhan Chan* party,[282] the *Tubul* and all the concerned persons who took part in the burial proceedings take bath, wash their hands and other parts of the body, signifying purification of defilements.

A feast called '*Kosana*' is normally hosted by killing a mithun, or pig or a cow whatever is available and an animal that can be easily afforded as soon as possible by the deceased's relatives Actually, '*Kosana*' is to be performed on the day of the burial itself. However, some people arrange on other day as is convenient to them. The '*Sangong*' (neck) of the sacrificial animal in this regard is given to the '*apu*' (maternal uncle).

(ii) 'Sen hut Thi' (Infant death): [283] The Thadous bury an infant's corpse as soon as possible under the floor within the café of the roof at the outer wall of the house parallel to the hearth of the family without any publicity and ceremonial rites.

(iii) 'Thi Sie' (unnatural death):[284] Any type of unnatural death called '*Thi Sie*', such as by accidental fall from tree, drowning, killed or murdered etc. irrespective of their social status including the chief does receive the least possible death rite. Such death is also considered as defiled, thereby prohibiting the dead to be brought to the village not beyond the village gate called, '*Khomol*', which is the entrance gate located before reaching the actual village site.

In contrast to this, the death of a person with fame, including the chief, received utmost possible elaborate death rites for a normal death. The brief death rites are such that the body is buried with food and drink, and with the skulls of animals, slaughtered for the funeral feast. It is particularly worth mentioning that at one time it was considered essential that a fresh skull of human victim sacrificed for the occasion, should adorn the grave of a chief.[285] It is amazingly true that a man-hunt is deliberately organized so as to complete the rituals for the purpose. This has persisted throughout history in different communities with some regional variations. At the time of erecting a dam or a house a human sacrifice was performed clandestinely. It was considered to be auspicious, as doubt, but loss of life could never be recompensated. So it was a negative practice not to be encouraged.

In consideration of the death rites of Thadous it is observed that the general principles of the rites are based upon the belief that the soul of a man continues to exist and it therefore transmigrates in some form or the other. In this connection it may be of interest to refer to the findings of Soppitt[286] wherein he stated that on the death of a man his spirit is believed to remain for a period of one full moon in the house he occupied when living, at the lapse of that time the soul departs to a village termed "the village of the dead", where it stays until it returns to earth (at the lapse of an uncertain number of years) in the body of a new born child. This belief system is an intrinsic part of Indian philosophy.

Old Kuki

Similar to the Thadous, Lushais, Lakher and Zomis, the old Kukis also buried their dead bodies at the village cemetery located outside the village except in cases of unnatural death for whom separate cemetery is located. This unnatural death including death in child birth are not given any death rites. Yet these different old Kuki tribes have slight differences in the detailed rituals, for example among the Aimols, a chief's corpse before burial, is carried round the village. The corpse is deposited with some cooked rice, *ju*, a dao, some meat, and a bow and arrow. It is also buried along with several cloths for a rich man and only one cloth in the case of a poor man. An animal is sacrificed and *ju* and rice is poured to the spirit of dead man for not creating trouble to the family.[287] However, the death in child birth and unnatural deaths are treated in different manner. In the case of death in child birth, before burial the husband has to host a feast by sacrificing a pig and the village performs '*Sherh*' for that day. In its burial, food and drink and domestic utensils are allowed to be placed along with the dead. The grave is dug exclusively with her household implements and just before the deposition of the corpse placement of the first stone or earth is done by the aged men and the work of filling the grave is done by young men. Then the *Thempu* incantates the charm following the singing and dancing by young men and women. The burial place of an ordinary death is carried out by men without using household articles, however the burial for an unnatural death is done outside the village i.e. in the jungle which is dug by people of 'grayed hair' and '*sherh*' is not observed in the village.

The Chothe practices burying the corpse at their cemetery, some distance from the village.[288] Over each grave a mound is raised[289] and fenced with a bamboo trellis work. A small post carved faintly to resemble the human form is placed over the gave of a man, while a hoe, axe, denotes the grave of a woman and on each grave rests a flat basket containing some flowers and a small jar of water. Behind each grave is a rough representation of a house raised some four feet from the ground, which is ornamented with flowers and some of the deceased clothes hung from it. Inside are placed a bamboo container full of *ju* and a small cup of which is filled with cleansed water and a handful of raw rice[290]. This is changed every third or fourth day till the *'Thi duh'* ceremony comes around in May when there is a feast and portion of meat and some *ju* are placed in each fresh grave. The Chothe death rite is distinctively prevalent among the other old Kuki tribes.

Among the Chirus, gunshots and beating of gongs are prevalent so as to indicate the death of a man and also the sacrifice of fowl, pig and goat at once. *Sherh* is observed for three days. In the deposition of corpse all personal belongings and even the combs are included. In addition to that the funeral feast is also hosted. During the *Sherh* period rice is placed in a small basket in the house and then thrown on the grave. The *Thempu* purifies the defilements by killing a fowl in the deceased's name on the third day. The other houses of the clan are purified by sprinkling of consecrated water or ju by the *Thempu* and in many cases the funeral party is similarly purified. These customs have been retained till this day. This act of purification is practised in major communities of .the mainland and even among those who have been marginalized over the many generations. This is one finding which brings our inferences closer to the assertion of common origin for all the Mizo group of people.

The prevalence of *sherh* is also found in the death rite of the *Kolhen*. The formalities vary for persons of different statuses. The corpse of Chief, "*Khullakpa's*" is carried three times round the memorial Stone from left to right which is to be erected as soon as possible when he is dead. In case of natural death the corpse is buried in the same manner as Lushai does, i.e., in front of the house. A bow and an arrow is placed in the grave. This is called *'Thickchiat'* and also is equivalent to the *'Lhamjuih'* among the Lushai.

The neck of the animal killed goes to the maternal uncle. A child death within ten days of its birth is buried under the caves of the house.

The Kom and Purum practise the digging of grave of the unnatural deaths by the son-in-law. It is said that the spirit of the dead lies out at the place where he met the death until it is appeased by an offering of tobacco leaves and rice.[291]

The *Tikhup* funeral is exactly the same as that of an ordinary Lushai.[292] The sacrificial animal's neck is received by the maternal uncle.

The Vaiphei dresses up the corpse and straps it on a bamboo frame, as the Lushais do and feast around it for three days, if food and drink suffice for so long. At the end of the feast the *Thempu* pour some *ju* down the throat of the corpse and bid the spirit to go in peace and the body is carried to the grave but if the deceased has attained *Thangchhuah*. however, it is first carried round the village. The household members of the deceased abstain from washing or dressing the hair till some wild animal has been killed. Some of these practices have been tempered today commensurate with the civilized ways of behaviour and refinement in our society.

REFERENCES

1. R.M. MacIver: Society: A Textbook of Sociology, New York, Farrar and Rinehart, 1945; p. 5.
2. Woodward Sutherland and Maxwell: Introductory Sociology: Oxford and IBH, Publishing Co., Bombay: 1961, p. 35.
3. Arnold Green: Sociology: McGrow-Hill Book Co. Inc., New York: 1956, p. 94.
4. Morris Ginsberg: Psychology of Society: Methuen, London (7th Edition) 1949, p. 122.

5. Gillen and Gillen: Cultural Sociclogy: The MacMillan Co. New York: 1950, p. 35.
6. Horton and Hunt: Sociology: McGrow – Hill, New York: 1968; p. 75.
7. A.R. Radcliff – *Brown and Daryl! Forde "African System of Kinship and Marriage"* 1950, p. 5.
8. A.R. Radcliff – *Brown and Daryll Forde: Op. cit.,* p. 46.
9. N.E. Parry: *"A Monograph on Lushai Customs and Ceremonies 1928;* p. 21. And it is through 'Pularim' or gossiping of youths, B.B. Goswami, "The Mizo Umest, 1979 p. 29, Nularim Offshoots.
10. N.E. Parry: *"The Lakhers"* 1932; p. 291.
11. Hmar Youth Association (H.Y.A.): *"Hmar Hnam Dan",* 1990; p.19.
12. Hrangthiawa and Lal Chungnunga: "Mizo Chanchin" 1978 ; p. 375 and J.D. Baveja: "The Land Where The Bamboo Floowers": 1970, p. 28.
13. Lal Biak Thanga: "The Mizos", 1978; p. 19.
14. Bimal J. Deb and Dilip Kumar Lahire: Lushai Customs and Ceremonies 1983; p. 35 and N.E. Parry: "A Monograph on Lushai Customs and Ceremonies", 1928; p. 35.
15. *N.E. Parry: "A Monograph on Lushai Customs and Ceremonies",* 1928; p. 35.
16. *Ibid.*
17. *Bimal J. Deb and Dilip Kumar Lahire: Lushai Customs and Ceremonies;* 1983; p. 35.
18. N.E. Parry: "A Monograph on Lushai Customs and Ceremonies" ;1928; p.36
19. J.D. Baveja: The Land where The Bamboo Flowers ;1970; p. 29
20. *Ibid.*
21. T. S. Gangte: *Op. cit.,* p. 79.
22. J.K. Dey and P.G. Dey; A Brief Outline of Physical and Social Anthropology, 1968; p.156.
23. T.S. Gangte: *Op. cit.*
24. *Ibid.*
25. A.R. Radcliff–Brown, 'Introduction' to the book entitled African System of Kinship and Marriage (1950), p. 75.

26. N.E. Parry: *Op. cit.,* p. 35.
27. Bimal J. Deb and Dilip Kumar Lahiri: *Op. cit.,* 34.
28. A dark blue cloth for burying people in.
29. It is known as "Nong a Pahaw" in Lakher customs.
30. A.R. Radcliff–Brown, *Op. cit.,* p. 75.
31. E.B. Tylor: On a method of investigating the Development of Institution: "Applied to Laws of Marriage and Descent" G.A.L. Vol. XXVIII.
31. J.G. Fraser: "Folklore in Old Testament" ;1919; Vol. II.
33. E. Westermarck: The History of Human Marriage: 1901; Vol. II.
34. W.H.R. Rivers, History of Melanesian Society: 1914; Vol. II.
35. A.E. Crawly: "Exogamy and the Mating of Cousins", Essays presented to E.B. Tylŏr, London;1907.
36. R.H. Lowie: "An Introduction to Cultural Anthropology" 1934; Primitive Society 1921.
37. B.Z. Saligman: Cross-cousin Marriage, 1925.
38. J.R. Swamton: "Contribution to the Ethnology of the Haida".
39. C. Hill Tout: The Natives of British America: 1907.
40. G.S. Ghurye: "Dual Organisation in India", J.R.A. I, Vol. LIII.
41. W.H.R. Rivers, History of Melanesian Society, 1914; Vol. II.
42. In Thadou-Kuki language.
43. 'Neihnu' in Gangte language.
44. J.K. Dey and P.G. Dey; A Brief Outline of Physical and Social Anthropology: 1968; p. 162.
45. T. Gougin, *History of Zomi,* 1984; p. 33.
46. N.E. Parry, *The Lakhers,* 1932; p. 293.
47. Vumson, Zo History: (Year of publication not given); p. 14.
48. The Institution of Primitive Society, 1963; p. 59. A series of broadcast talks by E.E. Evans Pritland, Reymond Firth, E.R. Leach, J.G. Peristiany, John Layard, Max Gluckman, Meyer Fortes and Godfrey Reinhardt.
49. L.B. Thanga, The Mizos, 1978; p. 22.
50. A.W. Davis, Gazetteer of The North Lushai Hills ;1915; p.13.
51. In Paite language, its spelling is Dan Thianga Kiteng as per V.D.Tombing, Molkoi, Churachandpur – interviewed on 18-5-2005.

52. Jamkithong Sitlhou, Thadou Puchon Pachon: 1967; p. 124.
53. T.S. Gangte: The Kukis of Manipur 1993; p. 82
54. It is the family council and in the Paite's custom is known as 'Inndongta'.
55. Rice beer.
56. The Gangte Custom Committee, Gangte Danpi ;1993; pp. 19-20.
57. William Shaw: The Thadou Kuki, 1928; p. 57.
58. *Ibid.*
59. N.E. Parry: *Op. cit.,* p. 24.
60. *Ibid.*
61. T.S. Gangte, *op. cit.,* p. 82.
62. *Ibid.*
63. T.S. Gangte: The Kukis of Manipur: 1993; p. 82.
64. *Ibid.*
65. T.S. Gangte: *Op. cit.,* p. 82.
66. J.H. Hutton in his footnotes at p. 58 in William Shaw's work on the Thadou-Kuki 1928; that appeared in the journal of Asiatic Society of Bengal (N.S.) XXIV, 1928.
67. T.S. Gangte, *op. cit.,* p. 58.
68. J.H. Hutton: Journal of Asiatic Society of Bengal.
69. Changsan is one of the Mizo tribes, dispersed among the Thadous and Hmars in Manipur while their main concentration is in Cachar and North Cachar Hills of Assam The Thadous, specially the Sitlhous regard them very highly treating that the Changsans are at par with them in terms of social hierarchical order among the Mizos.
70. C.A. Soppitt: A Short Account of Kuki – Lushai Tribes: 1893; p. 17, Reprint in 1976.
71. T.S. Gangte, *op. cit.,* pp. 83-84.
72. A special type of bamboo, called 'Saneibi' in Manipuri language.
73. J. Shakespeare: The Lushei Kuki Clans, Part. II: 1912; p. 160.
74. E.T. Dalton: Ethnology of Bengal: 1872; Reprinted in 1978 under the little "Tribal History of Eastern India", p. 47.
75. Holy Bible (King James Version): 1611; Genesis Chapter 29, Verses 10-30.
76. *Ibid.*

77. J.K. Bose, *op. cit.,* pp. 51-61.
78. *Ibid.,* pp. 60-61.
79. J.K. Dey and P.J. Dey: A Brief Outline of Physical and Social Anthropology, 1968; p. 161.
80. J.K Bose, *Op. cit.,* p. 72.
81. *Ibid.*
82. Based on my personal interview with N. Vijayalakshmi Brara on 17.8.06.
83. J.K Bose, *Op. cit.,* p. 71.
84. J.K Bose, *Op. cit.,* p. 71.
85. *Ibid.*
86. *Ibid.*
87. J.F. Mc Lennan: Studies in Ancient History, London.
88. Henry Maine, Early Law and Custom, 1883, London.
89. J.D. Mayne, A Treaty on Hindu Law and Usage: 1883; London.
90. H. Spencer: (i) Principles of Sociology, (ii) A short Rejoinder Fortnightly Review, 1877.
91. C.H. Starke, Primitive Family: 1896.
92. C.B. Tylor, Applied to Laws of Marriage and Descent, G.A., I.S. Vol. XVIII.
93. J.G. Fraser: (i) Totemism and Exogamy, 1910, Vol. II. (ii) Folklore in Old Testament, 1919, Vol. II.
94. E. Westermarck, History of Human Marriage: 1901, Vol. III.
95. K.P. Chattopadhyay: Glimpses of Tribal Life in North-East India: Institute of Social Research and Applied Anthropology, Ballyguage, Circular Road, Calcutta-19, 1980; p.74.
96. H.C. Das Gupta: Levirate in Ramayana, Man in India, Vol. VI, Nos. 2 and 3.
97. H.C. Das Gupta: Levirate in Ramayana, Man in India, Vol. VI, Nos. 2 and 3.
98. H.C. Das Gupta: *Op. cit.,* pp. 75-76.
99. *Ibid.,* p. 77-78.
100. *Ibid.,* p. 78.
101. H.C. Das Gupta: Levirate in Ramayana, Man in India, Vol. VI, Nos. 2 and 3. p. 78.
102. *Ibid.,* p.79.
103. *Ibid.,* p. 80.
104. *Ibid.,* p. 81.

105. *Ibid.*, p. 76
106. H.C. Das Gupta: Levirate in Ramayana, Man in India, Vol. VI, Nos. 2 and 3. p. 77.
107. J. Shakespear, The Lushai Kuki Clan, Part. II: 1912; p. 152.
108. Jayanta Bhusan Bhattacharjee: Cachar under British Rule in North East India: 1977; p. 219; Radiant Publishers, E-155 Kalkaji, New Delhi -110019.
109. J.K. Bose: Glimpses of Tribal Life in North-East India, 1980; p. 74.
110. J.D. Baveja, The Land Where the Bamboo Flowers: 1970; p. 25.
111. Lal Biak Thanga, The Mizos: 1978, p. 19.
112. N.E. Parry, A Monograph on Lushai Customs and Ceremonies: 1928, p. 24.
113. *Ibid.*
114. J.D. Baveja, The Land Where the Bamboo Flowers: 1970; p. 25.
115. J.D. Baveja, The Land Where the Bamboo Flowers: 1970, p. 25.
116. N. Chatterji, Status of Women in the Mizo Society,: 1975, p. 19.
117. J. Shakespear, The Lushai Kuki Clans, Part.I (Reprint in 1975), p. 50.
118. N.E. Parry, A Monograph on Lushai Customs and Ceremonies: 1928; p. 24.
119. Bimal J. Deb and Dilip Kumar Lahiri, Lushai Customs and Ceremonies: 1983, p. 24.
120. N.E. Parry, *op. cit.*, pp. 25 - 27.
121. G. Barkataki, Tribes of Assam,: 1969; p. 105.
122. N.E. Parry, A Monograph on Lushai Customs and Ceremonies:1928, p. 24.
123. 'Angkia' means house enter.
124. 'Puma' has the same significance of that other prices.
125. 'Nongcheu' is found to have exist only in the Lakher society.
126. 'Nangcheu' is equivalent to Niman or Niar, and it is sometimes replaced by 'Tini'.
127. T.S. Gangte, The Kukis of Manipur, 1993; pp. 92-93.
128. T.S. Gangte, The Kukis of Manipur, 1993; pp. 92-93.

129. *Op. cit.*, page 93.

130. *Ibid.*

131. *Ibid.*

132. *Ibid.*, p. 93.

133. C.G. Crawford, Hand Book of Kuki Custom: 1984, Reprint, pp. 2-3.

134. *It is also observed that the Gauhati High Court has undertaken a project on the customary laws of the Thadou-Kukis with special reference to the land holding systems, sponsored by the North Eastern Council, Shillong under the Directorship of Dr. J. Barooah, Law Research Institute Gauhati High Court, assisted by Mayonmi Shimray as Research Officer and Apem K. H. as Assistant Research Officer. It is found that the Research Institute has given a blanket acceptance to see the above marriage payment structure without slightest analysis on comment on the same.*

135. *William Shaw, The Thadou Kuki: 1928*, pp. 58 – 59.

136. J.H. Hutton, "Notes on the Thadou Kukis":1929; p. 59. Journal of the Asiatic Society of Bengal N.S. XXIV.

137. T.S. Gangte, *op. cit.*, p. 95.

138. *The contention of Gangte in regard to marriage payment of the Singson was confirmed from S.L. Singson, aged 70+, interviewed on 3.5.2004; Dr. Seikho Singsit, aged 58+ interviewed on 18-7-2006; Reverend Kaikhosei, aged 60+ interviewed on 7-4-2005 as informants.*

In order to further ascertain or otherwise Mrs. Lunkhoneng, aged 80+ was also interviewed on 30-9-2006 to share her personal experience as daughter of the chief of Lungthulien Village. She belongs to a Singson clan of the Thadou, Tipaimukh, Churachandpur District who married Thangkhopao in 1947 belonging to Kipgen of the Thadou claimed that she vividly remembered her marriage payment was 30 mihtuns.

139. William Shaw, The Thadou Kukis,: 1929, p. 63.

140. J.H. Hutton, Journal of the Asiatic Society of Bengal XXIV:1928.

141. J.H. Hutton, Journal of the Asiatic Society of Bengal XXIV:1928.

142. *Ibid.*

143. Information provided by Letkhojam Haokip, a clause causin of Chief of Chassad on 19-7-2005.
144. A.R. Radcliff – Brown, Introduction to the Book, African Systems of Kinship and Marriage: 1950, p. 51.
145. T. Gougin, History of Zomi: 1984, pp. 36 – 37.
146. Lutcha Vaiphei, Red Cross Road, Churachandpur, interviewed on 4-10-2005.
147. Vumson, Zo History (No year of printing is mentioned), p. 14.
148. J. Shakespeare, *Op. cit.,* p. 152.
149. J. Shakespeare, The Lushai Kuki Clans, Part.II ; 1912; p. 152.
150. Kingsley Davis: Human Society: 1981(Reprint), p. 409.
151. Lewis Henry Morgan: Ancient Society (Second Edition), 1958, p. 548.
152. Robert H. Lowie: Social Organisation: 1950, p. 146.
153. Hari Mohan Sinha and Dheeraj Narula: Legal Dictionary: 1993; p. 101.
154. Robert H. Lowie: Social Organisation,: 1950, p. 146.
155. Robert H. Lowie: *Op. cit.,* p. 147.
156. *Ibid.*
157. Robert H. Lowie: *Op. cit.,* p. 147.
158. Kingsley Dabis: Human Society, (First 2nd Reprint), 1981; p. 409.
159. G.D.H.Cole, "Inheritance" Encyclopedia of the Social Sciences, p. 36.
160. Kingsley Davis: Changing concepts of Marriage in Howard Beskar and Penben Hill (eds) Marriage and the Family: 1942, p. 103.
161. G.D.H. Cole, *op. cit.,* p. 36.
162. G.T. Garralt, An Indian Cmmentary (no date), pp. 27-33.
163. Chester G. Vernier, American Family Laws (Stanford; Standford University Press 1936; Vol. IV, pp. 113-116.
164. J.D. Baveja: The Land Where The Bamboo Flowers: 1970, p. 19.
165. N.E. Parry: *Op. cit.,* p. 82.
166. N.E. Parry: *Op. cit.,* p. 83.
167. N.E. Parry: A Monograph on Lushai Customs and Ceremonies: 1928, p. 84.

168. Lal Biak Thanga, The Mizos: 1978, p. 24.
169. N.E. Parry: *Op. cit.,* p. 88.
170. N.E. Parry: *Op. cit.,* p. 88.
171. *Ibid.*
172. S. Barkataki, Tribes of Assam: 1969, p. 91.
173. Eden Vansittart, Gurkhas,: 1915, p. 51.
174. N.E. Parry: The Lakhers: 1932, p. 286.
175. *Ibid.*
176. C.A. Soppitt: A Short Account of The Kuki –Lushai Tribes,: 1893, p. 16.
177. N.E. Parry: The Lakhers: 1932, p. 287.
178. Khup Za Go: Chin Chronicles,: 1988, pp. 32-33.
179. T. Gougin, History of Zomi,: 1984, pp. 45-47.
180. J. Shakespeare, The Lushai Kuki Clans, Part.II: 1912, p. 154.
181. C.G. Crawford, Hand Book of Kuki Custom, Reprint: 1984; p. 1.
182. *William Shaw: The Thadou Kukis,* 1928; p. 67.
183. *Bonita Aleaz: Emergent Women: Mizo Women's perspective; 2005, pp.46-47: Mittal Publishing House, A-110, Mohan Garden, New Delhi – 58. For details please see conclusion portion at pages 13-16*
184. Henri Labouret: La Parente & Plaisanteries on Afrique Occidentale, Africa, Vol. II, p. 244.
185. Mademircelle Deniese Paulme: Parenta & Plaisanteries et Alliance par le sang en Afrique Occidentale, Africa, Vol. XII, P. 433.
186. F.I. Pedler: Joking Relationship in East Africa, African, Vol. XIII, p. 170.
187. A.R. Radcliff-Brown: Joking Relationships, Africa, Vol. XIII – 3, 1940, pp. 195-210.
188. A.R. Radcliff-Brown: Joking Relationships, Africa, Vol. XIII – 3, 1940, pp. 195-210.
189. Mademoiselle Paulme: Parents & Plaisanteries et Alliance par le Sang on Afrique Occidentale, Africa, Vol. XII, p. 438.
190. A.R. Redcliff-Brown, African Systems of Kinship and Marriage: 1950; p. 57
191. A.R. Redcliff-Brown, *Op. cit.,* p. 29.

192. Mathew Chapter V, Verses 32 of the Holy Bible.
193. Mark Chapter X, Verses 11 & 12 of the Holy Bible.
194. Vidya Bhushan and R. Sachdeva, 'An Introduction to Sociology:1993; pp. 343-345.
195. Lunburg, Sociology, p. 133.
196. Martov and Hunt, Sociology, p. 216.
197. H. T. Mazumdar, Grammar of Sociology,: 1966, p. 582.
198. *Anderson and Parker, Society*, p. 144.
199. Vidya Bhushan and R. Sachdeva, *Op. cit.,* pp. 343-345.
200. Kingsley Davis, Human Society, (1981 – First , 2nd Rep.) p. 424.
201. The Word 'Hindu' under the Act includes a Buddhist, Jain or Sikh by religion and any person who is not a Muslim, Christian Parsi or Jew.
202. Scope of the Act: The Act, as its provisions reflect, does not simply codify the Hindu Law of Marriage or divorce but has affected important changes therein. It permits not only intercaste marriage but allows marriage between a Hindu, a Jain, a Sikh and a Buddhist. It has also reduced the degree of prohibited relationship in such a way as to allow marriage between relations who could not marry under the traditional Hindu law.
203. Robert H. Lowie, Social Organisation: 1950, p. 111.
204. J.K. Dey and P.J. Dey, A brief outline of Physical and Social Anthropology: 1968; pp. 167-168.
205. D.N. Mazumdar, Himalayan Polyandry,: 1962; p. 19.
206. S. Barkataki, Tribes of Assam, 1969, p. 88.
207. J. Shakespeare, The Lushai Kuki Clans, Part. I, 1912, p. 51.
208. N.E. Parry, *op. cit.,* p. 42.
209. J. Shakespeare, The Lushai Kuki Clans, Part. I, 1912, p. 51.
210. Literally means "the eating of cucumber" once a cucumber has been eaten, it has gone forever.
211. N. E. Parry, *op. cit.,* p. 44.
212. *Ibid.*
213. Lal Biak Thanga, The Mizos, 1978, p. 22.
214. N.E. Parry, *op. cit.,* 1928, p. 47.
215. N.E. Parry, *op. cit.,* 1928, p. 47.
216. S. Barkataki, *op. cit.,* p. 89.

217. J.D. Baveja, *op. cit.,* 1970, p. 29.
218. N. E. Parry, *op. cit.,* p. 343.
219. N.E. Parry: *Op. cit.,* p. 346.
220. N. E. Parry, *op. cit.,* p. 347.
221. C.A. Soppitt, A Short Account of Kuki Lushai Tribes,: 1893, p. 15.
222. C.G. Crawford, Hand Book of Kuki Custom (Reprint in): 1984, p. 8.
223. C.G. Crawford: *Op. cit.*
224. P.C. Misao, History and Customs of The Thadou Kuki: 1970, p. 38.
225. *Ibid.*
226. T. Gougin: *Op. cit.,* p. 43.
227. T. Gougin, *op. cit.,* p. 43.
228. J. Shakespear, The Lushai Kuki Clans: 1912, p. 154.
229. *Ibid.*
230. T. Gougin, *op. cit.*
231. *T. Gougin, History of Zomi,:* 1984, p. 43.
232. N.E. Parry, The Lakhers: 1932, p. 384.
233. *Ibid.*
234. *Ibid.,* p. 390.
235. Ginseppe Tucci, Tibet, Land of Snows: 1967, p. 154.
236. N.E. Parry, *Op. cit.,* p. 391.
237. N.E. Parry, The Lakhers: 1932, p. 386.
238. *Ibid.*
239. T.S. Gangte, The Kukis of Manipur: 1993, p. 89.
240. William Shaw, The Thadou Kukis: 1929, p. 51.
241. *Ibid.*
242. J.H. Hutton, Journal of the Asiatic Society of Bengal, N.S. XXIV, 1928, p. 51.
243. E.T. Dalton, Ethnology of Bengal – Tribal History of Eastern India: 1872, p. 47.
244. T.S. Gangte, The Kukis of Manipur:1993, p. 105.
245. J. Shakespeare, The Lushai Kuki Clans, 1912, p. 158.
246. *Ibid.,* p. 159.
247. J. Shakespeare, The Lushai Kuki Clans, 1912, p. 159.
248. J. Shakespeare, The Lushai Kuki Clans, 1912, p. 159.

249. *Op. cit.,* p. 160.
250. Sherh, means that the house is placed under profanity for a specific number of days, on the expiry of which it is considered as having been purified.
251. *Ibid.*
252. Raymond Firth, Human Types, 1958, p. 145.
253. *Ibid.*
254. Hindu Dharmashastras. Especially Manu's Dharmashastra and the provisions made therein have been codified in the Hindu Funerary rites.
255. Raymond Firth, Human Types, 1958, p. 145.
256. A. W. Davis, Gazetteer of the North Lushai Hills, 1915, p. 14.
257. The use of gun is quite recent but in olden days gongs were used to convey the message or beating of drums symbolized the gravity of the setretion in the village or the area.
258. The use of pugree is a main that contribution in the belief systems of the sun communities in the North East.
259. A.W. Davis, Gazetteer of the North Lushai Hills, 1915, p. 14.
260. N.E. Parry, *op. cit.,* p. 399.
261. N.E. Parry, *op. cit.*
262. *Ibid.,* p. 400.
263. N.E. Parry, *Op. cit.,* p. 420.
264. *Ibid.,* p. 406.
265. *Ibid.,* p. 407.
266. N.E. Parry, *Op. cit.,* p. 409.
267. *Ibid.,* p. 404.
268. N.E. Parry, *op. cit.,* p. 402.
269. *Ibid.,* p. 411.
270. T. Gougin, *Op. cit.,* p. 27.
271. *Ibid.,* p. 57.
272. T. Gougin, History of Zomis: 1984, p. 27.
273. Vumson, Zo History (No date), p. 17.
274. *Sing Khan Khai, Zo People And Their Culture,:* 1995, p. 131.
275. E.T. Dalton, Ethnology of Bengal – Tribal History of India: 1842; p. 47.
276. William Shaw, The Thadou Kukis: 1928, p. 53.

277. T.S. Gangte, *Op. cit.,* p. 107.
278. *Ibid.,* p. 108.
279. T.S. Gangte; p.109.
280. *Ibid.,* Its meaning is utterances of words of magic.
281. *Ibid.*
282. *Ibid.,* p. 111.
283. T.S. Gangte; p. 1129.
284. *Ibid.*
285. E.T. Dalton, Ethnology of Bengal Tribal History of India: 1842, p. 47.
286. C.A. Soppitt, A short Account of the Kuki Lushai Tribes: 1893, p. 12.
287. J. Shakespeare, The Lushai Kuki Clans Part-II: 1912; p. 165.
288. J. Shakespeare, *op. cit.,* p. 163.
289. It is a Buddhist practice. It shows the Buddhist influence on the Chothe group of people.
290. This practice is alien to the raising of Buddhist stupas for ancestor worship. Buddhist influence is explicitly seen being practised by the old Kukis.
291. J. Shakespeare, The Lushai Kuki Clans Part-II: 1912, p. 164.
292. *Ibid.,* p. 164.

5

Chieftainship Among the Meiteis and Mizos Societies

Traditional political life of the Meiteis and the Mizos is deeply rooted to their customary laws in their respective societies. The socio political institutions are closely entrenched with other institutions. Their system of political institution is based on Kinship relations and is termed as a mere "Social Organisation" distinguished from "Political Organisation" of civilized community[1]. Similar views were expressed by Durkheim[2] and Malinowski,[3] whose authority on the primitive people is undisputed. They contended that primitive State was not tyrannical, as is supposed to be, to its subjects because they were always a body of people related by bonds of kinship and relationship, by clanship and age grades and that they spoke of themselves as a group where practically everybody was related, in reality or fictitiously, to everybody else. Customary Laws governed and regulated these relationships and ties of fraternity which emerged thereof.

Schapera[4] contended that political system among primitive societies was based on kinship relation and that each tribe claimed exclusive rights to the land it occupied.* All people living therein were subjects to the chief, as head of the local Government, and only by moving away or migration could they escape his control. Outsiders might not settle in his territory without chiefs' permission, who rehabilitated them wherever he wished.** Thereafter, they, the settled outsiders, became his subjects. In case they disobeyed him they were expelled. He not only regulated the distribution and use of the land but also decided the fate of his subjects on the basis of customary laws.

MacIver[5] said with conviction that in primary sense a tribe was "community organized on the basis of kinship who usually claimed to have descended from a common ancestor" and that "tribal Government was characteristic of simple society" and "was equivalent to Primitive Government".

As a matter of fact, the study of Mizo and Meitei societies together is academically to our mind compatible due to the fact that though both are at different stages of societal birth, growth, development and civilization they have a common origin. Though the two societies are far apart from each other in all spheres of life, socially, politically and economically, the cultural legacies of the Meitei society can be studied deep into the historical period through their written documentary evidences, other materials available in oral traditions. Such evidences are recorded/

* The tribal areas are often governed for all practical purposes by the customary laws. Normally a Customary Law or the other had jurisdiction over the village administration, village officials and ever the village boundary. The authorities therefore exercised their customary laws over the villagers or their kinship based society whenever disputes arose or in due course of performing right rites and rituals.

** For details see the aspects of Yek and Salai formation in Meitei society especially with reference to the Muslim Pangals and the Brahmanas.

seen down into the antiquated period of pre-historical civilizational periods with the help of archeological excavations that have been carried out and some antique evidences, which can be claimed as far back as about more than two thousand years of Meitei civilization stretching into the ages of 'before Christ' periods. The Meitei society has long since gone through the processes of 'de-tribalisation' as can be observed in the evolution of chiefdoms that gradually resulted in the formation of the 'Meitei State' with the merger of the 'Seven-Salais' into the Ningthouja clan which assumed the dominant Royal authority at Kangla.

It needs to be highlighted here that Bhattacharjee[6] observed that in the early egalitarian societies inequality stratification started with the emergence of private property and interest groups whose political organizations were founded on territory and property, that State as a higher form of political organisation came into existence when economic relations were further sophisticated by privatization of property and extraction of surplus by the dominant groups in the society and that growth of such a situation strengthened authority of the rulers to assume the theory, 'divine right', which was more susceptible to contributing the 'Brahmanical myths' that propagated 'divine origin of the King'[7].

He was also convinced to attribute that social and polity formation processes in the North East India were more spontaneously influenced by its geo-political situation that readily absorbed pan-Indian traditions where a fine blending of Indo-Aryan and the Indo-Mongoloid traditions co-existed among tribal communities.[8] Bhattacharjee was also emphatic to say that emergence of States from indigenous and immigrant tribal social bases in the medieval history of the North-East region was significantly common as could be evidenced in the cases of Koch, Kachari, Meitei, Jaintia and Tripuri who were settlers since early times in the region.[9]

On the other hand, in the case of Mizo society, in particular and all the tribal societies in Manipur in general, it is not so. Sources are limited, shallow and often controversial enough to establish their exact state of antiquity though they may be so. The limitation is more apparent in empirical study when there are no material evidence to authenticate probable findings. Whatever scanty written materials available are from the British bureaucrats and anthropologists. We find that they do not go deep into the traces beyond their time of putting the records in writing. And these are the only documents available at our disposal to rely upon which unfortunately do not go beyond the 18th century, when the term 'Kuki' from which the word 'Mizo' was derived, first appeared according to Reid[10], when Mir Kasim, the chief of Chittagong, ceded the district to the British under Robert Clive in 1760 A.D. applying at the same time for a detachment of Sepoys to protect its inhabitants against incursions of the 'Kukis' as they were then called. This was soon followed with the first open attack against the British and their subjects dated as far back as 1777 A.D. since the days of Warren Hastings by the 'Kukis' when the Chins, the Thadous, the Lushais, etc. were included by the British under the said term mainly considering their distinctive similar characteristics.

Bhattacharjee said that they enjoyed considerable local autonomy, the Chiefs retaining their full traditional authority over their respective tribes and rules according to their own customary laws[11] and that the Rajas did not interfere in the internal affairs of the Chiefs, living under cordial relationships[12].

Dynamics of Chieftainship and Chiefdom

The synthesis that emerges from discussions of the various aspects of chieftainship and evolution of their chiefdoms, and the views of eminent scholars on the subjects, clearly recognizes the extreme complexity and interdependence of the sources of power in society and the forces of instability and division that constantly threaten to tear it apart. Of particular interest are long-term local and regional patterns of expansion and collapse. It goes without saying that to understand the development of chiefdoms, the ways in which finance, control and ideology empower an emerging ruling class has to be thoroughly examined. While the linear causality that was once felt comfortable with, has certainly outgrown, the new synthesis offers a rich and varied interpretation of socio-political process. The Meitei society offers a fertile field for necessary interpretation and analysis.

Loosely defined a chieftainship is "a centralized polity that organizes a regional population in the thousands" said Carneiro, and Earle.[13] The main characteristic is attributed to some degree of heritable social ranking and economic ratification. Origin of this polity, their development and their eventual collapse or transformation into states are its main features.

Kirch and Kristiansen[14] have opined that research is imperative to focus on sequences of long-term socio-political, economic changes documented archeologically and historically and that chieftainship vary in complexity and scale of development, simple and complex.

Steponaitis [15] convinces us that mode of financing is an important aspect for understanding the dynamics of Chieftainships. It is sine-qua-non.

Terence and Earle[16] are of strong view that in order to effectively finance dynamics of chieftainship structure of the institution, either group oriented or individualizing has to be ascertained, Colin[17] is of strong opinion that history of a particular type of chieftainship has to be thoroughly looked into so as to effect proper implementation of the development plan envisaged and inherent in it.

On ensuring these aspects, dynamism of chieftainships as political institutions can be understood and achieved. For this purpose outlining the various strategies with which rulers tried to extend and maintain political and social control through economic measures or even religious rites and rituals and the conditions that affected the success of these strategies need to be determined in the light of the customary laws which always remained an inseparable part of any society, tribal or otherwise, as an effective tool for social control. It appears that unstable and cyclical characters of most chieftainships were apparently inherent.[18]

A question arises relating to power relationships of followers' evaluation of the cost of compliance with the demands of leader relative to the cost of refusal as contended by Jonathan.[19] Jonathan strongly felt that construction of a complex polity required a leader to find a following to himself. Simply, he must control people's labour, and lead in difficult situations. Meitei history is replete with factional leaders – an unwanted factor, towards regional integration.

Johnson[20] has questioned as to what keeps such leaders from moving away from the centres of power and attraction. Historically we know larger groups do not form centres of power. Technological and social adjustments are necessary to concentrate and co-ordinate increasing numbers of people. The quality of leadership lies therein. The traditional answer to this question has been to point to the management functioning that leaders perform. Much of new-evolutionary thought since the 1950s has emphasized the function of leaders in maintaining their groups. To understand the evolution of chieftainship is to identify the new conditions created by technology or population growth that require central management for their effective and efficient operation. Often it is true but there are other parameters which must also be taken into consideration e.g. control and use of land for food production and settlement for new incumbents. The inheritance of land in the Thadou group is through patrilineal laws of primogeniture. All the land in a Thadou village often belongs to the Chief who exercises absolute power over it. He distributes the cultivable land to all the villagers at the beginning of every year after having consulted the village elders, Semang Puheng, for each elder represents different kin group in the village. Customarily speaking he is not compelled to abide by the decision of the Council of elders but the power of the council is real and irrefutable for the simple reason that the individual household has no right in land. He cannot alienate the plot of land nor transfer it when one has been allotted to him. The most important aspect is that the land is not inherited by the individuals. So the chief often enters into politics and tries to marginalize a section of the community which does not honour him or pay taxes as per the customary laws. The next result is that several families migrate to set up new settlements.

Population growth has received considerable attention since Ester's[21] work in 1965 on condition of agricultural growth which served as a catalyst in the most recent theories about the general synthesis of cultural evolution. Johnson and Earle[22] in their work on 'Evolution of Human Society' have contended that population factor has received little support as a prime mover. Drennan, Feihman and

Steponaitis have attributed the low population densities as revealed from the intensive surveys documented for the chiefdoms.[23] In every case customary laws have prevailed over constraints in demographic propagation in the tribal belts. However, in case of Manipur population has indeed been a prime mover since the seventeenth century. The substantial immigration of Muslims and the Brahmanas compelled the societal managers to reorganize the settlement pattern and the increase in the formation of the sub-sub-clans. It was a force, which developed into organized sectors and got channelized through the clan and the sagei/salai formations at the operative level.

Thus, we see that population increase is certainly associated with evolution of political systems in Manipur[24]. It is indeed a reminder of the universal processes of socio-political changes which are brought about through demographic explosions (migrations or otherwise).

Bargatzsky[25] has maintained that the environmental conditions are not something simply presented to a human population. Rather they are both cultural and natural and are constantly being modified by human intervention.

Manipur has been a fit case for such evaluation. For example, in the valley, the early concentration of social and economic activities including ceremonies, craft specialization, and the like attracted population to the center and made labour control possible. Although concentration of natural productivity was initially derived from soil, rainfall, vegetative cover, and the like, the resource base was quickly altered by human intervention – improved by irrigation, terracing and drainage by over-use and induced erosion. The two processes together had the effect of concentrating productive resources in limited zones that came to be owned by the elites of the seven clans.* In support of it, Thomas Earle has opined that some of this intervention may have been part of a strategy to increase economic control. More important is the fact that we must recognize the unforeseen consequences of the efforts of individual households and communities to improve their lot, and the role of customary laws which were exercised by the Chiefs of several enlightened clans, and the fact when sometimes the customary laws failed to resolve inter-village or inter-personal disputes recourse to negotiations were opted for. As such conflicts in law were settled through negotiations.

We know that ownership of the irrigation systems in Manipur is not known but it was the customary role of the king and his subjects in increasing the production and irrigational facilities, dredging of canals which was at a magnificent scale – an yearly ritual which ultimately had led to the emergence of the field system. This indeed was an attempt to control subsistence production through landownership. It may be recalled here that in pastoral chiefdoms such as those of Manipuri societies ownership of animals offered another basis of control.

Carneiro[26] has contended that warfare has been recognised as a common characteristic of chiefdoms with warriors used to conquer new communities and their tribute base and to intimidate communities reluctant to give up their full share to the overlord. His theory can be seen operative in the Manipur society. Meiteis expanded through conquest Inter-clan rivalry and their supremic rivalries. Interestingly, the potential for control based on military force seems quite limited and unstable for it happened

* The Khumans, the Angoms, Khaba Nganba, Luwang, Chenglei, Moirang and Ningthouja.

again and again. Warfare was prevalent but local chiefdoms were apparently unable to expand spatially to incorporate sizeable regional population. Many of the small Meitei polities remained politically independent of the expanding Meitei hegemony for a long time. Local clans like Moirang and the Angom seem to have been able to retain political autonomy by defending themselves in fortified locations virtually unassailable with the tactics that characterize chiefdoms.

Some other strategies in case of Manipur relate to ideology that legitimizes the position of leaders as necessary for maintaining the 'natural' order of the region. In many cases this involves the leaders' security connecting themselves to the past. Incorporation of social leaders into a religious pantheon of God like figures e.g. Thangjing, Marjing etc. seem to plant a community's leadership line on an eminence that dominates the landscape of the region.[27] It is a reflection of legitimizing social formations.

Equally important is competition for ties to a new ideology from outside, which acted as impetus to set off the ruling elite as a separate order,[28] for example, the warring elite of the Meiteis used such symbols as head hunting to define its status.[29]

Importance of ideology as a source of chiefly power has several historical examples. State ideologies derived from the Roman texts held by the church following collapse of Rome were used to "civilize" the invading barbarians and then to legitimize the emerging ruling system of small Italian city states. The influence of Hinduism on the Meitei Civilization as is often claimed by regional historians, is also a fact that Chiefdoms with their few high-status positions, are inherently competitive in their political dynamics. It is again more surprising that some chiefdoms are able to sustain themselves while others disintegrate. Here economic control would seem of paramount importance.

It is a fact that merger of the seven chiefdoms, which is now known as 'Meitei State' converting into a kingdom, was accelerated in the 17th century,[30] more in particular by consolidation of dominance of Ningthouja lordship over other six chiefdoms completed during Charairongba. However, it is interesting to note that the Moirang Chiefdom and the hill tribes continued to maintain their independent status all through despite the fact that they were defeated and subjugated in the 18th and 19th centuries.[31] The Moirang chiefdom was represented to the Royal Court of Ningthouja which had become Meitei Kingdom by their 'Ningthou' or 'Chief'.

Consolidation of Meitei 'Seven Salais' Created Myths for Marriage Codes and Ultimately Customary Laws

Having achieved his political objective to occupy the throne at Kangla that have covered the chiefdoms of Mangang, Angom and Luwang clan territories and defeat of the Khaba and Nganba, Nongda Lairen Pakhangba became the recognised legendary head of the Meitei confederation, Khumans and Moirangs still remaining outside the confederacy though they were very much part of social life of the Meitei society. This was no mean achievement on the part of Ningthouja Salai to bring the seven clans under the Meitei confederacy.[32]

Here it is expedient to highlight as to how the rites and rituals in regard to an occasion relating to coronation of a kind were performed, commen-surately with customary laws thereof. Having consolidated his position to confederate all the seven 'Salais' to constitute into Meitei State after the defeat of Khaba and Poireiton of Khaba Nganba and Khuman Chiefdoms respectively, Puleiromba, the Chief of

Angom Chiefdom, Luwang Langmaiba, a priest of Luwang Chiefdom, Ningthem Apanba of Mangang Chiefdom and many other leaders of Chakpa tribe, invited Pokhangba to Kangla, the ancient capital of the Meitei Kingdom[33]. To convey the invitation, according to Chakparol, Kansural, a leader of the Chakpa sent four persons, namely, Chakmaringba, Langmaringba, Mungmaringba and Ngangmaringba to Pakhangba[34]. They guarded Pakhangba during the coronation ritual proceedings as per customary laws.

Strictly following the rites and rituals as prescribed for the purpose by the Customary Law, Pakhangba performed a march between Heingang hills and Nongmaijing hills located to the northern part of north-east of Imphal along the Iril (Lilwai) river, passing through Lishi, Thangwai, Mucheng, Keihon, Naokel, Haomu, Tangkhul, etc. villagers of which accompanied him upto Kangla. The three Chiefs who invited him provided arms and weapons, and servants and attendants, as also officials like Pukhren, Nongthon, priest (Amai), poets, singers, torch bearers, swords-men, umbrella or parasol bearers, gold and silver, precious stones, clothes and food. [35]

At Kangla, Puleiromba, Luwang Langamba and Ningthou Apanba, the three Sorarens, greeted him with all necessary arms and weapons, and coronation robes and costumes. Even for the coronation ceremony all the people were invited when Pakhangba was formally coroneted to the investiture[36] accompanied by the queens.

Thereafter, the priests and Singers gave the 'regral' title of 'Tubi Yoinungda Nongda Lairen Pakhangba'[37]. The coronation took place, according to 'Sanglen Puba Puya' (reproduced by Manijao Singh, Shandrembi Chaisra), [38] on the 1st Saturday of the Meitei Month of Kalen (June/July).

Puleiromba, Chief of Angom, Khunthiba of Luwang, Ponglaben of Moirang and Arong of Khuman Clans drew water from Nongjeng Pond (Pukhri) on the Kangla and poured on the body of the King and the queen in compliance with provisions of the Customary Law. Scholars and priests, singers and poets, and 64 nobles were present in the coronation. The King and the queen were made to sit under the shade of 'Parasol' (light coloured thin umbrella) after having changed their dresses that were drenched with 'Nongjeng Pond' water. Puleiromba, the Angom Chief, presented Pakhangba his coronation robes. He was entitled to perform so, because of his higher ritual status than Pakhangba despite his titular secular position in the court of the latter. This was soon followed by the resounding noise of drum beatings. In the midst of unceasing drum-beat, the king and the queen were lifted to the royal 'Palanquin' (Kanglamen) to mark close of coronation investiture[39].

Now, it must be understood that there were good number of ethnic groups and tribes other than the clans of seven chiefdoms that constituted Meitei confederacy who accepted political supremacy of Ningthouja retaining at the same time their status of distinct clans within the greater Meitei societal fold.[40] Indeed, consolidation of Meitei confederacy was the greatest political support for Pakhangba and his Ningthouja Salai, which was now on the top hierarchical ladder of political achievement that reigned a Meitei Kingdom.[41] This prompted writers of later chronicles under the direction of rulers to describe Pakhangba as the head of seven clans and King of the Meiteis, though it led to the creation of myths, so as to mystify origin of the clans or 'Salais' bringing such mystic beliefs into marriage rules known as 'Yek Salai system' that formed clan exogamy, prohibiting marriage within the same 'Salai'. This ultimately resulted in drawing up of strict socio-religious codes which were given concrete shape that were incorporated in the common customary laws of the Meiteis.[42] Some believed that according to tradition 'Yek-Salai' was attributed to have been adopted during the reign of Pakhangba. And, 'Yek-Salai' stands for kinship relationship between members of clans, lineages and sub-lineages claiming a common ancestor.

During the course of our research with reference to the sources of history of Manipur which is basically history of Meiteis as is reflected in the Royal Chronicles, the coronation ceremonies of Meitei Kings after that of Pakhangba which had been discussed above in detail, reveals a set of customary laws which are the bases for the formation of Meitei State. It may appear theatrical but these laws have sustained the Meitei society through ages.

The customary laws relating to coronation of the Kings of Meiteis after Pakhangba as discussed hereinabove are crucial to his acceptance by the people. If customary laws had been violated at any stage the 'priest' and the 'Chronicle writers' are apt to refuse to accept them as genuine Rulers or Kings and therefore they are deprived of their status being mentioned in the royal chronicles, 'Ningthourel Lambuba'. This itself speaks volumes of importance of not only of coronation in the life of Manipuri Kings but also as part of customary articulation.

Place of Coronation

One spectacular dimension where importance of or indispensability of Customary Law articulation is the cave of KANGLA, believed to be the naval of 'Taoroinai' (Bodyguard and conveyance of Lord Pakhangba[43] It is also believed that the placenta and amniotic covering (Naopham and Naoyom) of the forefathers of the seven clans of the Meiteis are inside the Kangla cave[44]. That is why the cave is known as 'Melkhom Yaikhom' or 'Kangla Men'[45]. It is on this Kangla Men that the King sits in the ceremonial proceedings of coronation as per prescribed formalities and rituals of the customary laws pertaining to such solemned occasion. It is believed that as per oracular directive of Lord Pakhangba, incorporated in the formal rituals meant for this purpose in the Customary Law was performed at Kangla only from the time of King Naophangba till the last King Bodhchandra Singh. [46]

Shape of Coronation Chair

Customary laws relating to coronation spelled out that as per oracular instruction the coronation chair of Pakhangba was three legged with round shaped platform made in imitation of the circular shape of the sun and the moon[47]. Later on, the coronation chair was changed into an angular (four cornered) shaped platform as introduced during the reign of King Khagemba.[48]. The Kings coronated on such shaped coronation chair were Khunjaoba, Paikhomba, Charairongba, Pamheiba, Maramba, Chingthangkhomba, Talemkhomba and Mayangamba. During the reign of King Paikhomba some amendments and alterations were made under the directive of customary laws in respect of ceremonial part of the coronation in a moderate scale.[49] However, the rites and rituals of the coronation were so elaborate and grandeur from the coronation of King Naothingkhong as per direction of Luwang Ningthou Punshiba, the King of Luwang Principality.[50]

Under this innovative ceremonial coronation, ten Nobles of the royal court (Ningthou Panba Tara) fetched water from three canals and the Kings take bath with the water.

The King sits on a wooden seat made of UNINGTHOU plank. He collects water in a trough made of WANG wood.[51]

Another very significant feature is the indispensable Customary Law element in regard to the parts to be played by each 'Salai' and as also to ensure participation by several tribal groups as could be evidenced from different kinds of wood used in the construction of Kangla and of coronation platform, water to be drawn from different water-pools (lakes) belonging to seven different 'Salais', use of different designs of clothes both from the seven Salais of Meiteis and also from the tribal groups, such as, practice followed since the reign of Pamheiba for wearing of Tangkhul customary dress by the King during the coronation ceremony.[52] These are seen as attempts made to depict universal characteristics of the occasion so as to project the King as supreme authority of all the people living both in the Valley and the hills and in expression of solidarity and integration of societies with the blending commonality as the King of Manipur is.

The concept of divine Kingship of the Meiteis has it that the Meitei Kings got their divine power and strength from Supreme Being and as also from the ancestral gods of the clans through certain processes, such as, consecration, sacrifices at the time of coronation and the yearly ceremony of 'Cheithaba'. For this reason coronation of Kings is made as far wide participation of the seven Meitei Salais and as also the tribal groups to make it sure that coronation bears testimony of the multitude as per instruction of or in compliance of their customary laws.[53] In addition, as they are not actual during the Kings are to re-establish their solidarity with the divine forces as a mandate of the Supreme Being through consecration sacrifices at the time of coronation and the yearly renewals of 'Cheithaba'. They could not utilize their power beyond the jurisdiction of custom, tradition and culture of the Meiteis. In such societies legal norms and customary rules were highly respected by the Kings. Under these circumstances, the growth of certain legal codes such as 'Loyumba Shinyen' were favourable.[54] If the King acted against norms, mores and social institutions, there was every possibility to withdraw from them the mandate of Supreme Being who also represent the entire Meitei population through religio-cultural system[55]. By this, it is clear that coronation of Kings is one of the mandates of customary laws that has necessarily to be fulfilled.

Manipur from 18th Century to 1947

Manipur from 18th Century till 1947 witnessed different historical events which are very significant in many dimensions. It was a time turning point that shaped the society. During this period, several kings ruled who brought about changes in the traditional customs which had great socio-cultural impact. Several customary laws emerged therefrom. The following two great kings have been selected for brief discussion in this regard. They are (I) Garibniwaz, and (II) Bhagyachandra, whose contribution to the growth, development and innovation in various aspects of customary laws of the Meiteis had no parallel and cannot be marginalized.

(i) Garibniwaz or Gopal Singh or Pamheiba (1709-1748)

Garibniwaz ascended to the throne of Manipur on Wednesday 23rd Thawan (about August) 1709 according to the Royal chronicle though Pemberton and Gait contended that it was in 1714. Jhaljit Singh over-ruled their contention[56] on the ground that in such controversial issues, the Royal Chronicle should prevail. He abdicated the throne after reigning for forty years in favour of his son, Chit Shai on Wednesday the 10th May (Kalen), 1748.

Khelchandra maintained that the administrative decrees issued by him were incorporated in the customary laws of the Meiteis, claimed to become the first ever written constitution. 'Loiyamba Shilyen', 'Loina Shilon' and 'Phamlons'[57]. He subdivided his administration into four departments such as (i) Lourungshang (Revenue), (ii) Urungshang (Forest), (iii) Keirang (Civil Supply) and (iv) Justice.

As far as justice is concerned, Garibniwaz changed the customary law or traditional system[58] of dealing with justice. He made himself as the Executive Head while the rest entrusted upon the nobles. Thus, equal treatment through nobles was started.

He made the literary progress, such as the translation of Mahabharata into Manipuri.[59] He initiated a new religion under the guidance of one Shanti Das. As a matter of fact, adoption of Gotras of Hindu caste system in the Salais (Clan) system followed and the intermingling of Meitei festivals with Hindu festivals incorporated. These were done in accordance with the customary laws. Social stratification which was non-existent at all had come to exist and also the practice of Sati gained momentum.[60]

(ii) Bhagyachandra (1762 – 1798)

Bhagyachandra or Jai Singh or Chingthangkhomba ascended the throne in 1759.

According to Hiranya[61], he systematized the customary law in respect of traditional judicial order with special interest to revamp the administrative departments including Judiciary, such as given hereinbelow:

(i) Landai Kaibiron Shanglen;
(ii) Ngamdai Sat Nga Thaba Shanglen;
(iii) Cheirap (Court);
(iv) Kuchu,
(v) Gandiya Shinba Shanglen (department of religious affairs), and
(vi) Apan Shanglen (department of Women's affairs).

An outstanding feature of Bhagyachandra's reign was the preparation of calendar by Maniram Pandit Sidhanta and his associates based on the Customary Law that was called Kangleipak Sak or Manipur Era. It was started counting from 78 A.D. and was renamed as Chandrabda.[62]

Moreover, several socio-religious and also cultural events took place such as the adoption of Vaishnavism. And to that effect many aspects had been gradually started to evolve the Hinduised culture, the establishment of religious institution, the installation of Govindaji image and also the Ras Leela.[63] New customary laws related to the construction of the God's images and the materials of creation were formulated. Customary laws of worshiping animism underwent drastic changes.

Loyumba Shinyen: the Great Law Giver

Although the provisions as mentioned in *Loyumba Shinyen* are not followed by the ethnic groups, economic compulsions have lured them away from their traditional work. Yet in some cases especially in the rural areas these laws have come to stay. It was basically written to organize the division of labour and to avoid social conflict within the community and even outside it. The customary provisions of the *Loyumba Shinyen* should be discussed although it is of later date. It has a significance of its own.

Before 1709 A.D. there was monarchy according to *Chatlam Lutin*. Under the system, Nobility exercised tremendous influence over the King. However, they were bound by the rules of '*Chatlam-Lutin*', Law of the land. When Garib Niwaz ascended the throne in 1709 A.D. royal absolutism became a dominant rule. No one could violate command of the King. As such command of the King became the law. Therefore, to obey command of the King was to do justice. After Garib Niwaz, nature of law was a mixed and mediatory one in which supremacy of the rule of *Chatlam-Lutin* and the royal absolutism was blended. The King in consultation with the nobility enforced the rules of '*Chatlam-Lutin*'. Accordingly, justice was administered publicly. Thus so far as nature of '*Chatlam-Lutin*' is concerned, it appears to be supreme upto the reign of Charairongba (1697-1709). Because, no one, may he be the King, the priest, the noble or the servant, could transgress the rule of '*Chatlam-Lutin*'.

The Meiteis have their own Customary Laws. These laws are still in vogue or valid unless they infringe the provisions of the Constitution of India and any legislation enacted thereunder. Article VIII(3) of the Manipur Merger Agreement lays down that these customary laws shall be preserved.[64]

Lallup System

The Meiteis, and for that matter, the Mizos, have their own customary laws which shall be valid and preserved unless they infringe provisions of the Constitution of India as per Article VIII(3) of the Manipur Merger Agreement[65] and so also Chin Hills Regulations, 1818 in the Hill Areas of Manipur. Monarchy was the form of Government in early Manipur when the subjects venerated their King as the regent of God which was characteristic of Theocratic State wherein Law and Religion were so closely intertwined and blended that both could hardly be distinguishable from each other.

In those days, the King administered his country with a system called '*Lallup*' under which system was the entire Meitei population divided into Pannas, each Panna consisting of a number of families and tribes. The head of each family or tribe would select from his family or tribe the men who could render service, called '*Lallup*', to the King on behalf of the Panna to which they belonged. This system, according to Cheitharol Kumbaba, was in practice since the reign of King Loyumba.[66] It was pivot of the Government Machinery of the early Manipur. Lallup was abolished on September 29, 1892, the day of coronation of Sir Churachand Singh, which was substituted by an annual tax of Rs. 3/- per house.

Besides Lallup, there existed another system which assigned work allocation to each of '*Seven Salais*'. Such similar systems existed in other primitive communities as well. This system is called '*Yumnak Mashin*'. Khelchandra pointed out that another 'text' known as 'Mashin' has been added by the Editor of the published text. Added to this it is observed[67] that '*Loyumba Shinyen*' had been mixed up together with '*Mashin*' in '*Loina Shinyen*',[68] and further observed that despite a little confusion, '*Loyumba Shinyen*' and '*Mashin*', if read together, give a mine of information on the social and economic history of Manipur.

In the *Lallup* system, the male adult selected to render service to the King attends royal office, while the '*Yumnak Mashin*' attends to the work assigned to each '*Yumnak*'. Thus, all the '*Yumnaks*' of the seven *Salais* played their respective roles as assigned for specific work in the life and well-being of their society.[69] The names of *Yumnaks* or assigned surnames of each of the Salai are given below[70]:

Sl. No.	Name of Salai	No. of Yumnak	Sl. No.	Name of Salai	No. of Yumnak
1.	Angom	74	2.	Ningthouja	131
3.	Luwang	69	4.	Khuman	111
5.	Moirang	80	6.	Khaba Nganba	23
7.	Sarang-Leishangthem	50			

Incidentally, 'Salai' is derived from 'Sagei-Lai', ancestor of Lineage. Salai has been described by many as clan. Perhaps, this is not exactly so. S.N. Pratt (Religion in Manipur) traces the origin of the Salai to a tribal ancestor.[71]

In this system, there was a branch office called '*Khundin*'. This office looked after the men liable to 'Lallup' so that they performed their work well. The jurisdiction covers the whole State dividing into Pannas. In times of peace it worked for economic development of the State and in times of war it did military services. The liability to Lallup commences as soon as a man attains the age of seventeen when he also is entitled to cultivate one part of the land with tax in kind imposed by the King or Raja.

It is a royal edict (Constitution) and is an important historical document for the reconstruction of the social, judiciary, political and economic history of Manipur. It is also the first written Constitution of Manipur as promulgated by Meidingu Loyumba during his reign from 1074 to 1112 A.D.[72] and that the decree was issued reliably in 1110 A.D., according to Cheitharol Kumbaba.[73] The Constitution was in force with some modifications from time to time, codifying "... the ancient customary laws of Manipur. It embodied the traditions and customs that were followed by the Kings who reigned before Meidingu Loyumba", incorporating features, such as, the early Meitei polity, the land tenure system, the administration of justice and social organisation, "... besides throwing sidelights on various aspects of life. The Constitution also embodied both theological and legal norms".[74]

Whatever the King ordered was obediently complied with and followed by his subjects as if that was law provided, of course, without elements of disregard to traditions and customs that were then prevailing and that the form of Government as laid down in the Constitution was absolute Monarchy based on Theocracy.

Loyumba Shinyen was expanded further as innovative dimensions were added by the kings to effectively deal with such emerging situations during the reigns of Kyamba from 1467 to 1508, Khagemba from 1597 to 1652, Garib Niwas from 1704 to 1748, Bhagyachandra from 1763 to 1798 and Chourjit from 1803 to 1813. This expanded original text of the decree of *Loyumba* was published in 1975.[75] The decree deals with the distribution of occupation according to *Yumnaks*, assignment of duties to priests and priestesses, assignment of works for maintenance of abode of Village deities (Umanglais), creation of administrative departments (Loisang), duties and functions of Kings and Queens, royal etiquettes, titles and decorations awarded to the nobles, administration of justice, keeping of standard time. It was expanded also to include royal painters, court singers, procedures for delivery of royal children, feudal dues and services to be rendered by different tribes, etc.

Land Revenue

It was one of the main sources of royal incomes. Land records for which duties in cash were prepared and collected at the rate of hundred coins per PARI of land. As for virgin lands reclaimed for cultivation were also subject to payment of revenue at the rate of five hundred coins per PARI of land. Revenue in kind at the rate of sixty pots of paddy per PARI was exacted in case of unauthorized reclamation.[76]

Administration of Justice

The principles of criminal laws were very severe. Cattle-theft was punishable with mutation of the legs. Burglary was punished with mutation of the hands. Giving of false statement and false accusation were punished with deprivation of tongue. Indecency towards the queen or King was punished with deprivation of the eyes.[77]

Services of Pana

There were eight Panas under Meidingu Loyumba.[78] They were – Khongchalup, Nongmaillup, Angoubalup, Leichol-Lakpa, Tolongkhombalup, Khurailup, Lipphambalup and Khangjenglup. These Panas assist the King in his administration of the State. The King also distributes different works for performance amongst the sageis and the yumnaks covering all activities relating to social, economic, culture, religion, etc. etc. These structural patterns manifest existence of one's own constitution in embodiment of Customs and Customary Laws which are well codified in the form of 'Loyumba Shinyen'.[79]

Radical Changes in Customary Law

Anglo-Manipuri relation that started in the 1770s with the negotiation entered into with Varlest followed by the First Burmese War of 1824-26 gave birth to far-reaching consequences on the sovereign status of Manipur due mainly to the weakness of Manipur State. Conclusion of the Treaty of Manipur, 1833, with the British Government resulted to cede Cachar to the latter, and so was the lost of Kabaw-Valley in 1834 to Burma (then called Ava). This ultimately opened the way to the establishment of British Political Agency in Manipur which became the ear, the eye and the mouth of the British Government since 1836, and subsequently when Assam was placed under the Chief Commissioner in 1874, the Political Agent and all Officers in Manipur were under the control of the Chief Commissioner.[80]

Thereafter, Manipur gradually saw its entry into the hands of British who had become an interloper in the internal affairs of Manipur that resulted in the Anglo-Manipuri War of 1891 which indeed curbed the authority and independence of Manipur. Along with it the customary laws were also afforded. On attainment of majority when Churachand assumed charge of Administration[81] on 3rd Kalen (April-May), 1907, Manipur was already a vassal State under the British supremacy. For purpose of accession to the throne of Manipur, the British Government issued a SANAD to Churachand Singh, appointing him as the Raja of Manipur, tried and sentenced Tikendrajit, Thangal and others to death on the gallow.[82] The Political Agent of Manipur, who was the de-facto ruler, administered the State with the help of a Darbar headed by an Officer, designated as the President of Manipur State Darbar, appointed by the Government of Assam. But no Darbar resolution was valid without the assent of the Maharajah. However, regarding administration of justice, reference had to be made by the Political Agent of Manipur to the Government of Assam for necessary orders in cases when justice was believed to have not been done by the Darbar with prior consultation with the Maharajah.[83]

Even so, at the threshold of Indian Independence, before Manipur was integrated with the Indian Dominion, two Constitutional Acts, such as, the Manipur State Constitution Act, 1947, comprising of 58 Sections that laid down powers and functions of Legislature, Executive and Judicature as also the Fundamental Rights and Duties of the Citizens, and that of the Manipur State Hill People's (Administration) Regulation Act, 1947 for establishment of a responsible Government in the State were enacted.[84] In this regard it has to be understood that despite merger as per agreement signed for the purpose in Shillong on the 15th October, 1949, the Manipur State Constitution Act, 1947 was not repealed which is, therefore, supposed to remain in force.[85] But contrary to this, the Manipur Hill People's (Administration) Regulation Act, 1947 was not so.[86] The Regulation, in so far as it was related to the constitution and functions of Village Authorities and the administration of justice – both civil and criminal by court of Village Authorities – was repealed by the Manipur (Village Authorities in Hill Areas) Act, 1956.[87] The new Act brought in elements of democratic principles in the constitution of the Village Authorities which envisaged that Authorities of Villages which members were earlier nominated were now to be elected. A drastic change had taken place in the role of customary laws applicable in the society especially with reference to the coronation of the kings in Manipur. The theatrical aspects had taken a back seat.

Evolution of the Mizo Chieftainship (Through Customary Laws)

Chieftainship is a very powerful secular Institution based on kinship structure for the purpose of village administration which is the highest and independent political unit.[88] According to Customary Law, the office of Chieftainship is hereditary passing from father to eldest son among the Thadous and to the youngest among the Lushais.[89] In the case of Lushai, however, it has been changed from youngest to eldest in recent times.[90] It was very salutary as the process of fragmentation continued to erode not only the material possessions of the Chief but also the viability of his position as a chief.[91] It is associated with the concept of 'UPA' or man on the direct line of the senior descent.[92] The epithet 'UPA' is, therefore, conferred on a person by way of reverence, and a great deal of veneration is attached to it. 'UPA' is the only person who can become chief. Thus, 'chief' is synonymous with 'UPA'. Similarly, corresponding to 'UPA' the term 'NAOPA' stands for the junior man who cannot in the normal course of the customary law become the chief. He can become so only with the full consent of the chief, as also with the concurrence of Council of 'Ministers', or 'Elders' of the village, which is known as 'Semang-Upa', 'Pachong', or 'UPA' in Lushai collectively. Before a 'NAOPA' can become the chief, certain formalities and obligations are to be gone through as per Customary Law.

It must be said that under the circumstance there is no scope for growth of political leadership among the 'NAOPA' to become the 'Chief', unless specifically desired by the 'UPA' to develop and groom his 'NAOPA',[93] literally meaning younger brother, for leadership, or chief whatsoever.

Chieftainship manifests, therefore, in the rights and privileges handed down to the 'UPA' and these prerogatives are institutionalized in village organisation and the Customary Laws, through the system of Chieftainship called 'HAOSA' in Thadou and 'LAL' in Lushai to mean chief of the village and its Council of Elders (Ministers). Thus chieftainship has come to stay as an institution which is the perennial source of customary laws, and the mechanism by which such laws are interpreted in the social system that makes them a living force enabling to maintain their identity inheriting a rich cultural heritage.[94]

Administrative Structure and Functions (Wherefrom Customary Laws Flow)

As per the customary laws a village is an independent political unit among the Mizos and the Chief called HAOSA of the village and his Council of Ministers are the political leaders.[95] Administration of justice, enforcement of executive function, maintenance of social practices and customary law, including religious performances are the areas of village administration under the Chieftainship and his Council of Minister. Thus a Mizo village is an important administrative unit.

The village administrative organisation is normally structured as given below in the box, which normally leads to the exercise of power as vested with the customary law:

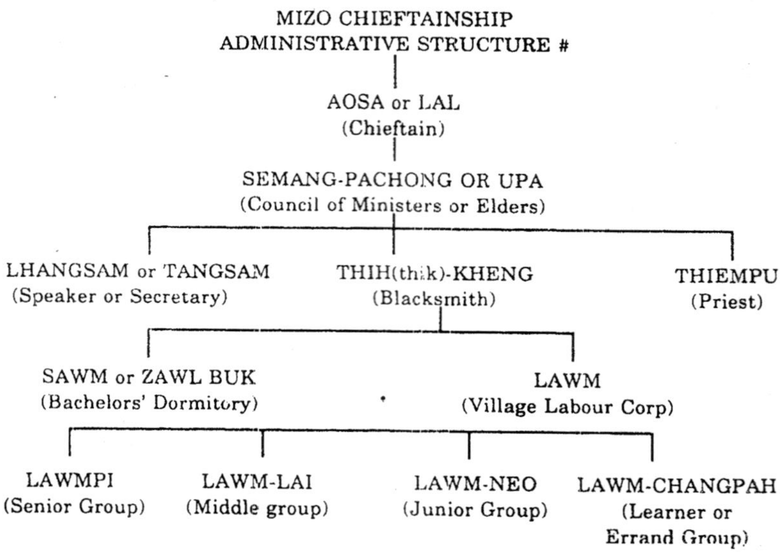

Fig. V (1)

Source: T.S. Gangte:

The Kukis of Manipur: 1993; p.126; Gyan Publishing House, New Delhi.

'Haosa' (Chief)

'Haosa' or 'Lal' is the office of the Village Chief. It is hereditary, passing from father to the son.[96] Among the Mizos, and unlike the Nagas, 'Haosa' has the absolute right of ownership over the entire land of the village.[97] The villagers have no right over the land whatsoever. Even if a villager, who is generally a 'Naopa' wishes to establish a new village, he can do so only with the permission of the 'Haosa'. The 'Haosa', howsoever, absolute his right over the land might be, normally allows, in consultation with his Council of Minister, [98] the villagers to cultivate and utilise as per their requirements. But the villagers have to pay to the 'Haosa' in return for such privileges in the shape of tributes called *'Changseo'*, even part of hunted games called *'Saleng'*.[99] *'Changseo'* is payable annually after harvest. The 'Haosa' is also entitled to free labour called 'Khuo-Tha'[100] of each villager once in a year.

Together with such rights, the 'Haosa' has certain obligations over the villagers. In return to the services rendered by the villagers, free of cost, and the tributes paid as token of loyalty, recognition, obedience and solidarity, the 'Haosa' has to protect their interests by providing security socially, politically and economically. It is also the bounden duty of the 'Haosa' to see that every villager is protected from external aggression and danger. Ideologically investigated it reminds us of Rousseau's social contract theory. The 'Haosa' system is indeed very similar to the Social Contract Theory of Rousseau,[101] who enunciates that rights imply duties. By this system both the villagers on the one hand and the 'Haosa' as the chief on the other, are in duty bound to fulfil their rights and obligations towards each other.

Many writers having a superficial knowledge about

the men and affairs try to draw a similarity between the 'Haosa' and the 'Zamindar' and often jump to a conclusion that the system of a 'Haosa' is despotic. Of course, there is sufficient room for a 'Haosa' to become a despot and tyrannical, but such things are rare. Despite such possibility of being so dreaded by the villagers, there are thousand and one ways by which such a situation can be averted due to interaction of forces within the system. The villagers are at liberty to leave the village and migrate elsewhere in case the 'Haosa' is found failing in his duty to protect interest of the villagers.

Notwithstanding the inherent defects associated with the 'Haosa' system which the Mizos cannot do away with the 'Haosa' system has come to stay as a perennial source of custom and tradition, in that, in spite of the onslaught of modernism and advancement in all walks of life, they are able to inherit a rich cultural and traditional heritage. The Haosa system has its bases on the proper interpretation of the customary law and tradition, and it is binding upon the people.

Unlike the Naga tribes of Manipur, who have no permanent and strongly established secular head of a village, the office of which is usually held by an elected man called '*Gaonbura*' for a specified term, similar to the Nuer tribes of Africa, who do not have a permanent Chief of the village other than the Leopard-skin clad Chief[102], who, though wields a great deal of influence and acts as a 'go-between' to settle disputes[103], the Mizos have a very solidly established institution of Chieftainship who, being the 'Upa' of a particular clan or lineage or sub-lineage, is considered to be the fountain-head of all customs and retainer of tradition, yet like the African Nuer, the Mizo political structure is segmented into lineages which are diverging branches of descent from a common ancestor.

Observations of Carey and Tuck[104] on the Mizo chief is interestingly worth taken note of. They said that Thadou chief might be wanting in qualifications and that there might be many of other families his superior in ability, but, unless he was physically quite unfit to his position, there was no danger of his being supplanted, and the usual course was for the elders and advisors to assist him in his rule. This was basic consideration of chieftainship which had a strong grip for efficient administration. The British knew it well and gave cognizance to it as part of their administrative machinery till 1947.

Today in India chieftainship has become a misnomer since this institution was abolished by an act of law. There exist two sets of people among the Thadou and Lushai Chiefs wherein the traditional leadership is provided by the chiefs and their clansmen. Sometimes they could not adjust to this new situation of abolished chieftainships. On the other hand, commoners saw a new ray of hope to move in their social hierarchy and asserted themselves through organized ethnic activities which came in direct confrontation with the Institution of chieftainship. This gave birth to the nomenclature, Mizo, in place of Lushai and controversy over the 'Kuki' terminology, mainly because of politicization of tribal society by the proletariats, resulting in emergence of new ethnic appellation and division of homogeneous cohesive village communities under the leadership of the chief into heterogeneous ethnic groups right from the village level to the highest social elites, aspiring for separate and multifarious identities.[105] One of the most serious social discordant notes that took place for reason mentioned above was between the Singson chiefs and the Hmar commoners which took place from mid 59 lasting till mid 60 that rocked the age-old social harmony and tranquility, resulting in the burning down of many Singson villages where Hmar commoners lived in peace under their Thadou Chiefs who dared not return to their villages till date. The damage done to the good relationship between the Thadous and the Hmars was due to non-conformity with the customary laws and was a direct manifestation of adverse influence brought about by modernism in the name of development. Summing up the situation, J.M. Raina,[106] the then Chief Commissioner of Manipur, attributed the main cause of conflict as the "Thadous relying too much on their past fighting and organizing capacities" on the one hand and the "docility and easy going nature of the Hmars", that confronted directly between the newly assumed 'aggressiveness of Hmars' under the prevailing new situation which the Thadou Chiefs "...too are not going to take it lying down" on the other. Notwithstanding, the system of 'Haosa' or 'Lal' could not be given a go-by.

Customary Laws Made Manifest

We are aware of the fact that the customs are not customary laws per se. They help us at the performance level. Rituals through constant usage may become part of customary laws because they need to be performed during the course of holding on to traditional values. Customary laws therefore emerge as an institution in itself which is referred to time and again. It has become part and parcel of the state/social system.

Semang-Pachong or Upa

The institution of 'Haosa' or 'Lal' presupposes the existence of 'Semang Pachong', in Thadou, or, 'Upa' in

Lushai, Council of Ministers or Elders of the Village. It has to work through the Council which assists in his day-do-day administration.[107] This Council is composed of persons of wisdom, integrity, knowledge of customary law and its interpretations etc. and is nominated by the 'Haosa'. Special representation is always given from the minorities and the poor villagers in the Council. The Council members assemble and make deliberations. They remain in office as long as the 'Haosa' is pleased. Social, political, economic, judicial matters etc. are dealt with by the Council.

The main mechanism through which the Council exercises its administration is interpretation of the customary laws.[108] The 'Haosa' as the Chairman or Head of this Council presides over the meetings. Members of the Council are exempted from payment of all kinds of tributes levied on the common villagers in token recognition of their services. [109]

Customary Laws govern appointments of officials and their powers till the offices exist. Officers are products of customary laws but not vice-versa.

REFERENCES

1. Lewis Henry Morgan: *Ancient Society*, London, 1877, pp. 65-67.
2. Emile Durkheim: *Elementary Forms of Religious Life*, London, 1915.
3. Boris Malinowski: *Freedom and Civilization, London: 1947*; pp. 263-266.
4. Issac Schapera: *Government and Politics in Tribal Societies,* London; 1963; pp. 14-15.
5. R.M. MacIver: *The Web of Government*, New York: 1965; p. 165.
6. J.B. Bhattacharjee: *Social and Polity Formations in Pre-colonial North-East India: 1991*, p.1, Vikas Publishing House Pub. Ltd, New Delhi.

6. *Ibid.*
8. J.B. Bhattacharjee: *Op. cit.*
9. *Ibid.*
10. A.S. Reid: Chin Lushai Land, Calcutta: 1893; pp. 5 - 7.
11. J.B. Bhattacharjee: *Op. cit.*, p. 72.
12. *Ibid.*
13. Robert Carneiro, and Timothy Earle: A Theory of the Origin of the State: Science: 169: and Earle Timothy: Chiefdoms in archaeological and ethno-historical perspective: Annual Review in Anthropology, 1987: 16: pp. 279-308.
14. Patrice Kirch: The evolution of the Polynesian Chiefdom: Cambridge, California University Press: 1984, and Kristian Kristiansen: The formation of tribal system in later European Pre-History "In Theory and explanation in archeology: The Southampton conference; Northern Europe, 1982: 4000-700 BC.
15. Vincas Steponaites: Locational Theory and Complex Chiefdoms: A Mississippian example: "in Mississippian Settlement Patterns": Edited by E. Smith, 1978: pp. 417-453, New York, Academic Press.
16. D'Altroy Terence and Timothy Earle: Staple Finance, Wealth finance, and Storage in the Inea Political economy, current Anthropology: 1985: 26: pp. 187-206
17. Renfrew, Colin: 1974: Beyond a subsistence economy: The evolution of social organisation in Pre-historic Europe "in reconstructing complex society": Edited by C. Renfrew and S. Shennan, pp. 1-9, Cambridge, Cambridge University Press.
18. Feinman Gary and Linda Nicholas, 1987: "Labour, surplus and Production – A regional analysis of Formative Oaxaca Socio-economic organisation" in Anthropological research papers.
19. Haas Jonathan: 1982, The evolution of the pre-historic state, New York, Columbia University Press.
20. Allen Johnson and Timothy Early: The Evolution of Human Society ; Standford, Standford University Press, 1987.
21. Boserup Ester: The conditions of Agricultural Growth, Chicago, Aldine: 1966.
22. Allen Johnson and Timothy Earle: *Op. cit.*
23. Richard Bradley: The Social Foundations of Pre-historic

Britain, London, Harlow, 1984. Several countries in the Oaxaca Valley of highland Mesoamerica, for the Black Warrior Valley of Alabama and for the Valle de la Plata in Columbia. Population density appears also to have been low for the early chiefdoms of southern England, said Richard Bradley.

24. Patrice Kirch: The population of the Polynesian Chiefdoms ; Cambridge, Cambridge University Press: 1984.On the Marquesas, population growth and resulting environmental deterioration created a susceptibility to drought that bound a local population to its leader and his breadfruit stores, contended Patrice Kirch. In Greece, population growth accompanied Mycenaean State formation and, following the precipitous "Dark Age" decline contributed to the emergence of the Polis, added Ferguson.
25. Thomas Bergatzsky: Culture, environment and the ills of adoptationism: Current Anthropology: 25: pp. 399-415; 1984.
26. Robert Carneiro: A theory of the Origin of the state: Science, 169 ; pp. 733-38: 1970.
27. Richard Bradley, 1984: The Social Foundations of pre-historic Britain, London, Harlow.
28. Kent Flannery: The Olmec and the Valley of Oaxaca. A modelfor international interaction in formative times, "in Dumbarton Oaks Conferenceon the Olmec": Edited by E. Benson, 1968; pp. 79-110,Washington D.C., Dumbarton Oaks and Mary Helms: Ancient Panama Austin: University of Texas Press, 1979.
29. Kristian Kristiansen: The formation of tribal systems in later European pre-history: 1982: Northern Europe 4000-500 B.C. in Theory and explanation in archeology: The Southampton Conference: Edited byh C. Renfrew, M. Rowland, and B. Seagraves, pp. 241-80, New York, Academic Press (1987) "From Stone to Bronze".
30. Unpublished work of Sanasam Amal: Socio-dynamics of chiefs and their chiefdom in the State formation in early Manipur (from the earliest time to the 16th Century AD) 2003: p. 220.
31. *Ibid.*
32. Gangmumei Kabui: History of Manipur Vol. One: Pre-Colonial period, 1991; p. 84.
33. Kh. Yaima: Pakhangba Phambal: p. 26-27.

34. Gangmumei Kabui: *Op. cit.*
35. Gangmumei Kabui: *Op. cit.*, p. 84.
36. *Ibid.*, p. 85.
37. Kh. Yaima: *Pakhangba Phambal*: p. 26-27.
38. Gangmumei Kabui: *Op. cit.*, p. 85.
39. Gangmumei Kabui: *Op. cit.*, p. 85.
40. *Ibid.*
41. *Ibid.*
42. *Ibid.*, p. 87.
43. Naoreoibam Indramani: Coronation of Manipuri Kings: *Sanathong Monthly Journal;* June 2001, Volume VIII No. 4; pp. 15-18: 8th Anniversary Publication.
44. Naoreoibam Indramani: *Op. cit.*
45. *Ibid.*
46. *Ibid.*
47. *Ibid.*
48. *Ibid.*
49. *Ibid.*
50. *Ibid.*
51. Naoreoibam Indramani: *Op. cit.*
52. *Ibid.*
53. M. Lokendra: *Divine Kingship in Manipur*: Proceedings of North-East India History Association: 10th Session, Shillong, 1989, p. 258.
54. *Ibid.*
55. *Ibid.*, p. 259.
56. R.K. Jhalajit Singh: *A Short History of Manipur: 1965*; p.144.
57. N. Khelchandra (ed): Phamlon (1987), Imphal.
58. *Upto the reign of Pitambar Charairongba, the kings administered justice sitting on a slab – their regular seat. Panthoibi Khonggoon Kangla Ningthouba thoudu nungpak wayenba.*
59. Gangmumei Kabui, *Op. cit.*, p. 258.
60. *Ibid.*
61. R.K. Hiranya, *Ningthou Ama Oina Bhagyachandra Sahitya*, Vol. 25, No. 49.
62. *Ibid.*

63. Gangmumei Kabui, *Op. cit.*, p. 76.
64. The Manipur State Merger Agreement to the Dominion of India dated the 15th October, 1949 in Shillong.
65. M. Ibohal, J.M.S.: The outlines of the Constitutional History of Manipur: Manipur before 33 AD: Manipur Past and Present, Vol. I, 1988; p. 293.
66. *Ibid.*, p. 294.
67. Gangmumei Kabui: *A Note on "Loyumba Shinyen" (1110 A.D.):* (The First Written Constition of Manipur): Manipur Past and Present, *Vol. I,* 1988; p. 307.
68. O. Bhogeshwar Singh: *Loina Shinyen, 1967, Imphal.*
69. M. Ibohal, M.J.S., *Op. cit.*, p. 294.
70. T.C. Hudson: The Meitheis, Neeraj Publishing House, Delhi, 1984, Reprint)
71. Gangmumei Kabui: *Social and Religious Reform Movement in Manipur in 19th and 20th Centuries:* Bulletin of History Div., JNU, Imphal 1974-75.
72. *Cheitharol Kumbaba,* p. 4.
73. N. Khelchandra Singh: *Ariba Manipuri Sahitya Itihas,* 1969, Imphal.
74. M. Ibohal, M.J.S., *op. cit.*, p. 295.
75. Khulem Chandrasekhar Singh: *'Loyumba Shinyen'* published by All Manipur Umanglai Laiharaoba Committee, 1975, Imphal; pp. 16-27.
76. M. Ibohal, M.J.S., *op. cit.*, p. 295.
77. *Ibid.*, p. 296.
78. Cheitharol Kumbaba: p. 8.
79. M. Ibohal, M.J.S., *op. cit.*, p. 295.
80. M. Ibohal, M.J.S.: *op. cit.*, p. 296 [as contributed in MANIPUR: published by Naorem Sanajaoba: Mittal Publications, Delhi.]
81. *Ibid.*
82. *Ibid.*
83. *Ibid.*
84. M. Ibohal, MJS, *op. cit.*
85. See Ram Manohar Lohia Vs. S. Sundram(S) AIR 1955. Manipur 41; also Heisnam Baruniton Singh Vs. Thokchom Ningol Heisnam Ongbi BHANI DEVI and others. AIR 1959, Manipur 20 (V.46.11).

86. The Manipur Hill People's (Administration) Redulation Act, 1947.
87. The Manipur (Village Authorities) Hill Areas Act, 1956.
88. T.S. Gangte: *The Kukis of Manipur:* 1993; pp. 125-126.
89. T.S. Gangte: *The Kukis of Manipur:* 1993; pp. 125-126.
90. Col. J. Shakespear: Lushai Kuki Clans: 1912; p. 42.
91. Mrs. (Dr.) N. Chatterjee: *The Mizo Chief and His Administration:* 1975, p. 2.
92. *Ibid.*
93. T.S. Gangte: *The Kukis of Manipur: 1993;* p. 125, Gyan Publishing House, New Delhi.
94. *Ibid.,* p. 127.
95. *Ibid.,* p.126.
96. T.S. Gangte: *Op. cit.,* p. 126.
97. *Ibid.*
98. Thangtindal: *Ancient Polity of the Gangtes:* 1988, p. 2.
99. Goulienthang: *A Short Chronological Account of Mizos*: 2001: p. 30.
100. *Ibid.*
101. Jean Jacqueu Rousseau: *The Social Contract:* 1712-1778.
102. E.E. Evans-Pritchard: NUER: 1940: p. 172.
103. *Ibid.,* p. 6.
104. Bertram S. Carey and H.M. Tuck: *The Chin Hills:* 1932, p. 201.
105. Andre Betteille: *Caste, Old and New:* 1969: p. 139, New Delhi.
106. D.O. letter No.51/1/60-Card. Dated Imphal the 18th June, 1960 from the Chief Commissioner, Manipur, addressed to P.R. Bahl, ICS., Joint Secretary to the Government of India, Ministry of Home Affairs, New Delhi.
107. T.S. Gangte: *op. cit.,* p. 124.
108. T.S. Gangte: *op. cit.,* p. 124.
109. Thangtindal: *Ancient Polity of the Mizos:* 1988; p. 3.

6

Social Structure of Meiteis and Mizos: Based on the Customary Laws

'Social Structure' is the basic concept for proper understanding of society. Since long, efforts have been made to define 'Social Structure', but no unanimity of opinion could be brought about. Spencer[1], was the first writer to throw light on the structure of society. He called society an 'organism' but his view was confused. Emile Durkheim also made a little attempt to define it. Nadel[2] said, "We arrive at the structure of society through abstracting from the concrete population and its behaviour, (the pattern or network for systems) of relationships, obtaining between actors in their capacity of playing roles relative to one another". According to Ginsberg[3], the study of social structure is concerned with the principal forms of social organisations, such as, types of groups, associations and institutions and the complex of these, which constitute societies.

Radcliffe-Brown[4] contended that components of Social Structure are human beings, and a structure is an arrangement of persons in relationships institutionally defined and regulated. A most renown Sociologist, Radcliffe-Brown[5] in his Presidential address to the Royal Anthropological Institute said that he was branded as belonging to the 'Functional School of Social Anthropology' and even as being its leader, or one of the leaders.

Defending himself, he hastened to add that the 'Functional School' as such did not exist, it was a myth invented by Malinowski who claimed to have, to quote him, "... bestowed by myself, in a way on myself", and referring to Lowie who announced that Franz Boas was the leading exponent of 'Functionalism' in the 19th century, Radcliffe-Brown did not agree to it saying that it was purely of chronological order. He claimed that if that was to be so, he should be placed either as the follower of Boas or the predecessor of Malinawski. Thus he concluded that the statement that he was 'functionalist' was to convey no definite meaning.[6]

It is of great interest that while the academic world was wrecked with controversial opinions on the subject matter Radcliffe-Brown[7] added certain factors in his definition of 'Social Structure' in the said Presidential address to the effect that 'direct observation' had revealed that " ... human beings are connected in a complex network of social relations. I use the term 'Social Structure' to denote this network of actually existing relations."

The term 'Social Structure' is used by some social Anthropologists and sociologists to refer only to persistent social groups, such as nations, tribes and clans, which retain their continuity, their identity as individual groups, in spite of changes in their memberships. Evans-Pritchard in the NUER, preferred to use the term 'Social Structure' in this sense. Certainly the existence of such persistent social groups is an exceedingly important aspect of structure. But Radcliffe-Brown[8] thought that it is more useful to include a good deal more than this under the term. Indeed, all social relations of person to person have to be accepted as parts of Social Structure. The kinship structure of any society consists of a number of such dyadic relations, as between a father and son, or a mother's brother and his sister's son. During the course of my field work we observed that in the Mizo society, the whole social structure is based on a network of such relations of person to person established through kinship connections in hierarchical orders.

Brown[9] includes the differentiation of individual and of class by their roles in his re-considered version of definition of social structure. He is convinced while stating that the differential social positions of men and women, of chiefs and commoners, of employers and employees, are just as much determinants of social relations as belonging to different clans or different tribes. We find it truly applicable to the two social entities – the Mizos and the Meiteis – who have been part of our research and scrutiny.

In this study of Social Structures of the Meiteis and the Mizos the concrete reality is understandable through the customary laws. For this purpose, it is necessary to investigate between structures as an actually concrete reality and the structural forms may be made clearer perhaps by a consideration of the continuity of the past Social Structure through time, continuity of which is not static, but there is a dynamic continuity, like that of the organic structure of a living body. Social structures have been retained through strict regulation of norms and social values.

Parsons[10] defined Social Structure as a term applied to the particular arrangement of the inter-related institutions, agencies and social patterns as well as the statuses and roles which each person assumes in the group. Similarly, Johnson[11] has expressed that the structure of anything, even society, consists of the relatively stable inter-relationships among its parts and that the term 'part' itself implies a certain degree of stability. Since a social system is composed of inter-related acts of people, its structure must be sought in some degree of regularity or recurrence in these acts. And we would add that this stability emerges out of the customary roles and power structure in family, or society of states.

Likewise, MacIver and Page[12] contended that it is the various modes of grouping that together compose the complex pattern of power in any Social Structure. We feel that in the analysis of Social Structure the roles of diverse attitude and interest of social beings must be revealed. Social Structure is composed of several groups like family, clubs, class, caste, state, community, etc. It can be treated both as abstract and as real. The difference is only of perceptions.

Firth[13] contended that study of Life in a community means organisation of the interests of individuals, regulation of their behaviour towards one another, and grouping of them together for common action. This grouping of individuals and groups and their togetherness creates power and leads a direction of purpose of their existence for the achievement of specific goals. Once the goal is achieved the togetherness starts getting dissolved and gradually the force and the power fritters away unless some new nobler issues are brought to the force and a new beginning has to be made. Thus new roles are assumed and newer heights are achieved. This game of group power play continues unabated till the group subsumes a role of cult. The relationships thus created between them can be seen to have some kind of plan or system, which may be called the 'Social Structure'. The ways, in which the relationships actually work, affecting the lives of individuals and the nature of society may be called their 'Social Function'.

Social Structure of a community includes different types of groups, which the people form, and the institutions in which they take part. When it is said of an institution it means certain sets of relationships arising from the activities of groups of people with a social end to accomplish. The Social Structure, both in regard to groups and institutions is based upon definite principles, such as, sex, age, locality, kinship, etc. which are among the most fundamental of all human societies.[14]

From the above discussion certain postulates emerge as essential features on the subject matter,

— that Social Structure is an abstract and intangible phenomenon;

— that individuals are units of associations and institutions which are units of Social Structure;

— that these associations and institutions are inter-related in a particular arrangement and thus create the pattern of Social Structure;

— that it refers to the external aspect of society which is relatively stable as compared to functional or internal aspects of society; and

— that Social Structure is a 'living' structure which is created, maintained for a time and changed.

which we shall try to look for in our research on the two communities under our purview.

II

MEITEIS

There are three major ethnic groups in Manipur. They are the Meitei (Hindu, Muslim and Sanamahi), the Naga and the Chin-Kuki-Mizo Groups covered by the term 'Mizo' under the present study. While the Naga and the Chin-Kuki-Mizo autochthones make their abode in the hilly mountains, the centrally located amphitheatre-like Imphal valley covering around hardly one-tenths of the total areas of Manipur with a preponderant number of two-thirds of the total population of the State, is occupied by the Meiteis. They are all of Mongoloid racial traits with some elements of Aryan straints. Historical perspectives being witnesses they were greatly influenced in their independent growth and development in varying degrees of cultural advancement and civilization of which the 'Meiteis' have an overriding edge against the Nagas and Chin-Kuki-Mizo tribes. The Meitei society had gone far ahead in the processes of de-tribalisation that entered into formation of Meitei State ultimately through the evolution of Chiefdom.

Origin of the Meiteis is shrouded in mystery and is highly controversial and speculative due to influence of Hindu religious faith and political ideologies of modernism. Hodgson[15] was convinced to say that Meiteis belong to the Moi Section of the Tai race and interpreted the word 'Meitei' as a combination and Kochin-Chinese 'Moy'and of Siamese 'Tai'. The blending of 'Moy' and 'Tai' thus resulted to 'Moytai', subsequently in corrupted form as 'Moitai' which was eventually called 'Meitei'.

Hudson[16] said that it was a derivation from a combination of two words, 'Mei' meaning 'man' or 'people' and 'Tei' signifying 'different' or 'Separate'. When the two words are reduced into an appellation it is deduced to mean 'different or separate people'. As in contrast to this, local rendering of the word, 'Meitei', is attributed to the concept of creation theory of man after the image of God, creator of mankind and the universe. Thus when the words 'Mi' meaning 'image' and 'Tei' as 'modelled' are combined they carry ultimately a literal meaning of 'image modelled' in likeness of God. During the course of our field work we found a new interpretation of the word prevalent among the Andro group of people. They believe that the origin of the word lies at the historical differentiation between them and others who had settled down in the valley – 'Mei': people, 'ateis': other. The other people referring to the group of settlers, who came from different directions, got amalgamated and gradually settled down in the different parts of the valley. As for the Andros – they have remained settled on the eastern part of the Nongmaiching and the last over 1500 years. The evidence of fire temple and the partial archaeological excavations carried out in this part reveals a settled village economy in situ for a considerable number of years. Therefore, their reference to the valley people as 'others' is more acceptable since it is a factual referral point, there is no speculative aspect added to it.

Yet, there is another theory of origin of 'Meitei' which is most profusely propounded by its protagonists and equally opposed staunchly by its antagonists is concept of 'Aryan origin'. The Aryan connection received unqualified patronage of the ruling Royal Family of the valley during the 18th century subsequently inducing the people to believe so. This was direct and immediate impact of acceptance of Hinduism and claim of the descent by the ruling dynasty from Babruvahana, a scion of the Pandava hero, Arjuna, of the Mahabharata, said Kabui.[17] He further asserted that despite best efforts of the great Brahminic Scholars with unqualified support of the royalty and the ruling elite could not establish that the Meiteis were either an ethnic group or a language family of the Aryan or Indo-Aryan racial stock. But it is a fact indisputably that there is historical truth that the Meiteis did assimilate Aryan elements in its fold, or vice-versa as Srinivas, propounded his theory of Pan-Hinduism which, as an absorbing aspect of assimilating local elements into the Hindu fold, is the catholicity of Hinduism. Hence, it is found that among the Meiteis there are Aryan elements in their society today. Such elements are Aryan colonizers, adventurers and immigrants who either came to Manipur or passed through it in the course of their colonization of or trade with south west China and South-East Asia, for Manipur used to be the route for trade and migration in the past, though it is no longer as important in modern times. Such elements are today represented in the Social Structure of Meitei society by the Brahmins and the Nongchup Haram immigrants from mainland India sections of the Meiteis, known as 'miscegenation Meiteis' from which section might have originated the theory of Aryan origin among the Meiteis. It goes without saying that major chunk of the elite Meitei circle belongs to these elements. Aryans not as a race but ass a cultural group refined and substantially improved genetically spread over large part of the subcontinent who acculturised many ethnic communities of assorted kind.

In contrast to the concept of 'Nongchup Haram' there emerged another theory of 'Nongpok Haram'[18] immigrants from the east, with which the Mon-Khmer and the Tai connections were established as evidenced from the Archeological excavations in recent times at Tharon cave in Tamenglong district. Existence of this element is believed to have taken its historical roots before Tibeto-Burman linguistic groups landed in Manipur and were amalgamated into various Meitei clan genealogies called 'Salais' and so also given due places into several lineages called 'Sageis' since the eighth century, more profusely in the fifteenth century and ultimately included the Hindu Gotras, when Hinduism was embraced as State religion. Such processes of assimilation were well recorded in the chronicles of Manipur[19]. These immigrants constitute the 'Nongpok Haram' in the hierarchical order of Meitei social structure.

The other element that impacted the Meitei Societal complex is the Tibeto-Burman racial trait. Grierson[20] attributed the Kuki-Chin (Mizo), Naga and Meitei as being of this linguistic group and included them in the sub-family of the Tibeto-Burman languages which he called as Kuki-Chin group. He however thought that the term was not very appropriate. It should have better been called Meitei-Chin linguistic group so that its coverage could be more specific and precise by sub-dividing them into Meitei on the one hand and the various tribes which were known under the names of Kuki and Chin on the other. However, he reconciled to the appellation of Chin-Kuki Group on the ground that there was no other proper name comprising all 'these tribes'. Chatterjee[21] was of strong view to identify this group of people with that of the Kiratas of the later Vedas and conjectured that these people must have settled together in the eastern region of India sometime in the beginning of the first millennium before Christ.

Thus the Kuki-Chin sub-family groups of Tibeto-Burman family and the Kirata connection theories have brought the indigenous ethnic groups of Meitei, Naga and Chin-Kuki-Mizo closer to each other. In this regard McCulloch[22] becomes closely relevant once again. In his search for the origin of Meiteis he was convinced to say that historically the valley of Imphal was once occupied by seven clans or Salai structure, such as Ningthouja, Luwang, Khuman, Angom, Moirang, Khaba-Nganba and Chenglei, which was also subscribed by Hudson.[23] Of these seven 'Salais', Meitei became more powerful and ultimately all of the seven 'Salais'amalgamated and accepted the name 'Meitei' as their common nomenclature.

McCulloch asserted that the Khumans came from the East where the Marings lived, the Meiteis and the Luwangs from the North-West where the Kabuis inhabited and the Moirangs from the south where the Kukis lived. By this, he established close relationship between the Meiteis and the hill tribes. Each of these clans is called 'Salai', and these seven 'Salais' are divided into a number of lineages called 'Sageis'. The origin as to how and when these seven 'Salais' came into being is shrouded in mystery. Each 'Salai' has a number of 'Sageis' or 'Yumnaks' and each 'Sagei' in turn is composed of several families. Unlike the Thadous, Lushais and Hmar whose 'Salais' and 'Sageis' are personal names of the founding progenitors, it is not so in the case of 'Meitei'. The 'Salais' and 'Sageis' are "... named after their trades or occupations, place of habitations, etc." said, Manikchand.[24]

According to Hudson[25], the number of 'Sagei' or 'Yumnak' of each 'Salai' varies as are found vide Appendix I pp.184-187 of his book, the Meitheis.

The number of Sageis as indicated in figures by Manikchand[26] is 465. Thus, there is a discrepancy in the total number of Sagei's as given by him with that of Hudson, numbering 448. These two total figures need to be checkmated and reconciled so as to establish the correct number of Sageis that actually constitute the Meitei Social Structure. However, as it stands now, since there is no detailed 'Sagei' list made available by Manikchand so as to authenticate the total figure of Sageis that he gave, obviously, detailed Sagei list as shown hereinabove are assumed as the valid number of Sageis. Therefore, for better clarity and verification number of sageis for each salai as given by Manikchand is shown hereinbelow:

Sl.No.	*'Salai'*	*No. of*	*'Sagei' (Yumnak)*
1.	Ningthouja, the . ruling Salai	—	125 (including Kanghujam, the lone Sagei of Ningthouja Ariba)
2.	Luwang	—	58
3.	Khuman	—	67
4.	Angom	—	62
5.	Moirang	—	67
6.	Khaba-Nganba	—	21
7.	Chenglei, Sarang Leishangthem	—	35

And, according to him there are altogether 465 Sageis of the original 'Meiteis' belonging to the seven salais. The founder of each Salai, progenitors, are as given below:

Sl.No.	*'Salai'*	*Name of Progenitors*
8.	Ningthouja	Nongda Lairen Pakhangba
9.	Angom	Pureiromba
10.	Moirang	Nganghunthok and Ngangningshing
11.	Khaba-Nganba	Thongaren
12.	Chenglei	Nungon Yumthangba
13.	Khuman and Luwang	Poireiton, a contemporary of Pakhangba.

It is a fact well known today that historically the nomenclature, 'Meitei', was for the first time used during the period of Ningthouja dynasty, when Nongda Lairen Pakhangba[27] assumed the seat of authority and wielded supreme powers within the realm of suzerainty of his dynasty with a view to consolidating unity and integrity of heterogeneous ethnic groups on a solid social structure, politically viable and socially vibrant with dynamism, further contended that there were two popular myths created in the 17th and the 18th centuries in order to explain origin of the seven clans,[28] while one myth was associated with the legends of 'Sanamahi' and 'Pakhangba' who were the two sons of a primordial father, Guru; shown in the form of a cattle in order to make them understand the 'creator', the other myth was concerned with the creation of seven clans, each clan representing limbs of the 'Guru',[29] within seven days so as to mystify origin of the clans which was proved otherwise with the historical evidences of existence of various ethnic groups with multiple heterogeneity that were found to have laid their footprints on the sands of time of Imphal Valley with diverse legendary backgrounds as against the existing Customary Law which prohibits marriage within the same clan. Members thereof constitute exogamous group.

III

MIZOS

We know that each kinship system, which is generally the base of Social Structure in a society, provides a set of dyadic relationships to each person so that he stands at the centre of a narrower or wider circle of relatives. During his lifetime the body of his relatives is constantly changing by deaths and births and by his marriage and the marriages of his relatives. These relationships, as we have argued earlier, place him in a role of increasing power to the benefit of his family and its positioning society.

The Mizos are divided into clans or sub-clans which are again divided into lineages. A lineage of any considerable size is further divided into branches, which are themselves smaller lineages and these are again sub-divided. For Structures having successive segmentations the term 'Polysegmentary' has been suggested. In other words, such a social structure is called 'Segmentary' type, which is very much prevalent among the Mizo Society.

For understanding Mizo Society, Social Structures of Thadou, Lushai and Hmar who are the dominant constituent groups with certain peculiar characteristics of their own representing the Mizos is necessary. Our research shows that unlike the Meiteis, the Mizo Clan system provides division into a number of distinct and separate groups, each having its own identity, such as, Thadou, Lushai, Hmar, Paite, Gangte, Vaiphei, Zou, Simte, etc. They all form the group which is 'Khul' or 'Khur' or 'Chhenlung' or 'Sinlung' origin. These several clans thus play important roles in the formation of the customary laws that govern their social, political and religious life.

It is true that there are numerous tribal groups under the 'Mizo' nomenclature and there is lot of reciprocity among them. Our research shows that the fundamental elements that constitute their Social Structures remain the same. Among these tribal groups patrilineal descent is observable in their society with segmental kinship system. We have observed that it is found existing to the minutest possible extent of clans, sub-clans, lineages, sub-lineages, etc in such a manner that every man and woman whether educated or not, is made conscious of his or her being a member of that particular group or clan or lineage within which he or she happens to be born. Such mentality having been developed with their accident of birth in a clan or lineage, they are idiosyncratic that every man and woman is obsessed with clannish hegemony that breeds parochialism in their outlook and approach, with abysmal narrow mindedness. Added to this, nomenclatures of all lineages, clans, sub-clans are personal names of the founding ancestors. Because of these factors, the disputes, such as, seniority issue between Doungel and his younger brothers erupted in their cordial relationship, tension and hostility prevailed with extreme antagonistic feelings against each other despite claiming themselves as close consanguineous relatives.

Before going to the specific problems of structural functioning of the Thadou Society, certain basic knowledge on their social structure need to be understood. As McCulloch[30] observed, the Thadous, and for that matter most of the Mizos, customarily pay much respect to their senior lineal descents, in token expression of which they present to the Chiefs of their particular branches one tusk of each elephant they may capture or kill, these chiefs again gave presents to their superior. They also pay, in bounden duty, 'Sating'[31], the topmost flesh portion of an animal captured or killed, that runs along the backbone as tribute, annually to their respective seniormost clan-head.

Their attention to genealogy, the distinction of clans, and the respect paid to their seniors are conspicuously made manifest in their day to day life-style. Out of these customary regulations may have sprung the only exclusiveness shown by the Thadous as to who would be entitled to use his 'comb' and 'whose comb' he might use. This is a very important matter among them. There is no religious 'importance' attached to it, but there is 'an indication of the superior status in respect of descent' or 'by connection of the estimation in which an individual is held' or 'holds himself' to be found in the persons to whom he would refuse his comb, or among whom his comb is common. It is also a fact that Thadous are very particular as to who is entitled to use whose comb and that social precedence among them may be tested by this. It is a significant customary law in order to maintain purity, sanctity and status of the family.

The Thempu, village priest, presents a newly married couple a comb each that man and wife only may use the same comb. As a matter of fact, Thadous believe and practice purity of comb and this is one of the peculiarities with which custom and tradition, the status and standing of a man in the social hierarchy is determined. The Changsan, Thangum or Lhangum clans which do not belong to the Thadou group claim themselves as belonging to some ancient races who were in existence before the former arrived on the earth's surface. They do not pay '*Sating*' to any Thadou groups. Thus, considering the Changsans as a people of respectable tribe the Sitlhou Thadous take women from them for wives, as was the case with the Meiteis and the Angoms.

Similarly, in much the same manner as Thadous are distinct from Changsans and Lhangums, so are the Changsans from Lhangums and vice-versa. Thadous are divided into eight main clans, such as, *Doungel, Sitlhou, Singson, Kipgen, Haokip, Chongloi, Hangsing and Touthang* bearing the names of their respective progenitors who are descended from their primogenitor ancestor called CHONGTHU, the genealogy of the clans reveal the customary respect which is mandatory from the individual members of the clan. There are many more sub-clans divided further from each of the eight clans, details of which are given in the Tabular form. Customarily they all bear testimony and allegiance to their clans, which bear the names of their progenitors. Above all these, interest, care, attention and regard given to their genealogy among the

Thadous is indeed amazing. This is very similar to what the Manipuris provide in every family a *'Mei-hou-rol'* or genealogical tree, such as, 'Salai' and 'Sagei', which appears a coincidence of custom worthy of notice. So the customary tradition of maintaining an acceptable and socially cognizable list of ancestors needed to be maintained in the past and it continues even today. It points towards a common tradition and origin though the take off stage in either case may have been differed for these practices. A closer investigation has to more similarities between them rather than dissimilarities.

Our research has helped in understanding the complex in-house structure of the several Kuki groups which comprise the nomenclature of the Mizos on the basis of customary laws. A critical study of certain specific cases has been made subsequently which throw much light on the common origin of their group of people.

Thadous

Herein we have attempted to look into some of the controversial issues which have remained problematic in the several Thadou groups due to maladjustment within the structural framework of their society and as also for sidelining the importance of applied customary laws.

McCulloch[32] did a meticulous study on the Social Structure of the Thadous which was published in the Journal of Asiatic Society of Bengal as far back as 1857 commencing from their primogenitor CHONGTHU to THADOU as shown in the tabular form below:

THE HOUSE OF CHONGTHU*

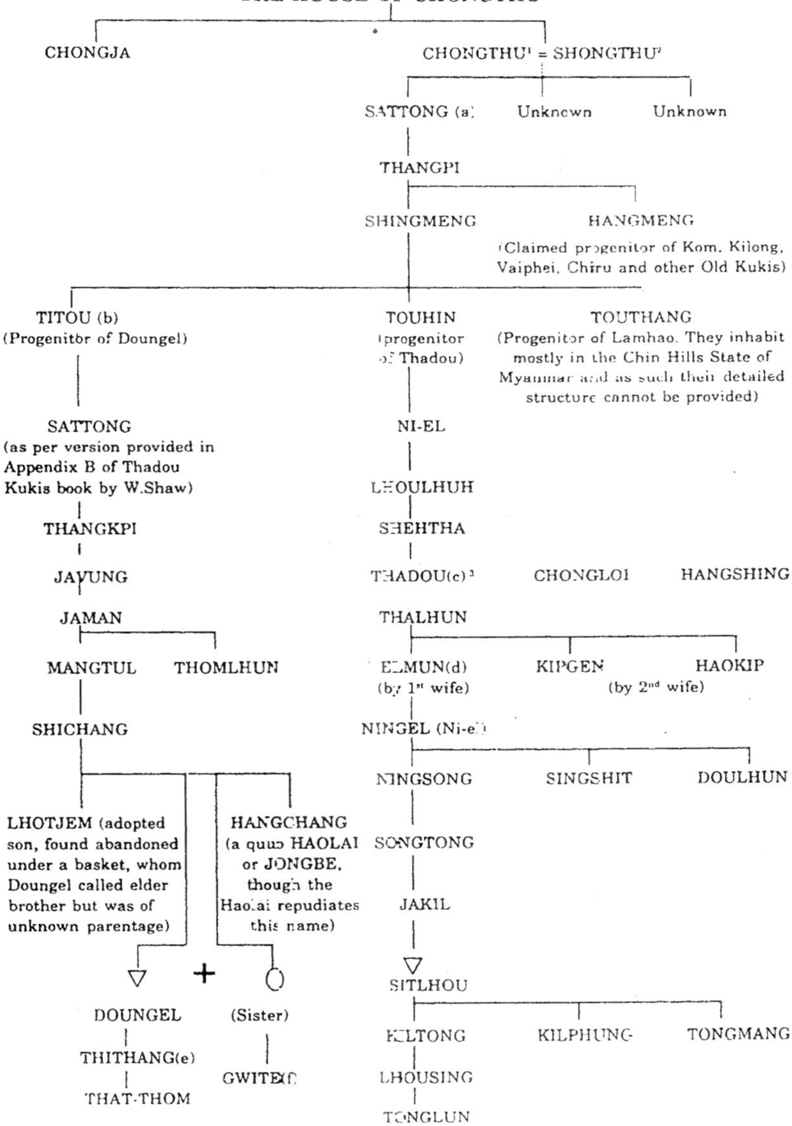

***Sources:** *Contd. to next page*

1. Wiliam Shaw: Notes on the Thadou Kukis, 1928, p.27 from Chongthu to Thadou
2. J.H. Hutton: Thadou Kukis, 1928, Appendix II from Shongthu to Chengjapao.
3. W. McCulloch: The Valley of Manipur: 1857: Appendix II, p.II – III from Thadou to Khotinthang

Continuation of House of CHONGTHU:

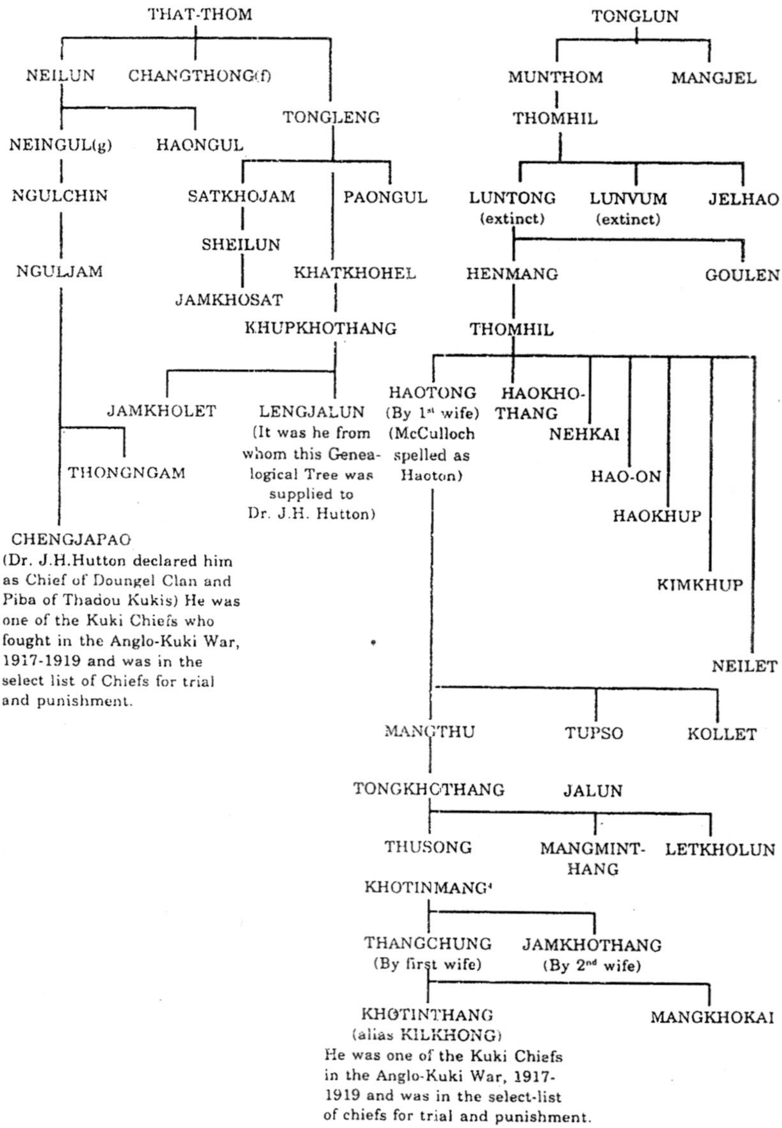

Source: 4 *William Shaw: The Thadou Kukis: 1929; p.33 from Khotinmang (Khodingmang) to Khotinthang.*

As has been indicated above that certain explanatory notes are to be highlighted on controversial issues, it is necessary that remarks (a), (b), (c) and (d) given above have to be taken up one issue after another that have given rise due to deviant behaviourial attitude against age-old rules as laid down by the customary laws. To begin with, the controversies relating to Sattong are taken up first.

(a) According to Shaw[33] as shown in his explanatory foot-note(a) of the genealogical tree from Chongthu to Thadou, he showed Sattong to have married Sheichin, a woman of Vanlai Village, which means the Village in heavenly abode. There were two other brothers of Sattong but their names have been forgotten as they went east and west and have not been heard of since. In his explanatory note(b), Hangmeng, the younger grandson of Sattong, was reportedly to have been confirmed by some Koms and others as their progenitor and further stated in his foot-note(c) that Titou was progenitor of the Doungel.

(b) Now, as customary laws of inheritance and succession, the Thadous give exclusive rights to the eldest son, Doungel being the eldest of the three sons, the genealogical tree of the Thadous has to be counted on the direct line of Titou whose descendants have now assumed the name of Doungel as their common appellation.

Shaw mentioned that pedigree of the Doungel is said to having not been accepted by the Thadous of other clans as the lineage had become extinct, "*Ingam*", in the true line and is now represented by the descendants of a slave. This controversy over the issue first started in the generation of Doungel himself, though not exposed openly, it remained latently current and contained explosive and potentially destructive traits.

This contention was not accepted by Hutton[34] who had refuted vehemently (after a lapse of sixty-one years) in 1928 when he made a review of what McCulloch had published in 1857.[35] While endorsing the truth of structural order from Chongthu to Thadou, he was sceptical to the alleged extinction of direct line of Doungel clan. In doing so he was vocal to say that he found the 'extinct' theory impossible to accept and alleged that it arose solely from the arrogant vapourings of Khotinthang alias Kilkhong, Chief of Jampi, a Sitlhou village, who as head of the Sitlhou clan would be Chief of all the Thadous if the Doungel clan were really extinct. No doubt, Hutton[36] contended the fact that Thadou himself, though a member of the cadet branch, has given his name to the whole tribe, has influenced others to this extravagant claim, but it is quite unacceptable. Hutton took the trouble of explaining his contention to the effect that even if the claim of head of the Doungel clan to an unblemished descent be rejected, there are plenty of Cousins whose family tree is unquestioned, not to mention Thomlhun and Haolái clans, both senior in descent in supersession to the Sitlhous and with unimpeachable pedigrees. It is unlikely, however, that there is any BONAFIDE DOUBT ABOUT THE LEGITIMACY OF Chengjapao's descent from Doungel, as otherwise the Cousins who reinstated Neigul's son Ngulchin would have claimed the Chieftainship for themselves.

In order to justify his stand, Hutton[37] provided the genealogical tree of the House of Doungel[38] and gave his verdict on the issue as found in the Journal of Asiatic Society of Bengal stating that pedigree of the Doungel had been so much pother about the illegitimacy of the line that represented Doungel.

He further contended to say that the theory of 'extinct',

INGAM, appeared to be based on the scandal caused by Neingul's marriage, and perhaps on doubts as to the real parentage of Ngulchin, but seemed really to arise from the arrogance of Khotinthang, Chief of Jampi Village, who probably really claimed precedence rather as the head of the lineal descendant of Thadou, which he was, than in any bonafide belief that the elder line was extinct. They were far from that, and if the Lotjems and the Guites were excluded, there were still members of the Thomlhun and Haolai clans with pedigrees every bit as genuine as Khotinthang's if less distinguished.

At this stage Hutton added to say that all these Doungel clans, however, are smaller numerically and poorer in possessions then their collaterals descended from Thadou and further stated that there was a story that Doungel had connection with a female Serow which he had caught in a snare. He let her go and the boy-child seen later with a Serow in the jungle and ultimately recovered was loved by his father and called 'Lushei' (a. lu, lun = much cherished), and from him were descended the Lushei tribes. The word 'Lushei' had ultimately been corrupted and later given a twisted spelling form as 'Lushai', which had become the generic name of the people who are now called 'Mizo'(Dulian speaking group).

It is difficult to correctly surmise as to what did Hutton actually wish to articulate out of this piece of legend, if not a myth, rather than a story. If we analyse his attribute of smaller numerical strength and poverty of Doungel clans than Thadou and the myth of 'Lushei' origin that he highlighted appear that it is an attempt to establish the blood relationship or consanguiuous relationship of 'Lusheis' with the 'Doungels', the combination of which preponderates over the Thadou clans. Be it as it may. Such conceptual postulate makes our research work on a much more stronger foundation that strengthens our efforts to synthesize our research findings that establish commonality in origin of the customary laws of the Mizos and their similarities or otherwise with that of the Meiteis.

And, in order to justify his decision and stand on the issue, he said that as per structural functioning of the Thadous Society "The Shithlo Chief, who contested the headship recently, used himself to pay 'Sathing' (sating is the correct spelling) to Chengjapao till 1918 and on taking the case into court in Manipur in 1928 had his claim to seniority laughed out at Court".

(c) In this connection, it is incumbent to recall the fact that as per findings of Shaw,[39] the progenitors of Doungel, Thadou and Lamhao (Touthang) are the three sons of Shingmeng whose names are respectively Titou, Touhin and Touthang. And, according to their custom the senior man called 'Upa' is given 'Sating', annual tribute of payment in recognition of being senior, by the younger brothers in hierarchical orders in the form of topmost portion of the flesh of animal that runs along the spinal cord (backbone). Now, therefore, in the present case of the three brothers, Doungel being the eldest of them, Thadou, the second brother, has to pay his 'Sating' to Doungel. Likewise, Lamhao alias Touthang being the third and youngest brother has to pay his 'Sating' to Thadou, his immediate senior. Touthang cannot have direct excess to pay to Doungel by-passing Thadou. It is breach of custom or structural order. Knowing this well, Hutton said that Kilkhong, Chief of Jampi, head of the Sitlhou clan of Thadous, " ... used to pay 'Sathing' (Sating) to Chengjapao until Kuki Rebellion (Anglo-Kuki War)", and further contended that the ground on which he alleged the line of Doungel having been 'extinct' was presumably due to that of Neingul's 'Misalliance', marrying a girl of inferior status belonging to Sheitul Village where he remained in shame. Hutton further argued that even if this were a legitimate ground, Chengjapao's descendants belonging to his cousins would have a prior claim to Kilkhong's, not to mention Chungul, Chief of Haolai Clan at that relevant point of time, as well as the head of the Thomlhun family, if the Guite, born of illicit relation with his sister, would be ruled out.

Hutton also sought opinion of former President of Manipur State Darbar, Duncan[40], and a senior member of the Assam Civil Service Cadre who had long experiences of administration as Sub-Divisional Officer among the Thadous gaining proficiency on customary laws of the Thadous and acquiring 'speaking knowledge' of their language for which he was given reward of extra-remuneration by the Government.

Counselling, Duncan offered was that the allegation that the Doungel line was 'extinct', INGAM, was based on a story that Doungel died without a legitimate issue and had omitted or deliberately not nominated to recognise his illegitimate offspring, Guite, and that Thadou was entitled to inherit under the circumstance, but refused his inheritance, which passed by default to a slave. Here, there are two elements of great importance to be taken into account. Duncan impliedly did not deny the theory of 'extinct' and gave ample indication that despite legitimate entitlement to the House of Doungel, refusal to assume so, on the part of Kilkhong, confirmed that law of inheritance had been defiled or contaminated that was passed by default to a slave.

Despite this, Hutton insisted that he suspected the INGAM theory to be of a recent invention of the Sitlhou and that the Lotjem claim of seniority to the Doungel clan in Court in 1928 on the ground that Doungel addressed their ancestor "elder brother" that was proved a failure, were evidences that supported the Doungel contention.

Hutton further gave a separate genealogical tree of Haolai as supplied by one Ehpu,[41] a minor chief of the Haolai family who was reportedly much concerned lest incorrect information be fed in by other informants. Ehpu was stated to have gone very far in his cups at the time of supplying the Haolai family structure and that Hutton did not have the opportunity to discuss whether he held to his version when sober.

It can be observed that the number of generation from Chongthu to Doungel was the same in each case, and many of the names were identical with the one constructed by McCulloch though not in the same order. The discrepancy was probably such as must inevitably arise between two versions of an account preserved only by oral tradition. It could also be observed that Ehpu's version agreed closely with that of the Sitlhou, who, however, made Hangmeng, the younger brother of Shingmeng the ancestor of Kom and other Old Kukis.

Yet, Hutton declared that Chengjapao, Chief of Aishan Village and head of Doungel clan as not only the most legitimate chief to the Doungel clan but also, to use his own rendering, "Head of the Thadou".[42]

It appears that the argument advanced by Hutton was entirely based on the question of seniority in lineal descent in the structural hierarchical order, sidelining the ground reality of dispute as to the issue of recognition and legitimacy over inheritance in terms of customary law. Duncan has rightly pointed out this fact. It must also be borne in mind that Thadou has not been Hutton further gave a separate genealogical tree of Haolai as supplied by one Ehpu,[41] a minor chief of the Haolai family who was reportedly much concerned lest incorrect information be fed in by other informants. Ehpu was stated to have gone very far in his cups at the time of supplying the Haolai family structure and that Hutton did not have the opportunity to discuss whether he held to his version when sober.

It can be observed that the number of generation from Chongthu to Doungel was the same in each case, and many of the names were identical with the one constructed by McCulloch though not in the same order. The discrepancy was probably such as must inevitably arise between two versions of an account preserved only by oral tradition. It could also be observed that Ehpu's version agreed closely with that of the Sitlhou, who, however, made Hangmeng, the younger brother of Shingmeng the ancestor of Kom and other Old Kukis.

Yet, Hutton declared that Chengjapao, Chief of Aishan Village and head of Doungel clan as not only the most legitimate chief to the Doungel clan but also, to use his own rendering, "Head of the Thadou".[42]

It appears that the argument advanced by Hutton was entirely based on the question of seniority in lineal descent in the structural hierarchical order, sidelining the ground reality of dispute as to the issue of recognition and legitimacy over inheritance in terms of customary law. Duncan has rightly pointed out this fact. It must also be borne in mind that Thadou has not been heard of an instance to have claimed precedence over his elder brother, Doungel. Our research shows that things have been twisted to build up more antagonism among the collateral cousins.

The controversy thus created between the descendants of Thadou and Doungel that raised its ugly head since the 18th century regarding unblemished pedigree of Doungel persists till today. Yet, it is interesting to note that in the midst of such controversial issue prevailing, certain junior clans of Thadou add more contradicting and complex problems. As a matter of fact, since Guite was born out of illicit relation of Doungel with his sister, he was rejected and as per Customary Law was not in the line of Doungel family. He was given treatment of a 'bastard' all the while.

Surprisingly, now different junior clans of Thadou such as, Kipgen, Haokip, Touthang, etc. have in recent past started payment of their annual tribute, 'Sating' to Guite by-passing Sitlhou and Doungel. This has heightened the tension that has been in existence between the seniormost and the second seniormost clans of the Thadou. It has promoted doubly the spirit of inter-clan rivalry and clannish hegemony among themselves that has rocked their relationship and unity. Things have been blown out of proportion.

Notwithstanding, it is incumbent that the status of Thadou in their structural hierarchy needs to be thoroughly brought to light, particularly in relation to certain values attached to social behaviours and attitudes. Based on the findings of McCulloch, Edward Tuite Dalton[43] described importance of 'comb' so as to make manifest of the value and status of person possessing and owning it. He said combs are very sacred things to the Thadous. It is very unlucky to lose them, and man and wife may use the same comb. When a man dies, the comb is buried with him and his near relatives break their combs and must go about with disheveled hair for a few days before they renew them. Value attached to such insignificant or minor aspect of life simply manifests the conservative and orthodox nature of the Thadous and rigidity or inflexibility of their custom and traditional heritage needs hardly be emphasised. Such sensitive issue as the dispute being discussed must on no account, therefore, escape serious consideration and cautious dealings.

Taking advantage of the situation certain sections of the Mizo tribes who are non-Thadou try to tease away some junior Thado clans from the fold of Thadou on the ground that they do not belong to the Thadou group, not being direct descendants of Thadou. Such junior clans thus won over are factions of Chongloi and Hangshing clans. These two clans are the younger brothers of Thadou. This campaign of disintegrating the Thadous can be observed being initiated by the non-Thadous who do not claim to belong to the descendants of CHONGTHU but were practically absorbed among the Thadous. In this regard, Shakespear[44] as an authority on Mizos (Lushai-Kuki-Chin groups) becomes very relevant who, convincingly through practical experience and thorough study said, "After many enquiries I am of the same opinion and have found pedigrees collected from various sources differ by slightly from that recorded by colonel McCulloch" and further stated, -

> "The main families of Thado are the Doungel, Shithloh (Sitlhou), (Singsit), Haokip, Kipgen, (Chongloi and Hangshing). The Doungel are descended from Thado's elder brother and therefore are considered as rather superior to the rest of the families".

(i) Shakespear further contended that the reason why Thadous have not been known by the name of Doungel was that *Thadou was a far greater warrior* and *killed more men*, that *Thadou was great in council and war* and that he retrieved the fortunes of the family, and *hence his name* has been adopted by them. Thus Thadou remains as the true clan name while Doungel, Sitlhou, Singson, Kipgen, Haokip, Chongloi, Hangshing and Touthang are the names of families which are further sub-divided as among the Lushais, into branches mostly named anonymously.[45]

(ii) Shakespear[46] also asserted that among the Thadous are found remnants of many other clans, which have been practically *absorbed*, having *adopted* not only *Thadou culture, customs and language but also their customary laws*. They are Lianthang (Lenthang) and his brother Thlangum (Lhangum) and Lunkim and his brother Changsan. The Changsans are sub-divided into eight families and are considered a clan of some standing, as is shown by the fact that Sitlhous would take wives only from Sitlhou and Changsan households.

(iii) Shakespear[47] further claimed that being derived by people themselves the following clans not descended from the 'bowel of the earth' or theory of 'Cave Origin' after the Thimzing episode have now to all intents and purposes been called Thadou. Most of them have also adopted the 'Sakhua' (religion) or domestic sacrificial rites of whichever family of the Thadou clan they have attached themselves to. Such clans are:

(1) Kulho, (2) Shongte, (3) Kullou, (4) Thangneo (Thangngeo),

(5) Han-ngang, (6) Hen-ngang, (7) Thangching (Thangjing)

Shongte and Kullou are reportedly brothers, the

former being the elder. They claimed to have emerged from Khulpi (Khul). Kulhou, Thangeo and Han-ngang are sons of Shongte. Shakespear further asserted that the name of Thadou was derived by the people themselves from the word "That", to kill and "dho" to war and that the term New Kuki which appeared so often in the records of Cachar and Sylhet in the middle of 19th Century and which had been adopted by Grierson in the Linguistic Survey of India might be taken as synonymous with Thadou.

(d) The question of Elmun is another controversial contentious issue which attempted to undermine Customary Law. Elmun is the son of Thalhun by *his first wife*. On the untimely demise of his wife, he had a *concubine* who begot Kipgen and Haokip as twin brothers. The eldest of the three brothers was Elmun whose descendants are in the direct line of seniormost Thadou clan now named as Sitlhou.

The oral tradition which has become a living legend in the backdrop of which it is believed to have unfortunately so happened that the first wife of Thalhun, the mother of Elmun died by accident in the hands of her husband. Thalhun out of shame and guilt fled his village leaving his infant son an orphan who was looked after by his two uncles, Chongloi and Hangshing. Meantime, Thalhun took a concubine, from the place where he took shelter, who gave birth to a twin, Kipgen and Haokip.[48]

After a few years, his son, Elmun, grew up and was able to look after the cattle and goat of the family, the two uncles of the boy considered necessary that their elder brother, Thalhun, should return to the village so as to look after the administration, the welfare of the villagers and his son before he attained adolescence. Thalhun, in compliance with the request of his brothers, returned to his village bringing his elder twin, Kipgen, along with him, leaving Haokip, the younger one, behind with his concubine. As per customary laws, however, Thalhun and Kipgen were not allowed to enter the house of the Chief of the village from where he killed his wife by accident and thus were made to live in a hut constructed at the outskirt of the village. Another significant action taken against Thalhun as laid down by the customary laws was that his name was *deleted* from the *genealogical tree* and *not counted* in the list of Chiefs enumerated at the time of religious rituals performed by the 'Thiempu', the Village priest, said Thangkhosei Chongloi, Chief of Khengjang Village and so also Haokhosei, Ex-Chairman, Kaithelmanbi Military Colony Village Authority.

It is interesting to note that there appeared, of late, a new version regarding existence of Elmun. A new version runs to the effect that being left behind at a very infant age by his mother, being deprived of the warmth and breast-feeding of a mother, Elmun suffered all kinds of diseases for which he expired.

On his return home, Thalhun was said to have *married another wife* as *arranged by* his two younger brothers and elders of *the Village Council* known as Semang-Pachong or Upa, who gave birth to a son whose *name was again given Elmun*. Now, this boy named as second Elmun is younger in age to his step brothers, Kipgen and Haokip. Therefore, Kipgen, the elder twin, should be in the direct line of Thadou occupying the seat of seniormost Thadou clan. This contention raised the eyebrows of elders and authorities or custodians of customary laws. As per customary law either the original Elmun if alive at all or the second

Elmun in the event of the alibi of second Elmun myth being afloat has slightest element of truth and an iota of ingenuity in the eye of Thadou customary laws who was born out of proper wedlock with the consent and knowledge of upholders of customary laws should always take precedence, being *born in the 'Khunpi'*, *'main-bed'*, the only *marital 'bed'* that *receive cognizance* within the *framework of customary laws*, meaning thereby *legally recognised 'bed'* for a married couple, over all other sibbings irrespective of age. The controversy thus created has added to the fragmentation among the Thadous out of all proportions.

It has to be brought home of the fact that in token expression of recognition and allegiance to one's own elder kindred, the junior kinsmen pay 'sating' annually to the former strictly on clan hierarchical order. Here, annual tribute payment of 'Sating' to senior clansmen is very significant as per customary laws. It cannot be paid at random by any person to senior clansmen as one wishes to do so. Hierarchical clan order of the genealogical tree of one's pedigree has to be religiously observed with reverential obeisance to customary laws.

Hutton in the Appendix B on the work of William Shaw on "The Thadou Kukis' gave a genealogical tree of the Doungel clan at pages 137-139. Therein he showed Doungel as the second son of the three sons and one daughter of Thithang and further showed Doungel as to have an illicit relation with his own sister who gave birth to Gwite.

In her effort to cover up her shame, Doungel's mother named the baby boy as Gwite which Hutton described, "So named after the sunlight, as his mother to cover her shame, pretended that her child was born from one of two eggs she had kept in a paddy bin where a ray of sunlight fell on them through a hole in the matting. It is, of course, only the Gwite who descend from Doungel (Dongngel) by his sister. Thithang was the son of a regular wife.

He ran away to Sheitul with a girl of inferior status and remained there in shame on account of his misalliance. His heritage was claimed by Haongul but the cousins objected and went to Sheitul and fetched back Neingul's son, Ngulchin,to succeed Neilun.

LUSHAIS

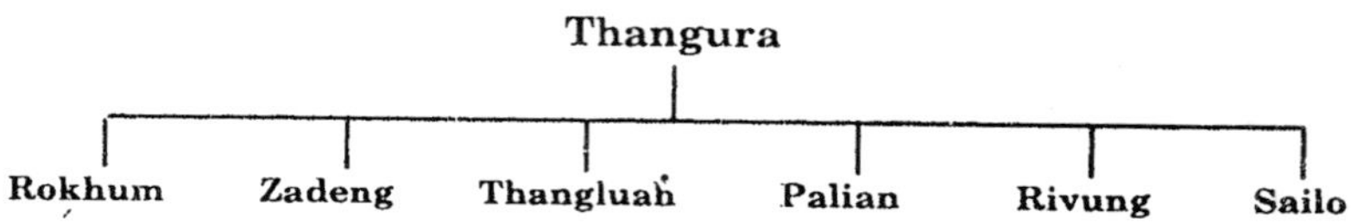

The Lushais in common with the Thadous and other Kuki-tribes, attach importance to their genealogies. And pedigrees, given at an interval of many years, and by persons living far apart, have been found to agree in a wonderful manner. From comparison of these genealogies and from careful enquiries lasting over many years, it is estimated that Thangura must have lived early in the eighteenth century. His first village is said to have been at Thangkua, north of Falam. From his lines sprung six chiefs[49], such as, 1) Rokhum, 2) Zadeng, 3)-Thangluah, 4) Palian, 5)Rivung and 6) Sailo.

There is no doubt that the Kukis, Chins and Lushais are all of the same race. There are reliable traces that the Lushais, the Kabuis and the Meiteis also are related. Playfair, in his account of the Garos pointed out many ways in which the said people resemble the Nagas. But Shakespear found that Garos also resemble very much with Lushais, Kukis and Chins. Yet Sir Charles Lyall found evidences of connection between Mikirs and the Kuki-chin-Lushai groups also. Thus said Shakespear that the term Kuki, like Naga, Chin, Shendu, and many others, is not recognised by the people to whom the British apply, yet, it has come to have a fairly definite meaning with which it has been understood to mean certain closely allied clans with well marked characteristics, belonging to the Tibeto-Burman stock. On the Chittagong border the term is loosely used to most of the inhabitants of the interior hills beyond the Chittagong Hill tracts. Likewise, in Cachar the term Kuki generally means some family of the Thadou or Khaotlang Clan, nowadays more popularly known as Hmar, though Khawtlang or Khcchung is very much current among the people themselves, locally distinguished as New and Old Kukis. In Mizoram nowadays it is hardly ever used having been superseded by Lushai, which also is ultimately replaced now by the term Mizo. In the Chin Hills and generally on the Myanmar border all these clans are called Chin.

The term Lushai now covers many clans,. It is the result of incorrect transliteration of the word 'Lushei'which is the name of the clan. It came to be used prominently in the 18th century and was responsible for the eruption into Cachar of Old Kukis at the end of that century and of the new Kukis half a century later.

The 'Lusheis' did not eject all the clans they came into contact with. They absorbed many of such clans among them who now constitute bulk of the subjects of the Thangur chiefs. Thus while 'Lushai' is used in this wider sense, 'Lushei' is used only for the clan of that name. Among the people themselves the 'Lusheis' are spoken of as 'Dulian' and the general population of the erstwhile Lushai Hills was spoken of as 'Mizo'. Thus Lushai Society has an organized base of 14 structures. They are called 'Family' with 'branches' similar to clans and lineages respectively. They are[50]:-

1. THANGURA the primogenitor of Lushei clan who begets six sons named as[51]:

(1) Rokhum, (2) Zadeng, (3) Thangluah
(4) Palian (5) Rivung, and (6) Sailo

All the Lushai chiefs of the present time belong to one of these branches which have become to be known as clans. These six brother chiefs have been added by one (7) Chenkhual. He is said to be a brother of Sailo probably a son of a concubine of Thangura, the ancestor of the 'Lusheis'. Chenkhuals had once independent villages, but are no longer looked on as chiefs.

1. PACHAO begets seven sons named as[52] –

(1) Charlal	(2) Chiawthliak	(3) Chhoalak
(4) Chonglal	(5) Darchao	(6) Lalbawm
(7) Lianthung		

The family of Pachuao as a clan name is said to be descended from the illegitimate son of Zadenga. Many heroes of whose prowess tales are current in the folk-lores of the Lushais, and their names appear among the branch names. They are[53] –

1) Durchaova, 2) Charlalla, 3) Lianthunga and 4) Lianghora.

In the family of Pachuao, three more branches sprung up believed to be from Vanpuia.[54] The branches are –

1) Liannghor, 2) Vanpuia-hrin, 3) Varchuan

3. CHANGTE: The Changte[55] clan has nine branches whose names are

   1) Darchun, 2) Pamte, 3) Viokngak, 4) Kawlche, 5) Padaratu, 6)Tumpha, 7) Lungte, 8) Ngakchi, 9) Chonglun.

It is believed that from some of the names of Changte's descendants, which are known as branches must have, in their migratory route, been delayed or taken temporary shelter in Burma on their sojourn to the erstwhile Lushai Hills, now Mizoram. This derivation is made in such a manner that one of the branches bear the name 'Kawlchi' must have indicated passing through 'Burma' for 'Kawl' stands for 'Burma' while 'Chi' stands for the family.

Similarly, the Changte family must have settled temporarily in Burma as another branch of the family bears the name of 'Ngakchi' which stands for 'waiting' that delayed movement of the family at one place under compelling circumstances.[56]

4. CHONGTE: The Chongte family as a clan hailed from a place called Muchhip[57], name of a hill. It has four branches called –

   1) Tuichhung, 2) Lungte, 3) Muchhip Chhuak, and 4) Pamte.

5. CHUACHANG: This clan is said to be composed of people with dark and fair skins or complexions.[58] They are believed to be descended from two brothers, the other being Chuaongo. It has three branches. They are –

   1) Chongchir, 2) Chongchhon, 3) Lathang,

6. CHUANGO: This clan is composed of seven branches.

They are descendants of Vanpuia.[59] They are said to have been very powerful and to have held a position similar to that now held by the Sailo clan. Their most powerful chief happened to be Vanpuia from whom this clan has been descended. They are:

(1) Vanpuia-tha, (2) Hlengel, (3) Hmunpel (4) Laller (5) Zongpau (6) Chumthluk (7) Aohmun.

7. HAONAR: This clan has four branches.[60] They are–
(1) Haothul, (2) Haobul, (3) Tuithang, (4) Shenlai.

8. HRASEL: This clan has four branches.[61] They are–
(1) Shelpuia, (2) Sontlunk, (3) Sumkhum, (4) Sazah.

9. HUALHANG: This family has eight branches.[62] This family is said to have sprung from two brothers, children of a 'Lushei' woman by a Poi or Chin father. They are said to have originated from a hole in the ground near the Sherpui rocks to the east of the Manipur river. The branches are –
(1) Chalhuk, (2) Sialchung, (3) Bialchi, (4) Chumkal, Khupao, (5)Fangtet, (6) Jaihlum, (7) Cherthang.

10. HUALNGO: This clan has five branches (lineages)[63]. They are descendants of the same parents with that of the Hualhang family with whom they lived together formerly in villages under Hualngo chiefs. On the rise of Thangur chiefs, a quarrel broke out and Hualngo were defeated by a combination of the Sailo, Zadeng and Pallian, and driven away across the Tiao and took refuse under the protection of the Falam chiefs, where their descendants still are, and are miscalled 'whenoh' by the Officers-in-

charge of the Chin Hills. The Hualhang deserted to the Thangurs, and are found scattered in the villages of their conquerors. The Branches are:

(1) Chalthleng, (2) Khupao, (3) Thuazol, (4) Cherput and (5) Bochung.

11. LUNGKHUA: The family of Lungkhua as a component clans unit of Lushai has five lineages.[64] They are –

    (1) Sialchung, (2) Ngalchi, (3) Ngalchung, (4) Phungchi, (5) Ngaphawl.

12. TOCHUNG: There are five lineages[65] of the Tochung family as given below:

    (1) Topui, (2) Chhakom, (3) Muchhip-chhuak, (4) Chemhler, (5)Tobui.

13. VANCHONG: This family of Vanchong has five branches[66]. They are –

    (1) Vanlung, (2) Sumkhum, (3) Chemhler, (4) Chengrel, and (5)Kaithum.

14. CHHAK-CHHUAK: This is smallest family unit having no branches. Meaning of the family is said to have "come out of the east". [67]

HMARS

There are as many as 27 clans, among the Hmars, according to Keivom[68] which constitute structure of the Hmar Society. Details are as given below:

1. LAWTHANG clan (Pahnom) has 10 sub-clans. They are –

(i)	Sielasung,	(v)	Varte,	(ix)	Chonsim, and
(ii)	Darasung,	(vi)	Thawmte,	(x)	Suomte.
(iii)	Lalasung,	(vii)	Parte,		
(iv)	Tungte	(viii)	Sungte,		

2. ZOTE clan (Pahnam) has 13 sub-clans. They are –

    (i) Chongvawte,
    (ii) Hriler,
    (iii) Pusiete,
    (iv) Salate (Salhmang)
    (v) Parate,
    (vi) Chonghau,
    (vii) Buonsung,
    (viii) Tlangte,
    (ix) Ngalate,
    (x) Darkhawlal,
    (xi) Chungtuol
    (xii) Hrangsote, and
    (xiii) Chuonkhup.

3. LUNGTAU has 14 sub-clans. They are –

    (i) Infimate,
    (ii) Mihriemate,
    (iii) Songate,
    (iv) Nungate,
    (v) Keivom,
    (vi) Lungchuong,
    (vii) Inhuoia,
    (viii) Tlawngate,
    (ix) Theisiekate,
    (x) Tamhrang,
    (xi) Pasulate
    (xii) Sielhnom,
    (xiii) Sunate, and
    (xiv) Intiate.

4. THIEK has 24 sub-clans and 5 lineages as given below:

    (i) Athu
    (ii) Amaw
    (iii) Buhril
    (iv) Tuolor
    (v) Thilsong
    (vi) Khawzawi
    (vii) Seihang
    (viii) Laldan
    (ix) Lalum
    (x) Hekte
    (xi) Ralsun
    (xii) Chonghekte
    (xiii) Kungate
    (xiv) Tuolte
    (xv) Hramte
    (xvi) Thhluchung
    (xvii) Selate
    (xviii) Taite
    (xix) Vankal has 3 lineages. They are: a) Pangote, b) Pangulte, and c) Khawlbuol
    (xx) Pakhumate has 2 lineages; they are: (a) Khumthur & (b) Khumsen
    (xxi) Thlihran
    (xxii) Hmante
    (xxiii) Tamte and
    (xxiv) Chawnnei.

5. KHAWBUNG has 8(eight) sub-clans and 2 (two) lineages as below:

    (i) Laesing,
    (ii) Muolphei,
    (iii) Pazamte,
    (iv) Pangumte,
    (v) Fente,
    (vi) Bunglung
    (vii) Riengsete
    (viii) Phunte has 2 lineages. They are: (a) Sierthung, (b) Siersak

6. KHUONGPUITHUR (Pakhuong) has 4(four) sub-clans as below

    (i) Khuongpui,
    (ii) Buongpui,
    (iii) Khelte,
    (iv) Hrangul,

7. FAIHRIEM has 12 sub-clans as shown below:

(i) Saivate, (ii) Tusing, (iii) Bapui, (iv) Khawhreng, (v) Khawlum, (vi)Tuallai, (vii) Dulien, (viii) Thlanhnung, (ix) Seihmar, (x) Sekong, (xi) Khawkhieng, and (xii) Seiling.

8. DARNGAWN has three sub-clans and 6 lineages as shown below:

(i) Ruolngul, (ii) Faiheng, (iii) Banzang lieng has 6 lineages as given below:

(a) Sonate, (b) Sinate, (c) Chonghmunte, (d) Famhoite, (e)Lamchangte, and (f) Fatlei.

9. LEIRI has 6 sub-clans as shown below:

(i) Neingaite, (ii) Pudaite, (iii) Pulamte, (iv) Puhuongte,(v) Putuolte, and (vi) Thlandar.

10. KHUOLHRING (Kholhring) has 10 sub-clans as shown below:

(i) Chungtheng, (ii) Lozun, (iii) Leidir, (iv) Lungen, (v) Midang, (vi) Pieltel, (vii) Thlamte, (viii) Milai, (ix) Rawlsim, and (x) Suokling.

11. DARLONG has six sub-clans and fifteen lineages as shown below:

(a) THIEKHAL has five lineages:
(i) Chonkal, (ii) Vankal, (iii) Kangbut, (iv) Hrawte, (v)Hmante.

(b) FALHREMHAI has three lineages. They are:
(i) Sathriem, (ii) Khawhren, (iii) Saihma.

(c) ZOTEHAI has three lineages. They are:
(i) Siete, (ii) Saite, (iii) Chonnet.

(d) HRANGCHELHAI has two lineages. They are:
(i) Khuoltu, (ii) Lawmte.

(e) NGURTEHAI has one lineage called Rante.

(f) BIETETE has one lineage called Fatlei.

12. HRANGATE has four lineages. They are –

(i) Hrangate, (ii) Hrangsote, (iii) Hrangdo and (iv) Hrangman

13. NEITHAM has five lineages as shown below:

(i) Chonghning, (ii) Singphun, (iii) Khawthang, (iv)Thangnawk and (v) Vaithang.

14. RAWITE has eight lineages as shown below:

(i) Pieltu, (ii) Sawte, (iii) Buite, (iv) Arro, (v) Zate, (vi)Hnungte,

(vii) Aite and (viii) Seldo.

15. PAUTU has two lineages as shown below:

    (i) Singate and (ii) Thungate.

16. NGENTE has ten lineages as shown below:

    (i) Chonghoi, (ii) Dosak, (iii) Dothlang, and (iv) Lailo, (v) Laitui, (vi) Laihring, (vii) Tuolngul, (viii) Zawngte, (ix) Zawhte and (x)Bawlte.

17. KHIENGTE has seven lineages as shown below:

    (i) Khupthang, (ii) Khupsung, (iii) Kumsang (iv) Khello

    (v) Muolnom, (vi) Lingbei and (vii) Chongte.

18. VANGSIE has six lineages as shown below:

    (i) Invang, (ii) Vanghoi, (iii) Dosil,(iv) Flukte

    (v) Theidu,and (vi) Zapte.

19. BIETE has thirteen lineages as shown below:

    (i) Nampui, (ii) Ngamlal, (iii) Thienglai, (iv) Daimei, (v) Hmunhring, (vi) Feilo, (vii) Fatlei, (viii)Chungngol, (ix) Tlungur, (x) Tamlo, (xi) Betlu, (xii) Sawnlen, (xiii) Khurbi-(a) Lienate.

20. CHANGSAN has nine lineages as shown below:

    (i) Zilchung, (ii) Hranhnieng, (iii) Zelhmang,

    (iv) Chailong, (v) Ngulthuom,(vi) Ngaesithuom, (vii) Kellu, (viii) Hrawte and (ix) Armei.

21. CHAWTHE has ten lineages as shown below:

    (i) Changfieng, (ii) Lienhna, (iii) Chongdang (iv) Halte, (v) Chonthik, (vi) Thamau, (vii) Chamte, (viii) Tamva, (ix) Hawnzong, and (x) Suonhoi.

22. CHAWROI has four lineages as shown below:

    (i) Lengkai, (ii) Tuipai, (iii) Saithuoiand (iv) Nisatarai.

23. HRANGKHOL has four lineages as shown below:

    (i) Penatu, (ii) Chawlkla, (iii) Phuoitong and (iv) Dumkher.

24. SAKACHER has ten lineages as shown below:

    (i) Neibawm, (ii) Bawmlien, (iii)Khewlum, (iv)Thingphum,

    (v) Keiphun (vi) Thirsu(vii) Zeitei, (viii) Sumtinkha, (ix) Telengsing and (x) Vaichei.

25. CHONGTHEI has four lineages as shown below:
    (i) Neichir, (ii) Hrechong, (iii) Luophuland (iv) Lamthik.

26. NGURTE has eight lineages as shown below:
    (i) Sanate, (ii) Pu Singathla, (iii) Saidangathla, (iv)Parate, (v) Saingur, (vi) Bangrang, (vii) Taite and (viii) Cheluon (Chirus).

27. There are other tribal groups who now are in between the Mizos and the Nagas. Despite the fact that they are originally, traditionally, culturally, linguistically, grouped under the Old Kuki fold, now Mizo, by academicians and British administration, these groups are politically motivated and made to claim as to belonging to the Nagas. They are in fact clans of the Hmar. Such people are Lamkang, Langrong, Pang, Muolthuom, Kaipeng, Bawng, Anal, Aimol, Chiru, Monsang, as per social structure of the Hmar.[69]

It may well be observed that social structures of the Mizos in respect of Thadou, Lushai and Hmar are based on the constituent units of clans called 'Phung' and lineages called 'Chang' as detailed given above. For better understanding, the number of clans and lineages of the three Mizo tribes taken up for purpose of this research work are given hereinbelow which are similar to the Meitei 'Salais' and 'Sageis' or 'Yumnaks':

THADOU

Sl. No.	*Name of Phung 'Salai' in Meitei-lon*		*No. of Chaang 'Sagei' in Meitei-lon.*
1.	Doungel	-	14
2.	Sitlhou	-	20
3.	Singson or Singshit	-	15
4.	Kipgen	-	20
5.	Haokip	-	19
6.	Chongloi	-	19
7.	Hangshing	-	13

8.	Touthang	- As they settle mostly in the Chin Hills state of Myanmar, it cannot be obtained for certainty with authority from responsible clansmen of seniority.

There are 120 'Chaang' or 'Sagei' among the Thadous for eight clans or 'Salai' as already given in the preceding pages.

LUSHAI:

Sl.No.	*Name of clan*	*No. of lineage*
1.	Thangura	- 6
2.	Pachaw (some spelled as Pachuao or Pachao)	- 14
3.	Changte	- 9
4.	Chongte	- 4
5.	Chu'achang	- 3
6.	Chuango	- 7
7.	Haonar	- 4
8.	Hrasel	- 4
9.	Hual hang	- 8
10.	Hualngo	- 5
11.	Lungkhua	- 5
12.	Tochung	- 5
13.	Vanchong	- 5
14.	Chhakchhuak	- This clan is the smallest unit of all the Lushai clans and it has no lineage.

There are 79 (seventy-nine) lineages and fourteen clans among the Lushais.

HMAR

Sl.No.	Name of clan		No. of lineage
1.	Lawithang	-	10
2.	Zote	-	13
3.	Lungtau	-	15
4.	Thiek	-	15
5.	Khawbung	-	8
6.	Khuongpuithu (Pakhuong)	-	4
7.	Faihriam	-	12
8.	Darngawm	-	9
9.	Leiri	-	6
10.	Khuolhring	-	10
11.	Darlong	-	21
12.	Hrangate	-	4
13.	Neihtham (included in Zote also)	-	5
14.	Rawite	-	8
15.	Pautu	-	2
16.	Ngente	-	10
17.	Khiengte	-	7
18.	Vangste	-	6
19.	Viete (included also in Vaiphei)	-	13
20.	Changsan (included also in Khongsai)	-	9
21.	Chawthe	-	10
22.	Chaawroi	-	4
23.	Hrangkhol	-	4
24.	Sakachek	-	10
25.	Chontlei	-	4
26.	Ngurte	-	8

There are as many as two hundred twenty-seven lineages for twenty-six clans among the Hmars.

These segmentary system of clans divided into a number of lineages called 'Phung' and 'Chaang' are amazingly found similar to that of the social structure of the 'Meitei' based on the same principle respectively called 'Salai' and 'Sagei' which are discussed earlier in this Chapter.

REFERENCES

1. Herbert Spencer: Principles of Sociology; 3 Volumes: 1897.
2. S.F. Nadel: The Theory of Social Structure, p. 12.
3. Morris Ginsberg: Reason and unreason in Society, 1932; p. 128.
4. A.R. Radcliffe-Brown: African systems of Kinship and Marriage:1950, p. 82.
5. *Ibid., Structure and Function in Primitive Society: 1952;* p. 188; reprinted from the journal of Royal Anthropological Institute, Vol. XXI, 1940.
6. *Ibid.,* Structure and Function in Primitive Society, 1952, p. 188.
7. *Ibid.,* p. 190.
8. A.R. Radcliffe-Brown: *African systems of Kinship and Marriage:* 1952, p. 191.
9. *Ibid.,* Structure and Function in Primitive Society: 1952; pp. 191-192.
11. Talcot Parson: Essay in Sociological Theory:1937; p. 80 and The Social Systems, 1951; pp. 182-200.
12. Henry M. Johnson: Essay in Sociological Theory,:1980, p. 89.
13. Robert M. MaC Iver: Society,:1945, p. 212.
14. Raymond Firth: Human Types:1945, p. 82.
15. Brian Houghton Hodgson: The Journal of Asiatic Society of Bengal: 1853.
16. T.C. Hudson: The Meiteis, 1908, p. 10.
17. Gangmumei Kabui: History of Manipur: Volume One; Pre-colonial period, 1991, p. 15.
18. A.B. Sharma: Pakhangba, 1952, and I. Ibungohal Singh: An Introduction to Manipur, 2nd Edition, 1963.
19. Gangmumei Kabui, *op. cit.,* p.17.
20. G.A. Grierson: Linguistic Survey of India ; Vol.III, Tibeto-

Burman Family; Part-III, Kuki Chin Group: General Introduction: 1904, p. 1.

21. S.K. Chatterjee: Kirata Jana Kriti; Contribution of the Indo-Mongoloid People to Indian Culture, Calcutta, 1950, p. 36.
22. Col. W. McCulloch: Valley of Manipur, 1857, p. 4.
23. Dr. T.C. Hudson: The Meitheis, 1908, p. 73.
24. Dr. Konsam Manikchand: The Evaolution of the Meitei State in an article under the book Manipur Past and Present, Vol. I by Naorem Sanajaoba; 1988, p. 147, Part. II.
25. T.C. Hudson: The Meitheis ; 1908, Appendix I, pp. 184-187.
26. Dr. Konsam Manikchand, *op. cit.*.
27. Gangmumei Kabui, *op. cit.,* p. 87.
28. *Ibid.,* p. 69.
29. Gangmumei Kabui, *op. cit.,* p. 69
30. Col. W. McCulloch: The Valley of Manipur: 1957; pp. 63-64
31. *Ibid.*
32. Col. W. McCulloch: The Journal of Asiatic Society of Bewngal, Vol. No. N.S. XXIV;1857,pp. 80 and the Social Systems: 1951, pp. 182-200.
33. William Shaw: The Thadou Kukis: 1928, p.27 where he gave the genealogical tree, which he called "The Lineage, from Chongthu to Thadou".
34. W. Shaw, *op. cit.*
35. Colonel W. McCulloch, *op. cit.,* p. 182-200.
36. Dr. J.H. Hutton, *op.cit.*
37. Dr. J.H. Hutton: Appendix B, *op. cit.*
38. *Ibid.*
39. *William Shaw*, *op. cit.,* p. 27.
40. Mr. Simon Jenkins Duncan: Journal of Asiatic Society of Bengal, N.S. XXIV, 1928.
41. Dr. J.H. Hutton, *op. cit.*
42. Appendix B: The Thadou Kukis of W. Shaw, 1928.
43. Edward Tuite Dalton: Descriptive Ethnology of Bengal: 1872; p. 47.
44. Col. J. Shakespear: *The Lushai-Kuki Clans, 1912,* pp. 187-190.
45. Col. J. Shakespear, *op. cit.*
46. *Ibid.*

47. Col. J. Shakespear, *op. cit.*
48. i) Jamkinthang: Thadou Tuchon Pachon; 1967, p. 41, Imphal
    ii) William Shaw: The Thadou Kukis: The Government of Assam, Shillong: 1929, p. 32; and
    iii) Dr. J.H. Hutton: Journal of the Asiatic Society of Bengal, N.S., XXIV, 1928.
49. J. Shakespear: Lushai – Kuki clans, 1912, p. 3.
50. Lt. Colonel J. Shakespear: The Lushai Kuki Clans: Part-I: 1912; London, Appendix 123-125. Reprinted by Tribal Research Institute, Govt of Mizoram, Aijawl, 1975.
51. Lt. Colonel J. Shakespear, *op. cit.*
52. *Ibid.*
53. *Ibid.*
54. *Ibid.*
55. Lt. Colonel J. Shakespear, *op. cit.*
56. *Ibid.*, p. 124.
57. *Ibid.*
58. *Ibid.*
59. Lt. Colonel J. Shakespear, *op. cit.*
60. *Ibid.*, p. 124.
61. *Ibid.*, p. 125.
62. *Ibid.*
63. *Ibid.*
64. Lt. Colonel J. Shakespear, *op. cit.*, p. 125.
65. *Ibid.*
66. *Ibid.*
67. *Ibid.*
68. Louis L. Keivom, *op. cit.*
69. Louis L. Keivom, *op. cit.*

Conclusion

Concrete acts acquire their meaning from norms and ritual representations which, in turn, find their justification in the general value commitments of society, values which – as Weber insists – ultimately involve non rational choices. This meaning is essential to social personality stability. We are concerned in this research work with the 'Customary Laws of the Meiteis and the Mizos in Manipur, the changes that took place at the decisive level of meaning and value, the basis of legitimations we have carefully attempted to bring out on the lower institutional level of the meaning system in customary laws wherein these changes were concealed behind ritual actions and the more formal aspects of religions and tribal life. Our attempt to find the several aspects of customary laws of both the societies and the widening gap between higher values and the forms of socio-political and religious expressions has been multi-dimensional. We have maintained in our research a reasonable amount of unbiasedness throughout.

As often done, we must not make the mistake of isolating these changes in the ideational realm from events taking place on the social and economic levels for during the course of our research we found out that the effect of actual modes of social organisation on the way the Universe is understood is never a simple outward projection of human relations. Sub-structure and superstructure interact in an intricate and often ambiguous fashion.

In our research we have attempted to discover the distinguished and the adaptive and integrative needs of the tribal and a non-tribal community in the light of their customary laws their genesis, growth and development into a realm of rules and regulations which could never be overstepped. The force of the customary laws in either society was valued and accepted uniformly. In their symbolization of cosmic forces the Meitei Gods and Goddesses and the Mizo Gods and Goddesses or the sprits of nature are found sufficiently similar in character to the Hindu deities and this allows us to speculate the impact of the Hindu belief systems on the indigenous cultural groups. In both the communities the sacrifice of animals is both a useful act and an obligation. It is often conceived in contractual terms, for the Gods have and of men just as men must ensure the cooperation or at least the non-interference, of supernatural forces. Ritual is understood here in as an elaboration of expressive forces and evaluative symbolism. The manifest purpose of the sacrifice is either to gain the assistance of the Gods or to placate them. Its apparent function in both the societies is essentially instrumental, as it is found in many other societies also. But here at least as important are the immediate gratification it provides and the possibilities for acting out psychological needs. We have maintained that the number of sacrifices and the rituals, the size and elaborate nature of these ceremonies in the Meitei and the Mizo societies reflect lavish spectacles of their chiefdoms and the more affluent members of the nobility rather than the simpler rites of the domestic hearth so important in later times. The concept of Sanamahi and the feasts of merit among the Meiteis and the Mizos are elaborate and distinctive.

We strongly feel that as the royal or chiefly ambitions swelled and the priestly power entrenched itself the sacrifices grew increasingly more complex and in number. In the interplay of priestly power and the common people and the sacrifice of animals or new philosophy got generated which reflected the desire of the masses to understand the processes of natural forces and use them in their daily life. We have investigated the primary relationship of man and animals with the ideology of the sacrifice: man's attempt to influence the sacred or the profane, to prevent the two from harming or even devastating one another as a result of improper contact. The precision of acts in sacrificing animals is a great reminder of its effects in the life after death when human souls are shown the passage to the Heaven by the souls of the animals he had killed and the one who has been immediately sacrificed for the purpose. Conducting the ritual was a demanding task, replete with intricates and detailed formulae. Some of these rites indicate definitely the important latent integrative function of the ritual when it was believed that power had to be restored or rejuvenated periodically through the sacrifice. With the importance of the emergence of royal or chiefly authority, the King assumed as one his duties to represent the tribe or the ethnic community at the sacrifice – for increasing the fertility and welfare of the community as well as his own magical potency through the public rituals. We know that sacrifice assumes a variety of forms and meanings but central to it is the 'sacralizing' of wealth in achieving the purposes of the sacrifant.

We maintain that several of the customary laws with the passage of time became part and parcel of the Mizo and Meitei social system. We have already discussed in detail in our chapters. The institutions of Joking relation, Mother's Brother's Daughter marriage, Konglo marriage, purification of rite of the bride and the groom before entering their conjugal home, etc. got deep-rooted in the Mizo psyche to the extent that without these rituals and their customary significance no marriage could be genuinely performed. Similarly, the performance of rituals as part of cleansing ceremony of persons who were involved in digging graveyard or who had participated in the burial service for the deceased or even in erection of memorial stone over graveyard of the deceased had become part and parcel of the Mizo Customary Laws.

Likewise, Customary laws relating to coronation of the Meitei Kings in their society was crucial to his acceptance by the people. If customary laws had been violated at any stage, the priest and the Chronicles refused to accept them as genuine rulers or Kings and therefore, they were deprived of their status being mentioned in the royal chronicles, 'Cheitharol Kumbaba' and 'Ningthourel Lambuba'. This itself speaks volumes of importance of not only of the coronation in the life of a Manipuri King but also as part of customary articulations in society.

Another very significant feature is the indispensable Customary Law elements in regard to the parts played by each 'Salai' and to ensure participation of several ethnic and tribal groups in bringing and contributing different kinds of wood available in their regions which were used in the construction of halls in Kangla and their participation in coronation-ceremony was essential. It was customary to collect water from different lakes belonging to the seven different 'Salais'. Use of different designs and colours on clothes both among the seven Salais of Meiteis and the tribal groups, a practice followed since the reign of Pamheiba, reveal the divergent cultural base. Wearing of Tangkhul customary dress by the King during the coronation ceremony was a demonstrative impact factor for the people to integrate. These are seen as attempts to depict characteristics of the occasion to project the King as supreme authority of all the people living, both in the Valley and the hills, in expression of solidarity and integration of societies. It was the blending of commoners in respective panas which the King cherished hence elaborate customary rites and rituals were developed.

Customary laws are so deep-rooted that after 1947 its impact was felt upon the conscious political, social and religious leaders. These customary laws had not been codified earlier but a kind of unanimity had existed which brought political acceptance of socio-cultural laws especially for performing public rituals. It also brought about a unified code of conduct for marriage and award of punishment to criminal activities like theft, murder, settling land disputes, looking into rights of ownership of land and dispensation of justice, etc.

Our research has brought to light the most important fact about the origin of the two – the Mizos and the Meiteis – as having a common origin. A folk song often sung at the Laiharaoba – a festival of the Meiteis reveals – that whether it be the settlers of the hills or that of the valley, both are of the same stock. The song,

> "CHINGDA TABA MAHAIGE, TAMDA TABA MAHAIGE, WAKON TANOI NOI ..."

when sung in its indigenous and primeval tune significantly expresses inseparable 'one-ness' and deep relationship that existed between the two groups of people.

That the Kingdom of Manipur, a segmentary state, had been in existence since the early Christian era constituted of the people belonging to the hills and the valley, cannot be denied the indigenous groups of people categoriesed as the TAM-MI (the people who settled in the valley) and the CHING-MI (the people of all groups irrespective of their indigenous ethnic divisions settled in the valley or those who remained in the hills) because of their customary laws and socio-political common terminology found in their respective administrative units is also a fact.

Two dissimilar societies emerged from a homogeneous but complex society on account of the British manipulations who emphasised upon dissimilarities instead of similarities in cultural traditions, language and religious rites and rituals. The policy of divisiveness created a psyche for differences amidst the tribal groups. These two groups were further alienated when Hindu Vaishnavism was accepted in Manipur which gradually developed strong grip over the Meitei society under the royal patronage. Subsequently the King declared Hinduism as State religion during the reign of King Charairongba in the 17th Century and converted the Meiteis into a part of the pan-Vaishnav culture. This alienation was further aggravated when the hill people adopted Christianity in the early part of 19th Century. By this time orthodox Hinduism was firmly entrenched in the Meitei society.

Our research clearly shows that with the advent of Christianity the traditional belief system that had provided the hill people with a link, albeit tenuous, with Meitei society ended. The new religion discouraged the hill people from observing their traditional ceremonies and festivals as they were considered by the Christian Missionaries to be 'Paganistic and primitive'. The rich culture and traditions of the hill people became relics of the past. The role of religion in shaping the present and future of the people were denied thereafter, in one way or the other. Though Christianity did not pose any challenge to the dominant

Meitei society, the latter refused to acknowledge the new and alien religion. The 'new' ways of life of the Christianized converts among hill people was ignored by the dominant Meitei society, and the two societies diverged on different parts ignoring their common traits in their cultural history.

Thus, the two great world religions contributed in no small measures in the causes for 'drifting away' of the two groups of blood-fraternity. Politics, subsequently kept them at 'daggers drawn' against each other despite their inherent 'one-ness', traditionally, culturally, linguistically in terms of customs and customary laws.

In the policy of the Government of India as provided for under Article 244 of the Indian Constitution we find some of the customary laws being assimilated. Some noteworthy features in this regard are that the said policy of the Government of India,

(i) is not an innovation but merely an extension of the old policy pursued by the British Government;

(ii) it is a provision for setting up the Tribes Advisory Council to advice for the welfare and advancement of Scheduled Areas formerly called Excluded Areas;

(iii) it is to set up the First Scheduled Areas and Scheduled Tribes Commission in 1961, called the Dhebar Commission, to suggest a guideline for practical policy for the tribals; the second Commission under the Chairmanship of Dilip Singh Bhuria along with 10 other members having been appointed on the 18th July 2002 to recommend measures for implementation of provisions contained in the 5th and 6th Schedules of the Constitution and to suggest measures for making self-government, social and economic advancement of tribals more effective.

Consequent on announcement of five principles as laid down by late Jawaharlal Nehru, former Prime Minister of India, in 1958, Panchayats (Extension to Scheduled Areas) Act, 1996 was enacted which stressed that –

(i) State legislation shall be in consonance with the Customary Law, social and religious practices and traditional management practices of community resources;

(ii) A Village shall ordinarily manage its affairs in accordance with traditions and customs;

(iii) Every Gram Sabha shall be competent to safeguard and preserve the traditions and customs of the people, their cultural identity, community resources and the customary mode of dispute resolution.

Thus we find that the administrative systems were directed to study and realize the value of customary laws from which human beings gradually learnt that a particular mode of behaviour and conduct are conducive and beneficial to collective living. The Hindu laws as applicable in India today are nothing but codification of most of the pre-1955 different customary laws relating to marriage, inheritance, adoption, guardianship, etc. It has encompassed a large chunk of existing customary laws.

In retrospection we find that subsequently, the five principles for administration of tribal areas as enunciated by late Pandit Jawaharlal Nehru, as far back as 1958, has gained more force, validity and relevance. Keeping this in view, the Planning Commission of India set up a Working Group to study "Impact of new laws on the traditional tribal societies in the North-Eastern India".

Our study too, enforces the facts that it is necessary to take into consideration two structurally different modes for settling disputes - one by negotiation and compromise, which is the way of Customary Laws as are prevalent among tribal societies and the other that of adjudication and penal imposition, which is the way of courts of law. Our conclusion in this regard is quite clear that the customary laws are more humane in certain areas and quite effective in some others. And so efforts have to be taken to compile and look into existing customary laws to remove uncertainty, ambiguity and possible misapplication through ignorance or inadvertence at certain levels. We strongly feel that the cultural identity and rich heritage of the two ethnic communities be preserved, though it is the duty of the peer groups.

During the course of our field work we found introduction of Cr.P.C. and C.P.C. in the hill areas has caused considerable inconvenience to the tribals in general and the Mizos in particular and that the delay has resulted in complicating procedural laws which have shaken the faith of the tribals in the very system of administration of justice. Today (since 1983) we have felt that supplanting their customary laws would lead to erosion of authority of the indigenous tribal institutions. This weakening of social control pattern would result in confusion and imbalance. We are also convinced that insurgency and youth delinquency in these areas and communities can be attributed to some extent, to a hasty and ill conceived replacement of the indigenous system of administration of justice by a totally alien and unfamiliar system. Subsequently, we are convinced that the Village Authorities Act, 1956 had failed to command the same respect as the traditional Village Authorities and as also the District Council which was constituted under the District Council Act, 1971 had failed to meet the needs of the tribal societies. We worked among the Mizos and the Meitei institutions to find out why the strongly felt traditionally constituted Village Authorities should not be entrusted not merely with judicial powers but also with all developmental work and that why Village Authorities should be constituted on the traditional lines and wherever possible elections based on franchise be avoided. We observed that laws are not being imposed on the tribals particularly in matters relating to their social and economic life, e.g., land, forests and social practices. Also, their traditional system of administration of justice, civil as well as criminal, should not unnecessarily be disturbed, that is to say that the customary laws be given a chance once again for we have found that of late several cases have been resolved under the customary laws of the ethnic communities quite peacefully. And it is hoped that it will be long lasting.

Historically we would like to state categorically that Mizos who are Kukis of Mongoloid race of the Tibeto-Burman group of tribes, belong to the mountainous region of our country. They could be of the Kirata family. The original home of these people was in the hilly region. And it is unquestionable because their tradition, myths, legends and historical facts based on research all point to it. But it is extremely difficult, perhaps impossible, to definitely give the correct date of their settlement and beginning of their migration. Therefore, to this aspect of the Mizo history, no conclusive research can presently be made.

Having found their new homes in Burma, the Kukis are believed to have been there for a number of centuries. Unlike other Kiratas who reached Assam following the course of Brahmaputra river and still others who reached the other hill areas through mountain passes, the Mizos alike the Kukis arrived in their present habitats in the Lushai Hills through the present Chawnchhim, popularly known as Champhai or Champa, the capital of the Mahajanapada of Anga. Some scholars have claimed that their main route appears to be the land route via what is popularly known as Rihdil, the Rih Lake. But it seems certain that when they moved westward they moved in small numbers, one group under the command of one Chief moving from one place to another. That is why they are often attributed nomadic characteristics. However, we strongly feel that the Kukis of the Lushei ranges, now known as the Mizos had reached the present habitat through Bangladesh and Meghalaya.

Among the Mongoloid tribes whom the classical writers and modern authors refer to as Kiratas who found their ancient settlements in the plains and the hills of Assam with whom the Ahoms had contacts with the Mizos had no part to play because they were distinctly different from them. But, it is certain that some sections of the Chin group might have had contact with them because many accounts are given about the Chins in Hindu literatures. The Mizo groups who are now found in North Cachar of Assam are those, as pointed out earlier, who migrated back from Tripura via the Cachar valley and finally arrived in the hills. They had been employed in the Barak valley as Kuki Levy by the Cachar Rajah in putting down their adversaries. Therefore, certainly several groups of the Kukis had contact with the Meiteis, as customary laws reveal a common origin.

In our studies we have extensively pointed out that in early societies custom was the main vehicle of legal development. In the mainland, while moulding the ancient Hindu Law, the commentators and the text writers have by and large included the prevalent customs in their early writings. For example, the Srutis and Smritis have strongly recommended that customs be followed. Manu declared that it is the duty of the King to decide all cases according to principles drawn from local usages. When the Smritis fell out of date in relation to the needs of the contemporary society, commentaries adopted the Smriti-law, by the process of interpretation, to bring it to accord with customs which had roots in the then society. Even today, the personal laws of the Meiteis have been recognised by judges as such and are embodied in judicial decisions.

Nevertheless, with the advancement and development of society, coupled with the increasing mobility of the people, and maturity of the legal system, time has come when a uniformity of law becomes imperative. Some of the features of the traditional law are thus bound to be out of harmony with contemporary social conditions and facts of life. It has been strongly felt to modify the laws in certain circles and adopt them to meet modern exigencies and circumstances.

Our study on the Social Institutions of Meiteis and Mizos opened a Pandora box of stark revelations of extreme contrasting statuses of womenfolk of unilaterally very strong patriarchal system of society, based on patrilineal descent kinship with patrilocal marriage. The customary laws of the two societies are poles apart in their treatment of women in regard to inheritance and succession.

While the Meiteis who are predominantly Vaishnavite Hindus provide proper laws for inheritance and succession to womenfolk with a sense of care, love and affection, the Mizos relegated their womenfolk to the lowest ebb of social hierarchy treating them with utmost impunity and contempt.

In the birth of a female child in a family is considered arrival of an 'unwelcome guest', attributing the child as having been born 'with abundance of misfortune to the family', and, still worst and confounded is the fact that there exists no provisions in their Customary Law for womenfolk for inheritance and succession. A perpetual subjugation of large chunk of population was denied a status of well being which contributed to such social participations. Hence, emancipation of women for upliftment and empowerment of women in Mizo society has been an equally uphill task.

Yet commonfolk women's struggle for all round improvement of their status is amazing. Herein the name of Aleaz is relevant, who has highlighted the efforts of Mizo women to uplift their status through organized Associations, like -

1. Mizo Hmeichhe Tangrual Pawl

Founded in 1946, the objectives of which are –

(i) to request the Government authorities to accept the concept and precepts of a "Will" made before death should be made valid and that the people should be acquainted with the idea;

(ii) to divide family property into two equal parts between the families of the husband and the wife in the event of death of the husband before having any issue;

(iii) to allow a female child who has no brother to inherit her father's properties;

(iv) to condone a woman who had sex after the death of her husband without treating her as having committed adultery; and

(v) to allow children to live with either the father or the mother in case of divorce.*

Obviously, we feel that all the contentious issues within the Mizo customary laws and constraining the position of women have been incorporated in the objectives of "*Mizo Hmeichhe Tangrual Pawl*". A special State Legislative Assembly was convened to consider the abovementioned issues for review of Mizo customary laws affecting women rights. The Organisation also pressed home the fact to the District Council as adopted in the General Assembly of the Organisation in 1956 for certain amendments relating to 'bride-price'. Yet, no substantial changes, except marginal ones, could take place. Important issues, such as laws of inheritance and succession could not receive patronage for amendments and womenfolk remained deprived of property rights. Later, due to emerging political scenario, the activities of the Organisation could not be strengthened and invigorated. However, gradually, it took to other welfare activities, such as, health and sanitation in public and private areas, popularized art of weaving, established maternity and child welfare centres, tailoring centres, homes for motherless babies, working women's hostels and such other enterprises were taken up, thereby gaining gradual predominance in welfare orientation activities. The state accepted these and strengthened the empowering of women movement on the basis of their little rights vested in them through the customary laws.

2. The Mizo Hmeichhe Insuikhawm Pawl (MHIP) or Mizo Women's Federation

This Organisation was also established in 1946 and today it is the largest and the most active Organisation for

* *For details see Bonita Aleaz : Emergent women : Mizo Women's perspective, 2005.*

women in Mizoram. It looks after Orphanages. It gained momentum and has achieved a status of recognised autonomous body under the Central Social Welfare Board ensuring greater attention of the Ministry of the Central Government in welfare activities of women and children, unlike the customary laws wherein we find that children whose mother had expired at childbirth were put in graves of their mother whose dead body was found over the infant to bring death to the child – the cause being the mother herself.

The environment thus enumerated was bound within the structures of patriarchal society. Hence, education had generated consciousness among women recipients. It had successfully broken the traditional barriers. Womenfolk in Mizo society have yet a long way of struggle to go to achieve desired goal of upliftment and empowerment. Nonetheless we are witnessing today a great social change not only among the Mizos but also among the Meiteis whose customary laws had been moderated by the influence of the Hindu customs and Vaishnavite influences of social governance. However, when we deeply look at the status of women in the Meitei society we feel that though liberated and omnipotent the Meitei women still need social security and more human treatment at the hands of the male partners. The customary laws need to be reinterpreted in present time, in both the societies in a rationalized manner.

As we go through the constitution and function of Chieftainship among the Meitei and the Mizo societies we find that it clearly manifests sustainability of customary laws under trying situations. The dynamics of evolution of Chiefdoms of the Meiteis ultimately led to the formation of 'Seven Salais' (there may be more) to merge into a Meitei State under a royal dynasty called 'Ningthouja'. As against it, despite a very strong autocratic secular base Chieftainship among the Mizos have, through the legacies bequeathed to them by the Kukis, there appears a very weak base of segmentary type of authority that deprives them elements of evolutionary mechanism. Chieftainship among them remains dormant mainly due to inter-clan hegemony and inter-village rivalry that bring their customary laws which remain confined to a narrow ambit.

The dynamics of 'Loyumba Shinyen' is another glaring instance among the Meiteis. As the 'first written Constitution' of the Meiteis it withstands enactment of the Manipur State Constitution Act, 1947. It was not repealed under the Manipur merger agreement signed on 15-10-1949 in Shillong. It continues to survive since it is not in contravention with the Constitution of India. In broad perceptions it reveals the concept of division of labour much regard in the past to streamline collective responsibility and understood effort. Unlike this, with the promulgation of the Manipur Hill People's (Administration) Regulation Act, 1947, the first target it aimed at was abolition of traditional Chieftainship of the Mizos that prompted the Government to introduce the Manipur (Village Authorities in Hill Areas) Act, 1956, mainly with a view to do away with the traditional Village Authority called 'Chieftainship' which was followed from time to time with amendments of the Act with more stringent provisions, the latest being "the Manipur (Village Authorities) in Hill Areas (Amendment) Act, 1983. It simply manifests partisan approach of the Government towards the indigenous institutions, such as, Customary Laws, of the Mizos. This effort was supplemented with the introduction of District Council Act, 1971 which had failed to meet the needs of the tribal societies. Above all, these measures of the Government had weakened the social control pattern that resulted in confusion and imbalance and failed to command the same respect as the traditional Village Authorities enjoyed.

We are reminded of the fact that when people live together certain rules are required to be framed for guiding their conduct so that conflicts and clashes can be avoided. Evolution and enforcement of such rules provide an interesting example of the process of structural differentiation. We have abundantly highlighted this aspect in our work.

Traditionally, each Mizo Village used to be a separate sovereign State under a Chief who was supreme in all respects, though on a miniature scale. Justice was administered at his dispensation under the guidance of his Council of ELDERS called UPA or SEMANG-UPA as the case may be, interpreting Customary Laws as per relevance to the case concerned. Residence of the Chief was the Court-house and proceedings of the case were drawn therein along with all round drinking of the home-made 'rice-beer' called ZU. This was the highest court of justice at the Village level. There was no appellate court in the village. In case the unsuccessful litigant wished his case re-heard, he/she might do so by approaching a more powerful Chief for review of the decision thus already arrived at. If the approach was entertained, it might be heard who would accept him as a subject and take up his quarrel on the terms agreed upon. Shakespear described two such customary penal systems of the Mizos as:

(a) Offences in respect of property :

A fine of one Mithun was liable to be imposed for a theft of rice, clothes, guns, brass-pots, domestic animals and wild animals or birds which have been killed or trapped irrespective of the actual value of the article stolen; and

(b) Offences connected with mortal beings:

Originally punishment in these cases rested with the aggrieved party or his relatives, who were allowed to exact summary vengeance. Thus, a husband was at liberty customarily to kill an unfaithful wife and her paramour. He may as well be killed in return by the family of the victim in vengeance or retaliation. He could, however, escape by taking permanent refuge under the protection of the Chief.

Shakespear said that shortly after British authorities extended their powers in the North-East, two boys deliberately killed a man in open broad daylight, who, they were told, had murdered their father many years before. It took place in the middle of the village, "and apparently attracted but little attention". Also if a man after committing murder ran into the Chiefs compound and touched a pillar no harm could be done to life. The punishment could be determined by the Chief only.

Another proceeding of trial with slight variation is current among the Mizo tribes today. It is that when one takes a case to the Chief for a trial, a date for hearing is fixed. On the day thus fixed, the Chief along with one or two of his Council of Elders, UPA (Mecha in Lakher), goes to the house of one of the parties in the dispute generally to that of the plaintiff, and appoints two or three Elders of his Council along with a representative of the Chief to go to the house of the other party. The proceedings start with handing all round of ZU. Then the party in whose house the Chief is seated places his side of the case. Thereafter, the Chief nominates a member of his Council, ELDER, to hear the case in details who will go to and fro between the parties in the litigation. The Chief discusses in full detail of the case with his full-house Council of ELDERS which often leads to further discussion with endless 'comings' and 'goings' between the two houses of litigants until at last the Chief and his ELDERS come to a final decision.

Thus, with the pronouncement of his orders the case comes to an end. It so happens, very often than not, that the greater the amount of ZU or 'rice-beer' is served by the parties the longer is the case as the Chief and his ELDERS are quite ready to continue the proceedings indefinitely provided they are supplied frequently with ZU, and so cases sometimes last two or three days. The Britishers had tried in the past to get rid of the customary ZU practice but could not prevail upon the Lushei Mizo Chiefs and the common people and ultimately failed in their persuasion. The Customary Law prevailed but however they were able to get rid of an obnoxious customary practice called the Kelmi Charm.

Following declaration of the final decision of the Chief, in case either of the two parties was not satisfied, sometimes recourse to the trial was taken by ordeal of 'diving into the water'. For this purpose an ELDER or UPA of his Council was appointed to supervise the diving contest proceedings. In the process, the ELDER appointed for the purpose took the parties to a stream which was dammed to form a pool wherein both the parties would be made to stand at equi-distance from him with the same level of depth of water surface. He will place each of his hands on the heads of the contending litigants. He will then submerge both of them simultaneously. Whoever emerged first from under-water would be declared as defeated party, the result of which is accepted compulsorily by one and all including the Chief as per traditional belief of customary laws which maintain that howsoever the person may be expert in swimming and diving 'aquanaut' or art-dexterity, cannot stand for long under the water in case he used fault-play or cheated the jury. It was justice done in a natural way but help taken from the chief.

Such was effectiveness and dynamism of Chieftainship, in both the societies. The evolution of Meitei Chieftainship to ultimate transcendence of seven Chiefdoms into an independent Kingdom was based on customary laws. The promotion of Meitei State coupled with the steadfast grip of Mizo Chieftainship over its people, despite its stagnant nature of being a dormant state, only speaks volumes of their indispensability.

With this in the backdrop and its past glorious history, we feel that Chieftainship of any sort or system must on no account be sidelined or marginalized in the name of growth, advancement and development of society. Chieftainship is the symbol of the tribe he belongs to and has an identity thereof whose place of significance is deep rooted in the psyche of the people he represents which inevitably lasts longer than one could surmise. Many of the divisive acts have happened which reveal the fact the chiefs could have controlled it much effectively in their respective domains.

Our research has revealed that even as pagans the Mizos and the Meiteis had many excellent qualities and affection for children is one of such noble qualities. Towards the younger members of the family, both parents are indulgent to a fault in both the societies. Respect to the aged and elderly people by their younger generation has not diminished even when all the materialistic achievements or advancements and economic progress has been made by the Mizos or the Meiteis. It is indeed an effect of their customary laws.

At the end it must be said that it was not only the need to fill historical lacunae that led us to supplement the institutional approach and that of history of ideas with a psychological-cultural method but that we were attracted towards the customary laws for understanding the sociology of law prevalent in order to have a better understanding of their culture and tradition which have got recorded in their history.

Glossary

1.	Ai Kawnpui Sial	=	Pre-Christian sacrifice for success in hunting.
2.	Angkia	=	Price in marriage-payment in Lakher custom.
3.	Angong	=	Neck
4.	Apanbi	=	The second wife of the king.
5.	Aphei	=	Adultery committed by wife.
6.	Apu	=	Maternal uncle.
7.	Becha	=	Male relative of the man.
8.	Changsan or Jensen	=	A Mizo tribe mainly confined in Cachar and North Cachar Hills, is also dispersed among the Thadou and Hmar in Manipur
9.	Chatlam Lutin	=	Customs and usages.
10.	Chengluk Nungshang Hanba	=	Rite performed on the fifth day after the wedding by the bridegroom's party
11.	Fatlam	=	Youngest son.
12.	Gopi keh	=	Bamboo split of *bambusa balcoa* = *Saneibi*
13.	Haija-Chatchaba	=	Request for engagement by the bridegroom's party.
14.	Hanjinnaba	=	Re-union or reconciliation.
15.	Haosa / Lal	=	Chief of Semitic people of ancient Palestine including the Jews and Arabs and Assyrians.

16.	Hebrew	=	Semitic language of the ancient Jews, modern form of this used especially in Israel.
17.	Hmeifa	=	Concubine.
18.	Hri	=	Disease
19.	Hrupathlie hasala	=	Adultery committed by husband.
20.	Imungnaba	=	Persons of common maternal grandfather.
21.	Incontrovertible	=	Indisputable, indubitable.
22.	Ingam	=	Extinct.
23.	Inndongta	=	Family council in Paite custom.
24.	Keng-puna or miningpuna	=	Name giving ceremony.
25.	Khainaba	=	Divorce.
26.	Khawchhiar	=	Village writer
27.	Khibah	=	Necklace of beads.
28.	Khichang	=	A single big bead
29.	Khumpui	=	Big bed
30.	Konglo	=	Waist earning
31.	Kosana	=	Feast hosted by killing a mithun or pig or cow by the deceased family.
32.	Kukisthanan	=	Land of Kuki
33.	Kut	=	Festivals of harvesting and new arrivals of crops and vegetables.
34.	Lai-Chaklon Katpa	=	Annual dedication of food to the deity of clan.
35.	Lallup	=	System to administrate by the king with the help of Panna from which selected men to render service i.e. free labour to the king for 10(ten) days in every 40 days.
36.	Leimakhubi	=	The third wife of the king.
37.	Leimarel	=	The first wife of the king.
38.	Longchang	=	Beads

39.	Lugunthangba	=	Ceremony of taking or wearing sacred thread.
40.	Luhongba	=	Marriage
41.	Lukhra	=	Widow
42.	Lutom-Laisui	=	Very important and compulsory items in the marriage payment.
43.	Maithiman or migepman	=	Adultery price by the adulterer to the aggrieved husband.
44.	Malang khot	=	A married woman's devotedness to her children and husband and his side.
45.	Man	=	Marriage payment
46.	Mane-Matung-Inba	=	Marriage with father's sister's son in the case of bride or mother's brother's daughter.
47.	Mangkat	=	Bride payment.
48.	Mankang	=	Extra and additional marriage-payment for daughter.
49.	Messiamic Judaism	=	Orthodox Judaism.
50.	Mou	=	Married woman
51.	Murky (Murkier)	=	Gloomy, thick, dirty, suspiciously obscured.
52.	Niar	=	Paternal aunt's share in the marriage-payment.
53.	Niyoga	=	An obligation to the widow without male issue at the time of her husband's death to get married with the younger brother of the deceased husband.
54.	Nong a Pahaw	=	Preferential marriage in Lakher custom.
55.	Nongcheu	=	Part of marriage-payment which goes to mother in Lakher custom.
56.	Nularim	=	Courting of girl.
57.	Nupi Chenba	=	To elope girl.

58.	Nupi Maral or Thuam	=	Women's property/dowry/stridan
59.	Paigen	=	Leather decorated belt.
60.	Palai	=	Go between
61.	Pathien or Lalpa	=	God
62.	Pawi/Mara/Lai	=	Lakher or Marring
63.	Pee-dinnaba	=	Persons belonging to different yek-salais from a common grandmother.
64.	Pen-tinnaba	=	Persons having a common maternal ancestor.
65.	Per se	=	Latin phrase meaning 'of its own' or 'alone'.
66.	Ponve	=	Petticoat/lungi or phanck.
67.	Potloi	=	Decorated garment put on by the Meitei bride in modern system of marriage. It is also a costume of Manipuri Rasa worn by the Gopis.
68.	Pularim	=	Gossiping of youths.
69.	Pusum	=	Maternal share in the marriage payment in Lushai custom.
70.	Putative Judaism	=	Reputed Judaism.
71.	Radiedo	=	Ear piercing ceremony on the ninth days for a girl child and tenth day for a boy child.
72.	Reutang	=	Inheritance in Lakher custom.
73.	Rokhawm	=	Inheritance in Lushai custom.
74.	Ru	=	Death due
75.	Sagei / yumnak	=	surname
76.	Sahmahei	=	Fermented rice
77.	Sakhua	=	God
78.	Sawm	=	Dormitory
79.	Sel	=	Mithun
80.	Senhut	=	Childhood death upto the age of three years. (Soren in Manipuri)

81.	Shairuk-tinnaba	=	Belonging to the same clan or lineage.
82.	Sherh	=	Placing of a house under profanity for a specific number of days on the expiry of which it is considered as having been purified.
83.	*Sine quo non*	=	Indispensable condition or qualification.
84.	Sumtansha	=	Agreement reached upon
85.	Thaw	=	Become genial; become warm enough to lose numbness; become less cold or stiff in manner.
86.	Thiempu	=	Priest.
87.	Thih-Kheng	=	Blacksmith
88.	Thi-pha	=	Natural death
89.	Thi-sie	=	Unnatural death
90.	Uire	=	Adultery
91.	Vis-à-vis	=	In a position facing one another person occupying corresponding position in another group: social part.
92.	Wa loithokpa	=	Confirmation of divorce.
93.	Wai	=	Measurement of one fist.
94.	Yek-Salai	=	Kinship relationship between members of clans, lineages and sub-lineages, claiming a common ancestor.
95.	Zawlbuk	=	Bachelor's dormitory.

Appendices

APPENDIX-I

Persons Interviewed

1. Dr. Sheikho Singsit, at his residence at Tuibong, Churachandpur on 18-7-05
2. Dr. V.S. Varughese from Kerela at present Ashram, Delhi, Gopinath Bardoloi Airport, Guwahati, 8-4-05
3. Emunah, Gush Katif, Israel, 6-3-06
4. Ksh. Bimola Devi at her office, M.U. on 7.7.06
5. Latkhojam Haokip, while he visited our residence, Old Lambulane, on 19.7.05
6. Lutcha Vaiphei, Red Cross Road, Churachandpur, Churachandpur,on 4-10-06
7. Lianzella, Mizoram University, Mizoram, Hotel Brahmaputra, Guwahati on 3.4.2005
8. Lunkhoneng Kipgen, daughter of the Chief of Lunthulien, Tipaimukh, Churachandpur on 30-9-06
9. N. Vijayalakshmi Brara, at her Shillong residence, On 17.8.06
10. N. Memcha Devi, aged 50 years at Leimaram, on 4.7.2005

11. N. Nobinchandra Singh, Lairikyengbam Leikai, at my residence, Old Lambulane, on July, 2006
12. Ningthoujam Ningol Nungleppam Ongbi Tombi, aged 51 years, Pheiyeng, Singda Dam on 5.10.2005
13. Rev. Kaikhoisei at his residence, Old Lambulane on 7-4-05
14. Rev. Renghang, aged 65 years, while visiting at my residence, Old Lambulane on 17.7.06
15. S.L. Singson (aged 70), Old Lambulane on 3-5-04.
16. Th. Rampiyari Devi, Thiyam Leikai, Kwakeithel, Imphal, on 24.4.2005
17. Thao Anita Chothe, aged 21 years, Bishnupur District, Ward No.2, Lamlangphui, on 3.2.06.
18. Thao Nabadwip Chothe, aged 47 years, Bishnupur District, Ward No.2, Lamlangphui, on 22.6.06.
19. V.D. Tombing at Molhoi, Churachandpur on 18-5-05.

APPENDIX-II

Questionnaire

1. What is your name?
   (i) Sex:
   (ii) Age:
   (iii) Community:
   (iv) Address :
2. What do you mean by:
   (i) Tradition:
   (ii) Culture :
3. Are custom and customary law important elements/factors in your society? If yes, give reason.
4. Is religion an adverse impact on Customary Law of your society? If so, give reason.
5. When did Customary Law established?
6. What are the importance and significance of Customary Law?
7. Who inherit ancestral property as per your Customary Law?
8. Woman's right property is recognised by your society. "Yes" or "No"
9. "Upliftment of women is the issue of this present." Comment.
10. The role of chieftainship in sustenance of Customary Law shows its indispensability to uphold traditional and cultural heritage. Do you agree?(i) "Yes" or "No"(ii) Give reason.
11. Solidarity and Unity in your society had been disintegrated by external elements. Do you agree? If so, give elements thereof.
12. What are merit and demerit of Hinduism/Christianity?
13. Have you transformed yourself by professing Hinduism/ Christianity? If "Yes", give the implications.
14. Has Hinduism/Christianity affect your tradition, culture and customary law?
15. Do you agree that the Meiteis and the Mizos have a common theory of origin? If "Yes", what are the proofs?

Bibliography

Agrawal, R.K. (1982), *Hindu Law,* Allahabad.

Aleaz, Bonita (2005), *Emergent Women,* Mittal Publication, New Delhi.

Allott, Antony N. and Gordon R. Woodman. (eds): (1985), *People's Law and State Law,* The Bellagio Papers Dordrecht, Foris.

Bacon, Elizabeth E., (1969), 'Tribe' in 27 *Encyclopaedia Americana.*

Barkataki, S., (1969), *Tribes of Assam,* National Book Trust, N. Delhi.

Baveja, J.D., (1970), *The Land Where The Bamboo Flowers.* Secretary, Publication Board, Assam, Gauhati.

Becker, J.C., (1989), *Seymour's Customary Law in Southern Africa,* 5th Edition, Juta, Cape Town.

Benedict, Paul R., (1972), *A Conspectus, Cambridge.*

Bennett, T.W., (1995), *Human Rights and African Customary Law under the South African Constitution.* Juta, Cape Town.

Bennett, T.W., (1991), *A Source of African Customary Law for Southern Africa,* Juta, Cape Town.

Beteille, Andre, (1976), *Caste: Old and New,* New Delhi.

Betram Carey, and Tuck, H.N., (1976), *The Chin Hills,* Vol. I & II Firma KL.M. Pvt Ltd. Calcutta.

Bhattacharjee, J.B., (1977), *Cachar under British Rule in North East India,* Radiant Publishers, New Delhi.

Bhattacharjee, J.B., (1991), *Social and Polity Formations in Pre-Colonial North East India.* Vikas Publishers, Delhi.

Bhowmick, P.K., (1969), *Some Aspects of Applied Anthropology,* Institute of Social Research, Lake Town, Calcutta.

Bhusan, Vidya and Sachdeva, R., (1993), *An Introduction to Sociology,* Kitab Mahal, Allahabad.

Bimal, Dev J. and Lahiri, Dilip Kumar (1983), *Lushai Customs and Ceremonies,* Mittal Publications, Delhi.

Bose, J.K., (1980), *Glimpses of Tribal Life in North East India,* Institute of Social Research, Lake Town, Calcutta.

Bowles Gordon, T. (1984), *The People of Asia,* Weidenfield and Nicolson, London.

Bradly, Richard, (1984), *The Social Foundations of Pre-Historic Britain,* Harlow, London.

Britanica Encyclopaedia, (2005), Vol. 13 Encyclopaedia Britanica India Pvt. Ltd., N. Delhi.

Brown, R., (1873), *Statistical Account of Manipur,* K.M. Mittal Sandskaran Prakashak, Delhi.

Brown, Radcliff, A.R., (1950), *African System of Kinship and Marriage,* Oxford University Press, London, New York, Toronto.

Brown, Radcliff, A.R., (1964), *Structure and Function in Primitive society.* The English Language Book Society, Cohen and West Ltd. London.

Burkitt, M.C. (1929), *Our Early Ancestors,* Cambridge, London

Canter, Richard, S., (1980), *Dispute Settlement in Zambia,* in Nadar and Todd, London.

Carter, James, (1989), *Law: Its Origin, Growth and Function,* Allahabad.

Chakravorty, B.C. (1964), *British Relations with the Hill Tribes of Assam since 1858,* Firma K.L. Mukhopadhyay, Calcutta.

Chatterjee, N. (1925), *Status of Women in Mizo Society,* Tribal Research Centre, Aizawl.

Chatterjee, N. (1975), *Jawlbuk as Social Institution in the Mizo Society,* Tribal Research Centre, Aizawl

Chatterjee, N. (1975), *Mizo Chief and his Administration,* Tribal Research Centre, Aizawl.

Chatterjee, S.K., (1974), *Kirata Jana Kriti*, The Asiatic Society, Calcutta.

Chaudhury, P.C., (1987), *The History of Civilization of the People of Assam to the 12th Century,* A.D. Spectrum Publication, Guwahati.

Christoph Von Furer Hai-mendrof, (1966), *South Asian Societies,* Sterling Publisher Pvt. Ltd., Delhi.

Cohen, Jonathan and Hart, H.L.A., (1950), Symposium: *Theory and Defintion in Jurisprudence.* Aristotelian Society, Prodeedings, Supplementary. Vol. 29, Problem in Psychotherapy and Jurisprudence. Harrison, London.

Cole, G.D.H. (1954), *Encyclopaedia of Social Sciences,* London.

Colin, Renfrew, (1974), *Beyond Subsistence Economy,* Cambridge University, Press.

Crawford, G.C., (1984), *Handbook of Kuki Customs,* Directorate, PGT and STY, Manipur, (Reprint).

Crawley, A.E., (1907), *Exogamy and Matting of Cousins,* London.

Dalton, E.T., (1872), *Descriptive Ethnology of Bengal*, Originally published by the Office of the Superintendent of Govt. Printing, Calcutta.

Damant, G.H., (1875), "Notes on Manipur Grammar". *Journal of Asiatic Society of Bengal*, Vol.XLIV, p. 178.

Das Gupta H.C., Levirate in Ramayana, *Man in India*, Vol. VI, Nos 2 & 3.

Davis, A.W., (1987), *Gazetteer of the North Lushai Hills*, Matero Company, Delhi.

Davis, Kinsley, (1972), *Changing Concepts of Marriage and Family*, Havard Basker and Penkenfill.

Dey, J.K. and P.J. Dey (1968), *A Brief Outline of Physical and Social Anthropology,* Indian Book Publishing House Company, Calcutta.

Diwan, Paras (1978), Customary Laws of Punjab Publication Bureau, Panjab University, Chandigarh

Durkheim, Emile (1915), *Elementary Forms of Religious Life*, Macmillan, New York.

Esther, Boserup (1966), *The Conditions of Agricultural Growth*. Chicago.

Evans Pritchard, E.E. (1940), *The Nuer*, The Clarendron Press, London.

Evans-Pritchard, E.E., Raymond Firth, E.R. Leach, J.G. Peristian, John Layord Max Gluckman, Mayor Fortes, Godfrey Lienhardt, (1963), *A Series of Broadcast Talks, Institution of Primitive Society,* Basil Blackwell, Oxford.

Fernandes, W., (1981), *Caste and Conversion Movements in India,* Indian Social Institute, New Delhi.

Firth, Raymond, (1958), *Human Types,* the New American Library of World Literature, Inco, New York, USA.

Frazer, J.G., (1919), *Folklore in Old Testament*, Vol. II, London.

Frazer, J.G. (1910), *Totemism and Exogamy*, Vol. II London.

Gait, Edward Sir, (1981), *History of Assam*, Gauhati.

Gangte, T.S. (1993), *The Kukis of Manipur*, Gyan Publishing House, New Delhi.

Gerini, G.E. (1909), *Researches on Ptolemy's Geography of Eastern India*, London.

Gillen and Gillen (1950), *Cultural Sociology*, The MacMillan, Co., New York.

Ginsberg, Morris, (1947), *Reason and Unreason in Society*, Longman, Green and Co., London.

Gluckman, Max, (1965), *The Ideas in Barotse Jurisprudence*, New Haven, Connecticut Yale University Press.

Goswami, B.B. (1979), *The Mizo Unrest: A Study of Politicisation of Culture*, Aalekh Publishers, Jaipur.

Gougin, T. (1984), *History of Zomi*, Churachandpur.

Goulienthang (2001), *A Short Chronological Account of Mizos*, Lamka.

Green, Arnold (1956), *Sociology*, McGraw Hill Book Co., Inc. New York.

Grierson, G.A. (1904), *Linguistic Survey of India Tibeto-Burman Sub Family*. Reprinted by Motilal Benarsedas, Delhi.

Griffiths, Anne, M.O. (1997), *In the Shadow of Marriage: Gender and Justice in an African Community*, University of Chicago Press, Chicago.

Hardiman, Scott, *Gazetteer of Upper Burma and the Shan States*, I & II.

Hart, H.L.A. (1954), Definition and Theory in Jurisprudence, *Law Quarterly Review*: 70.

Harvey, G.E., (1945), *History of Burma,* London.

Hayes, J.C., (1982), *Modern Europe to 1870*, Surjit Publications, Delhi.

Hmar Youth Association (HYO), (1990), *Hmar Hnam Dan Sinlung,* Society Publication No. 11, C.C. Pur.

Hodgson, Brian Haughton (1953), *Journal of Asiatic Society of Bengal.*

Holleman, J.F. (1952), *Shona Customary Law with reference to Kinship, Marriage – the family and the Estate*, Oxford University Press, Cape Town and New York.

Holy Bible, Deuteronomy 4:27-28 and 28:64.

Holy Bible, Leviticus 26 : 12.

Holy Bible, Mark Chapter X, Verse 11- 12 .

Holy Bible, Mathew Chapter V, Verse 35.

Horton and Hunt, (1968), *Sociology,* McGraw-Hill, New York.

Hrangthiauva and Lalchhungnunga (1978), *Mizo,* Chanchin Lalriana and Sons, Brara Bazaar, Aizawl.

Hudson, T.C. (1906), *Thadou Grammar,* Shillong.

Hudson, T.C. (1975), *The Meiteis,* Delhi, (Reprint).

Hutton, J.H. (1928), *Footnotes on William Shaw's book on The Thadou Kukis*, Shillong.

Ibohal, M., The Outlines of the Constitutional History of Manipur: Manipur before 33 A.D. in N. Sanajaoba, *Manipur Past and Present,* Vol. I (1988), Mittal Publications, Delhi.

Ibungohal, L.M. & Khelchandra, N. (1967), *Cheitharol Kumbaba,* Imphal.

Jain, M.P. (1972), *Outline of Indian Legal History,* Bombay.

Jamkithang (1967), *Puchon Pachon,* Imphal.

Johnathan, Haas (1982), *The Evolution of Pre Historic State,* Columbia University Press, New York.

Johnson, Allen & Earle Timothy (1987), *The Evolution of Human Societies*, Stadford University Press.

Johnstone, J., (1971), *My Experiences in Manipur and Naga Hills*, Vivek Publishing House, Delhi.

Kabui, Gangmumei (1991), *History of Manipur*, Vol-I: Pre-Colonial Period, National Publishing House, Delhi.

Kabui, Gangmumei (1985), *Anal: A Transborder Tribe of Manipur,* Mittal Publication, Delhi.

Kabui, Gangmumei, *Genesis of the Ethnoses of Naga and Kuki-Chin*, Naga Students Federation.

Kamkhenthang, H. (1988), *The Paite, A Transborder Tribe of India and Burma,* Mittal Publications, Delhi.

Kantorowicz, Hermann (1958), *Definition of Law*: Edited by A.H. Campbell, Cambridge University Press.

Keivom, L. (1990), *Hmar Tolung: A study of Hmar History*. Eastern Standard Offset and Letter Printing Press, Keishamthong, Imphal.

Khuplam, Milui Lenthang, (1905), *Manmasi Chate (Kuki Chin-Mizo) thulhun kidang masa,* Hill Tribals Councils (HTC) Moreh, Manipur, India March.

Khup-za-Go (1988), *Chin Chronicles,* Churachandpur.

Kirch, Patrice, (1984), *The Evolution of the Polynesian Chiefdom,* Cambridge, California.

Kuanga, Rev., (1989), *The Role of Christianity in Socio-economic Life of Mizos,* Aizawl.

Kunstadter, Peter, (1967), "Burma" in *South-East Asian Tribes, Minorities and Nations,* Peter Kunstadter, Princeton University, N. Jersey, U.S.A.

Kusum and P.M. Bakshi (1982), *Customary Law and Justice*

in the Tribal Areas of Meghalaya, The Indian Law Institute, New Delhi.

Lalbiakthanga (1978), *The Mizos: A Study in Racial Personality,* United Publishers, Gauhati.

Lalbiaktlaunga (1989), *Theological Trends in Mizoram,* Aizawl.

Laldena Christian Missions and Colonialism: A study of Missionary Movement in NEI with particular reference to Manipur and Lushai Hills, 1894 -1947, (1988), Shillong, Vendrame Institute.

Laldena, (1995), *Hmar Folk Tales*, Scholar Publishing House, New Delhi.

Lalthangliana, B. (1979), *History of Mizos in Burma,* Zawlbuk Agencies.

Lehman, F.K. (1980), *The Structure of Chin Society*, Tribal Research Institute, Aizawl, (Reprint).

Lewin, T.H., (1984), *Wild Races of South Eastern India,* Mittal Publications, Delhi.

Lewis, *International Encyclopaedia of Social Sciences,* Vol. XVI, pp. 146-150.

Lianzualla, P.L., (1989), *Towards a Tribal Theology: The Mizos Perspective,* Tawmngaihna in Aizawl.

Llewellyn, K.N. and Hoebel, E.A., (1941), *The Cheyenne,* Way Norman (Oklahama).

Long, James, (1955), *Analysis of the Rajmala or the Chronicles of Tripura,* Gauhati, (Reprint).

Lowie, R.H., (1966), *Social Organisation,* Routledge and Kegan Paul, London, (Reprint).

MacIver, R.M. & Page, C.H. (1950), *Society,* Macmillan India Press, Madras.

Mackenzie, Alexender, (1979), *North East Frontier of India,* Mittal Publications, Delhi.

Maine, Henry, (1897), *Ancient Society,* London.

Malianawski, B., *Forces of Law and Order in a Primitive Community* in K.C. Meek, *Law and Authority in a Nigerian Tribe*, XIII, Footnotes: 3.

Manijao, N. (1964), *Chingda Satpa Ingellei,* Imphal.

Manikchand, Konsam, (1988), *The Evolution of Meitei State: Manipur Past and Present*, Vol. I. Mittal Publications, Delhi.

Marshall, H.I. (1929), *The Karen People of Burma,* University of Columbia, Ohio.

Mayne, J.D. (1983), *A Treatise of Hindu Law and Usage,* London.

Mazumdar, D.N. (1962), *Himalayan Polyandry,* Asia Publishing House, Bombay.

Mazumdar, H.T. (1966), *Grammar of Sociology,* Asia Publishing House, Bombay.

McCall, A.G. (1949), *The Lushai Hills District Cover,* Maranatha Printing Press, Aizawl.

McCree, John Surgeon, *Asiatic Research*, Vol. VII Asiatic Society of Bengal, No. NS.XXIV.

McCulloch, W., (1980), *Valley of Manipur,* Gian Publication, Delhi.

McKenzie, J.R. (Ed.), (1986), *The Uncivilized Races of Men*, Vol. VII. Daya Publishing House, Delhi, (Reprint).

McLennan (1996), *Studies in Ancient History,* London.

Miller, R.A., (1986), *Sino-Tibetan: In Trends in Linguistic,* Vol. 5. Scneak Mouton and Co, The Hague

Misao, P.C., (1970), *History and Customs of the Thadou Kuki,* Imphal.

Morgan, Lewis Henry (1958), *Ancient Society,* Bharati Library, Calcutta.

Nadar, L. (1965), "Law in Culture and Society," 67 *American Anthropologist.*

Nadel, S.F. (1953), *Anthropology and Modern Life*, Australian National University, Canberra.

Palit, D.K. (1983), *The Sentinels of the North East,* Palit and Palit, Delhi.

Pandey, S.N. (1985), *Sources of the History of Manipur and Adjoining Areas,* National Publishing House, Delhi.

Parratt, Saroj Nalini, (1980), *The Religion of Manipur,* Firma KLM (Pvt) Ltd., Calcutta.

Parry, N.E., (1976), *The Lakhers*, Firma KLM (Pvt) Ltd., Calcutta (Reprint).

Parry, N.E., (1976), *The Monograph of Lushai Customs and Ceremonies,* Firma KLM (Pvt) Ltd., Calcutta (Reprint).

Parsons, Talcott (1951), *Essay on Sociological Theory and the Social System*, London.

Paton, George Whitecross, (1972), *Jurisprudence*, Oxford University Press, London. (Reprint).

Quareshi, F.A., (1951), *Christianity in the South Eastern Hills of South Asia: Social Impact and a Political Implication*, Bangladesh University Press, Dacca.

Ray, Animesh (1958), *Mizoram Dynamics of Change,* Pearl Publishers, Calcutta.

Ray, J. (1958), *History of Manipur,* Calcutta.

Reid, Robert (Sir), (1983), *History of the Frontier Area Bordering on Assam, 1883-1941*. Eastern Publishing House, Delhi.

Report of Assam Government (1987), Physical and Political Geography of the Province of Assam. Matero Company, Delhi (Reprint).

Rinnel, J. (1800), *Chief Engineer of Bengal Lepsia.*

Rivers, W.H.R., (1914), *History of Melanesian Society*, Vol. II Cambridge.

Romila Thapar (1914), *A History of India*, Vol. I, Penguin Books, New Delhi.

Rousseau, Jean Jacqueus, (1778), *The Social Contract Theory,* London.

Rowlin (1972), *The Mountainers of Tipra*, Asiatic Society of Bengal (Reprint).

Roy Burman, B.K., (1970), *Demographic and Socio-Economic Profile of Hill Areas of North-East India,* Census of India, 1961.

Roychoudhury, R.N. (1983), *Tripura Through Ages.*

Sangeramano, Fr., (1883), *A Description of the Burmese Empire* (Translated by William Tandy' D.D. Rome) Allen and Co., Rome, Reprinted at Government Printing Press, Rangoon.

Sangkima (2004), *Essays on History of Mizos,* Spectrum Publications, Gauhati.

Sangkima, (2004), *A Modern History of Mizoram*, Spectrum Publications, Gauhati.

Sarkar, A.K., (1988), *Summary of Salmond's Jurisprudence*, M.N. Tripathi, Bombay.

Sarojini Devi, Kh. (2005), *British Political Agency in Manipur 1835-1947,* Linthoi Publication, Imphal.

Schapera, Issac, (1955), *A Handbook of Tswana Law and Custom*, Oxford University Press (Reprint).

Scoff Welfred, H., (1912), *Principles of the Emythean.*

Seligman, C.G., (1925), *Cross-Cousin Marriage,* Man.

Shafer, Robert, (1966), *An Introduction to Sino Tibetan,* Otto Harrassowitz Weisbaden.

Shakespear, J., (1912), *The Lushai Kuki Clans,* Part – I & II, London.

Sharma, A.B. (1952), *Pakhangba*, Imphal.

Shaw, William (1929), *The Thadou Kuki*, Shillong.

Shinni, Ronald, J.L. (1998), *Comparative History of the Nagas*.

Simons, H.J. (1968), *African Women: Their Legal Status in South Africa*, Northwestern University Press, Illios.

Sing Khaw Khai (1995), *Zo People and their Culture. Khampu Hatzaw*, New Lamka, Churachandpur.

Singh, Angahal (1965), *Yaithingkonu*, Imphal.

Singh, Bhogeshwor, O. (1967), *Loina Shinlon,* Imphal.

Singh, Bhogeshwor, O. (1968), *Ningthourol Sheireng,* Imphal.

Singh, Budhi, Ch. (1994), *Whence and When,* Imphal.

Singh, Chandra, M. (1974 Oct), "Meitei Luhongba: An Essay" in the *Cultural Integration*, 3rd issue, Imphal.

Singh, Chandra, M. (1972), *Panthoibi Khongkul*, Imphal.

Singh, Ibobi N. (1968), *The Manipur Administration (1709-1900)*, Imphal.

Singh, Ibotombi, M. (1976), *Khupchup Cheini Yong,* Imphal.

Singh, Ibungohal, L. (1963), *Introduction to Manipur,* Imphal.

Singh, Jhalajit, RK, (1965), *A Short History of Manipur,* Imphal.

Singh, Khelchandra, N. (1966), *Chada Laihui,* Imphal.

Singh, Khelchandra, N. (1967), *Naothingkhong Phambal Kaba,* Imphal.

Singh, Khelchandra, N. (1979), *Lam: Sahitya* (May-August). Imphal.

Singh, Khelchandra N. (1972), *Ariba Manipuri Itihas* (Seisak), Imphal.

Singh, Khelchandra N. (1993), *Savapati Bhasan,* Imphal.

Singh, Khulem Chandrasekhar (1975), *Loyumba Shinyen,* All Manipur Umanglai Laiharaoba Committee.

Singh, Kirti M. (1983), *Meitei Customary Law,* Lanmei Thanbi. Imphal.

Singh, Konthoujam (1985), *Manipuri Puya,* Imphal.

Sinha, Hari Mohon and Narula Dheeraj (1993), *Legal Dictionary,* Allahabad Law Agency, Allahabad.

Snodgrass, JJ., (1826), *Narrative of the Burmese War,* London.

Soppitt, C.A. (1976), *A Short Account of Kuki-Lushai Tribals: An Outline Grammar.* Firma KLM Ltd., Calcuta (Reprint).

Spencer, Herbert, *Principles of Sociology.*

State Kala Academy (1994), *Sagei Salairon,* Imphal.

Stewart, R. (1929), *A Slight Notice of the Grammar of Thadous. Journal of Asiatic Society of Bengal,* Vol. XXIV.

Stone, Julius (1964), *Legal System and Lawyers & Reasoning,* Stanford University Press.

Stone, Julius (1966), *Social Dimensions of Law and Justice,* Stanford University Press.

Suba, Rao, Venkata, G.C. (1984), *Jurisprudence and Legal Theory*, Eastern Book Company, Luchnow.

Sutherland, Woodward and Maxwell, R. (1961), *Introductory Sociology,* Oxford and IBH Publishing Co, Bombay.

Swamton, J.R. (1984), *Contribution to the Ethnology of the Haida*, American Museum of Natural History, *Men-* VIII.

Thangtindal (1988), *Ancient Polity of the Gangtes,* Lamka.

Thanzauva, K. (1989), *Theory of Zawlbuk: Towards a Tribal*

Theology: The Mizo Perspective, Mizo Theological Conference with the help of Eastern Theological College, Jorhat, Assam.

The Gangte Custom Committee (1993), *Gangte Danpi,* Churachandpur.

Tombi, M. (1975), *Cultural History of Kangleipak,* Imphal.

Tout, C. Hills (1907), *The Natives of British America,* New York.

Tucci, Ginseppe, (1967), *Tibet, Land of Snow* (Translated by J.E. Stapleton Driver), Alek Books Ltd, London.

Tylor, E.B. (1978), "*Applied to Law and Marriage and Descent,*" *G.A. J.S.* Vol. XXVIII.

Vansittart, Eden (1987), *The Gurkhas,* Matero Company, Delhi (Reprint).

Vernier, Chester G. (1936), *American Family Laws,* Vol. IV. Stanford University Press.

Vincas Steptonaites (1978), *Locational Theory and Complex Chiefdoms: A Mississippian example in Mississippian settlements pattern* Academic Press, New York.

Vioglin and Vioglin (1964-65), World Languages appeared in different volumes of *Anthropological Linguistics*.

Vumson, *Zo History*, Vumson, C/O T.N. Thawnga Venglku, Aizawl.

Weil, S., (1991), *Beyond the Sambatyon, The Myth of the Ten Lost Tribes,* Tel Aviv, Israel.

Westermarch, E. (1922), *The History of Human Marriage,* Vol. III, The Appleton Book Company, New York.

Wilk, Stanley (1976), "Custom" in *Encyclopaedia of Anthropology,* 113.

Zaithangchhungi, (1990), *Israel – Mizo Identity*, J.R. Bros' Offset Printer, Aizawl.

Zamzachin, G., (1992), *Paite Tanchin*, Rainbow's End, Sanjenthong, Imphal.

A good number of eminent scholars and authorities on law and their classic works on various aspects of law have been taken advantage of in the main text of the subject matter and their names have been utilized as references. Their names together with the titles of their varying works have been also included in the Bibliography. However asteric(*) marks are given to indicate important books on law which have bearings upon their work for understanding the concepts of sociology of law and law *per se*.

Anderson, James, N.D. (1963), *Changing Law in Developing Countries*. Praeger, New York.

Cohen, Morris R, (1961), *Reason and Law Studies in Juristic Philosophy*. Free Press, Glencoe-Ill.

Davis, F. James (1962), *Society and Law*, Free Press, New York.

Durkhiem, Emile, (1960), *The Division of Labour in Society*, Free Press, Glencoe-Ill.

Durkhiem, Emile, (1958), *Professional Ethics and Civic Morals*, Free Press, Glencoe-III.

Ehrlich, Cugen, (1913), *Fundamental Principles of the Sociology of Law*, Havard University Press.

Friedman, Wolfang, (1959), *Law in Changing Society*, University of California Press, Berkeley.

Guvitch George D., (1947), *Sociology of Law*, Routledge, London.

Hall, Jerome, (1952), *Theft, Law and Society*, Indianapolis, Indiana.

Hazard, John N., (1960), *Settling Disputes in Soviet Society. The Formative years of Legal Institute*, Columbia University Press, New York.

Hoebel, E. Adamson, (1961), *The Law of Primitive Man: A Study of Comparative Legal Dynamics*, Havard University Press, Cambridge, Massachusett.

Kirchheimer, Otto, (1961), *Political Justice: The use of Legal Procedure of Political Ends*, Princeton University Press.

Lev, Daniel S., (1965), *The Lady and the Banyan Tree: Civil Law Change in Indonesia*, American Journal of Comparative Law.

Llewellyn, Karl N., (1962), *Jurisprudence: Realism in Theory and Practice,* University of Chicago Press.

Llewellyn, Karl N. (1960), *The Common Law Tradition Deciding Appeals*, Boston.

Malinawski, Bronislaw (1961), *Crime and Custom in Savage Society,* Routledge, London.

Malinawski, Bronislaw (1945), *The Dynamics of Culture Change: An Inquiry Into Race Relations in Africa,* Yale University Press, New Haven.

Plucknett, Theodore F.T. (1956), *A Concise History of the Common,* Butterworth.

Radcliff-Brown, A.R., *Law Primitive* Vol. 9; pp. 202-206, Macmillan, New York.

Timasheff Nicholas (1939), *Introduction to Sociology of Law*, Havard University, Cambridge.

Weber, Max (1954), *Law in Economy and Society,* Edited with the introduction and annotation by Max Rheimstein. Havard University Press, Cambridge, Massachusett.

JOURNALS/SEMINAR PAPER/ARTICLES AND RECORDS

Published Work

Akbar Ahmed, BBC Programme on 28.8.2006 at 9 a.m. (*Asia Today*)

Angoubi, H. Vs Nongmaijing Sharma, A.I.R., 1953(B)

Beatson Bell, Nicholas, *Proceedings of the Foreign and Political Department*, Government of India, No. 8856P dt. Sept., 27, 1920

Botham, A.W.C., C.I.E., I.C.S., Chief Secretary of Assam, Letter No.9242.P , Political Department, dated 05-10-1920, Secretary to the Government of India.

Chatterjee, Suhas, Early History of Mizos: *Proceedings of North-East India History Association,* 9th Session, Guwahati, 1988

Chattopadhyay, K.P., "Contact of People as Affecting Marriage Rules" *Presidential Address,* Anthropology section, Indian Science Congress.

Chaudhury, N.D., The Early Inhabitants of North-East India with special reference to Mizoram, Paper presented in the *International seminar* on 7-9 April, 1992, Aizawl.

Chauton, S. Vs. Sanabam Lalit Singh, D.C.A. No. 146 and D.C.A. No. 102.

Codification Committee, Manipur Customs, 1960 pp. 29-30.

Cole, W.G.H. Cal., Political Agent Manipur Confidential Letter No. DO.5c dt. 17th March, 1917 addressed to B.C. Allen, ICS, Special Officer, Government of Assam, Shillong.

Fienman, Gary and Linda Nicholas, "Labour Surplus and Production – A Regional Analysis of Formative of Oaxaca socio-economic Organisation" in *Anthropological Research Papers* – 1987.

Ghurye, G.S., Dual Organisation in India, J.R. A. I., Vol. III.

Heisnam Baruniton, Singh, Vs. Thokchom Ningol Heisnam Ongbi Bhani Devi and Others, A.I.R. 1959, Manipur 20 (V.46.11).

I.L.O., "The Evolution of Labour Dispute Settlement procedure in certain African countries in 91(2), *International Labour Review*, 1965.

Keary, Henry, Gen, G.A. Letter No. 1762, *KPM*, dated May, June

Kent Flannery, The Olmec and the Valley of Oaxaca- A model for international interaction in formative times, "in *Dumbarton Oaks Conference on the Olmec*" Edited by E. Benson, 1968, pp.79-110, Washington D.C. Dumbarton Oaks and Mery Helms : Ancient Panama Austin : University of Texas Press, 1979.

Kristian, Kristiansen, The formation of tribal systems in later European pre-history : 1982 Northern Europe 4000 – 500 B.C. in *Theory and Explanation in Archaeology: The Southampton Conference:* Edited by C. Penfew, M. Rowland, and B. Seagraves, pp.241-80, New York, Academic Press (1987) "From Stone to Bronze".

Labouret, Henri, *La Parents & Plaisenteries on Afrique Occidentale,* Africa Vol. II.

M. Lokendra Singh, An Article "Devine Kinship in Manipur" – *Proceedings of North East India History Association* (Tenth Session) Shillong, 1989.

Madammercelle Demise Pauline, Parent & Plaisentaries at Alliance par le sang an Afrique, *Africa* Vol-XII.

McCulloch, W., *The Journal of Asiatic Society of Bengal*, Vol. No.NS.XXIV, 1857, p.80 and Social Systems, 1951, pp.182-200.

Micholas, Linda and Gary Finman, Labour Supplies and Production – A regional analysis of formative Oaxaca Socio-economic organisation in Anthropological Research Papers.

Naoreoibam Indramani, Ningthou Phambal Tongba (Coronation of King) ; *Sanathong*, Vol. VIII, No.4 – June 2001 (8th Anniversary Publication)

Parker and Anderson, *Sociology*.

Parson, Talsot, *Essay on Sociological Theory and The Social System,* 1951.

Pedler, E.G., Joking Relationship in East Africa, *Africa,* Vol. XIII

Robert Carneiro and Timothy Earle, A Theory of the Origin of the State :Science 169. Chiefdoms in archaeological and ethno-historical perspective; *Annual Review in Anthropology,* 1987; pp. 279-308.

Sangkima: 'Oral Sources of Mizo' – Paper presented at the *Seminar in sources of History of North-East India* organized by ICHR – NERC, Guwahati on Marc 12, 2002.

Sangkima: The coming and settlement of Myanmese in Mizoram : Paper presented in *National Seminar on cross border movement of people*, 24th April, 2002.

Sangkima: A Study of the Mizos with reference to their early Home: Paper presented at International seminar held on 7-9 April, 1992 on the *Studies on the Minorities Nationalities of North-East India: The Mizos.*

Section 13(a), The Indian Evidence Act, 1872

Section 32(4), The Indian Evidence Act, 1872

Sections 48 and 49, The Indian Evidence Act, 1872

Simon Jenkins, Duncan, *Journal of Asiatic Society Bengal*, N.S. XXIV, 1928

Singh, M. Chandra, Meitei Luhongba : An essay in the cultural integration; 3rd issue.

Singh, S. Raghumani, Jurisprudential Study of the Interaction of Meitei Customary Law and Hindu Law (Thesis submitted to Kurukshetra University) in 1985.

Singh, Sanasam Amal, Social Dynamics of Chiefs and Their Chiefdoms in the State Formation in Early Manipur – Thesis submitted to Manipur University, Canchipur in 2003.

Terrence, D. Altroy and Timothy Earle, "Staple Finance, Wealth finance and Storage in the Inca Political economy," *Current Anthropology*; 26; 187-206

Thomas, Bergatzsky, "Culture, Environment and ills of adaptationalism." *Current Anthropology* : 25, pp. 399-415, 1984.

Vijayalakshmi Brara, N., Religious Movements and Cultural Synthesis in Manipur : An observation and the Manipuri Hinduism – Globalisation and the Changing Scenario of Cultural Interaction : Manipur Experience – Centre for Manipuri Studies, Manipur University, Canchipur, Imphal on 3-4 March, 2005.

——The Manipur State Merger Agreement to the Dominion of India dated the 15th October, 1949 in Shillong.

——The Manipur Hill Peoples (Administration) Regulation Act, 1947.

——The Manipur (Village Authority) Hill Areas Act, 1956.

——The Kuki Cultural Festival Committee, 2006 – Chibai 21st Century (A Commemorative Souvenir of the First Ever Kuki Cultural Festival, 2006) – Diamond Offset, Churachandpur.

——The Extra-ordinary Gazette of Manipur, Notification No.1/15/54 dated 17 January, 1957; Vol. No. 6-E-4, Imphal, Thursday, April, 1957.

Sources:

Damodar Singh, W., Merger of Manipur with the Dominion of India – *Sangai Express*, 27-9-06 and 29-9-06.

Gangte, T.S., Origin, Concept and Growth of Kut Souvenir, 1985.

Higgins, J.C., Letter No.KPM/37/198 dated 11-01-1919.

Hiranya, R.K., Luwang – a paper submitted to SRI of Manipur Studies in a seminar on History of Manipur to 1500.

Hussain, W., Migrating to the promised Land – The Telegraph, Calcutta, 24-11-91

J.M. Raina, the Chief , D.O.letter No.51/1/60 dated Imphal, the Commissioner, Manipur, 18th June, 1960 addressed to P.R. Bahl, ICS, Joint Secretary to the Government of India, Ministry of Home Affairs, New Delhi.

K.N.A., Social Organisation at the Point of Kuki National Assembly

Khan, Ghulam Vs. Chirag Bibi, 43 PR, 1916.

Lavy, V. Benjamin, Letter, dt. Feb, 1984, General Secretary of Manasseh People, Shinlung - Israel, NEI, Mizoram to Chief Rabbiset Council, Israel, 1984.

Memo No., C.M-20/G.S./N.S./ML&LR/89 dated 19th September, 1989.

Muharram Ali Vs Barker Ali, 12 Lah; 286, 1936

Narendra, M., Sarang Leishang: Seminar Paper on History of Manipur to 1500 A.D. Sponsored by S.R. Institute, Imphal, 1985 (Dec).

Ratiram Vs. Shararam, L.R. 900

Resolution, No.1 of the Kuki National Assembly meeting held at Thingkhanphai Village, Churachandpur (then Manipur South District from 19-22 January, 1960.

Rose Mary Zoramchhuani, Peace and Prosperity Sans, *Telegraph*, North-East, 30th June, 1997.

Samra, Myer, The Tribes of Manaseh, Judaism in the Hill Areas of Manipur and Mizoram, Man in India 71(a), 183-202

Sawmminlam, Tukbesawm Tribe, Kangpokpi.

Subhir Ghosh, Mizo Accord: The Cry of Thunder Now So Distant: *Telegraph*, dt. 30th June, 1997.

Index

N

O

P

R

S